PAUL

A Man of Grace and Grit

Publications by Charles R. Swindoll

ADULT BOOKS

Active Spirituality

The Bride

Compassion: Showing We Care
in a Careless World

The Darkness and the Dawn

David: A Man of Passion
and Destiny

Day by Day

Dear Graduate

Dropping Your Guard

Elijah: A Man of Heroism
and Humility

Encourage Me

Esther: A Woman of Strength
and Dignity

The Finishing Touch

Flying Closer to the Flame

For Those Who Hurt

God's Provision

The Grace Awakening

Growing Deep in the Christian Life

Growing Strong in the Seasons of Life

Growing Wise in Family Life

Hand Me Another Brick

Home: Where Life Makes Up Its Mind

Hope Again

Improving Your Serve

Intimacy with the Almighty

Joseph: A Man of Integrity
and Forgiveness

Killing Giants, Pulling Thorns

Laugh Again

Leadership: Influence That Inspires

Living Above the Level of Mediocrity

Living Beyond the Daily Grind,
Books I and II

The Living Insights Study Bible—
General Editor

Living on the Ragged Edge

Make Up Your Mind

Man to Man

Moses: A Man of Selfless Dedication

The Mystery of God's Will

The Quest for Character

Recovery: When Healing Takes Time

The Road to Armageddon

Sanctity of Life

Simple Faith

Simple Trust

Starting Over

Start Where You Are

Strengthening Your Grip

Stress Fractures

Strike the Original Match

The Strong Family

Suddenly One Morning

The Tale of the Tardy Oxcart

Three Steps Forward, Two Steps Back

Victory: A Winning Game Plan for Life

Why, God?

You and Your Child

MINIBOOKS

Abraham: A Model of Pioneer Faith

David: A Model of Pioneer Courage

Esther: A Model of Pioneer Independence

Moses: A Model of Pioneer Vision

Nehemiah: A Model of Pioneer Determination

BOOKLETS

Anger

Attitudes

Commitment

Dealing with Defiance

Demonism

Destiny

Divorce

Eternal Security

Forgiving and Forgetting

Fun Is Contagious!

God's Will

Hope

Impossibilities

Integrity

Intimacy with the Almighty

Leisure

The Lonely Whine of the Top Dog

Make Your Dream Come True

Making the Weak Family Strong

Moral Purity

Our Mediator

Peace . . . in Spite of Panic

Portrait of a Faithful Father

The Power of a Promise

Prayer

Reflections from the Heart—A Prayer Journal

Seeking the Shepherd's Heart—A Prayer Journal

Sensuality

Stress

This is No Time for Wimps

Tongues

When Your Comfort Zone Gets the Squeeze

Woman

CHILDREN'S BOOKS

Paw Paw Chuck's Big Ideas in the Bible

A Man of Grace and Grit

PAUL

Profiles in Character from

CHARLES R. SWINDOLL

W PUBLISHING GROUP™

www.wpublishinggroup.com

A Division of Thomas Nelson, Inc.
www.ThomasNelson.com

Published by The W Publishing Group, P.O. Box 141000, Nashville, Tennessee 37214

Swindoll, Charles R.
    Paul: a man of grace and grit : profiles in character from Charles R. Swindoll.
       p. cm.—(Great Lives from God's Word)
    Includes bibliographical references (p.).
                        ISBN 0-8499-1749-2
    1. Paul, the Apostle, Saint. 2. Christian saints—Turkey—Tarsus—Biography
    3. Christian life—Evangelical Free Church of America authors. I. Title.
    BS2506.3.S95   2002
    225.9'2–dc21
    [B]   2002016734
              SPECIAL EDITION: ISBN: 0-8499-9057-2

Printed and bound in the United States of America

02 03 04 05 06 07 BVG 9 8 7 6 5 4 3 2

DEDICATION

With enduring gratitude for the many who have
mentored me during my formative years,
I wish to dedicate this book to four of them who made
significant contributions in areas of my greatest need.

RICHARD NIEME, now deceased, who
taught me how to overcome stuttering,
so that I might speak in public without fear.

HOWIE HENDRICKS, who taught me
how to study the Bible and communicate its message,
so that I might accurately handle the Word of truth.

J. DWIGHT PENTECOST, who taught me
how to stand firm in hard times and trust God, regardless,
so that I might be a minister who finishes strong.

RAY STEDMAN, now deceased, who
taught me how to be real and enjoy the ministry,
so that I might be a shepherd who encourages the sheep.

As I look back and remember the things these mentors taught me,
it occurs to me that it was more who they were
than what they said that won my heart.
Each one stands out in my mind as a man of grace and grit.

CONTENTS

INTRODUCTION

Paul: A Man of Grace and Grit

S everal treasured biographies line the shelves of my personal library—
some written a century or more ago. Though their pages have yel-
lowed through time, their print painfully small, their paragraphs
long, and their prose often flowing tediously across each page, like a band
of faithful friends, these volumes stand ready to spring to my aid at a
moment's notice. Each one offers a depth of insight into the lives of the
great individuals about whom they report that inevitably rekindles my own
passion for such straight-thinking courage and clarity of expression so rare
in much of modern writing. To me, these books are of priceless value.

Josiah Gilbert Holland's biographical work, *The Life of Abraham
Lincoln,* is a classic example. Dated 1866, the year after the assassination
of America's sixteenth president, this leather-bound jewel has been a source
of much pleasure and inspiration for me through the years. In my opinion, the 544-page masterpiece would qualify as the original *Mr. Holland's
Opus.*

It was in the preface of his work on Lincoln, however, where I found words that helped sustain me in my effort to complete this sixth book in the series, Great Lives from God's Word.

While struggling with the colossal assignment of treating in a few chapters a subject as magnificent and impressive as the life and ministry of the apostle Paul, Holland's words describing what he "aimed to do" and what he did not "aim to do" steeled me for the task. Acknowledging the impossibility of composing an exhaustive treatise covering every detail of the events surrounding Abraham Lincoln's monumental and enduring life, he wrote, "I have tried to paint the character of Mr. Lincoln, and to sketch his life, clinging closely to his side."

That is precisely what *I* aim to do in the pages that follow.

It is mainly Paul's character I wish to paint in this mere sketch of his life, clinging closely to his side through the dramatic events that unfold in the pages of Scripture. As in each preceding book in this series, we'll allow the Word of God to guide us in our quest to grasp the enormity and significance of this remarkable man and his story. And what a fascinating story it is! I know of no other person in the Bible, aside from Christ Himself, who had a more profound influence on his world and ours than Paul—an individual whose life seems best summarized in the title I have chosen for this book, *Paul: A Man of Grace and Grit.*

My well-worn dictionary defines grit as "firmness of mind or spirit . . . unyielding courage in the face of hardship or danger." I love that! There's no better description of this man from Tarsus, whom God used to play such a major role in turning the world upside-down for Christ in his generation. Tough, tenacious, and fiercely relentless in his determination, Paul pursued his divine mission with unflinching resolve. The man modeled grit like no other soul mentioned in the sacred Scriptures.

But his message and his style, as we shall see, were also marked by grace. This one, who himself claimed to be the least of all saints and the chief of all sinners, understood and explained grace better than any of his contemporaries. It isn't difficult to understand why. He never got over his own gratitude as a recipient of it. God's unmerited favor, His super-abounding grace, reached down to him in all his self-righteous zeal, crushed his pride, drove him to his knees, softened his heart, and transformed this once-violent aggressor into a powerful spokesman for Christ. A man with that much grit needed that much grace. Not surprisingly, grace dominated Paul's message and ministry to the final moment of his life.

Hopefully, some of both will begin to seep into our lives as we cling closely to Paul's side. An enormous supply of each is desperately needed as we face the uncertain challenges of the future.

Before we embark on the journey, however, I must express my gratitude to those who have encouraged me in the writing of this sixth biblical biography. First, my heartfelt thanks to my editor and long-time friend, Mark Tobey. Though busy with his own writing demands and deadlines, Mark accepted the challenge of working with me as I struggled at times to portray in flesh and blood the person of Paul. A character *that* profound with a mind *that* deep wrapped in a life *that* colorful seems best kept at a distance, admired as a saint framed in stained glass, and left aloof. Mark helped me gently remove Paul's halo without diminishing his influence.

I am also deeply indebted once again to Julie Meredith for her tireless and diligent efforts in securing permissions for material I've borrowed for this volume—a task she never fails to tackle with a smile.

I'm also grateful for David Moberg and Mark Sweeney, Lee Gessner and Ernie Owen of The W Publishing Group, who have continued to believe in the Great Lives From God's Word series. Each man, in his own way, has encouraged me to keep putting my pen to my pad, to stay at these biographies, and not grow weary in well doing. Their gracious, persistent prodding has resulted in yet another completed work.

I should certainly mention the wonderful congregation of Stonebriar Community Church in Frisco, Texas. It is not only my privilege to serve as their pastor, it was my joy to present these portraits of Paul first to them in a series of messages I delivered on Sunday mornings during most of the year 2001. Their enthusiastic response and frequent words of affirmation, suggesting that I write these thoughts in a book, fueled the fire of determination within me when my own energy would have scarcely sustained a flicker of resolve.

Finally, to Cynthia, my wife of almost forty-seven years, I express my deepest feelings of love and gratitude. Her model of affection and faithfulness to me, her relentless pursuit of excellence, and her unselfish dedication to the goal of making it possible for me to communicate God's truth and its application have motivated me to remain passionate about the same objective. Another of the many tangible results of her commitment to me is this book you now hold in your hands. Without her encouragement, seeing the project through to the end would not have occurred.

And now, let's step into the imaginary time tunnel together. Let's travel far back to another place in another era. Let's allow ourselves to focus our attention on this one man's life, clinging closely to his side. Hopefully, as a result, our lives will change and never again be the same.

—CHUCK SWINDOLL
Dallas, Texas

A Man of Grace and Grit

PAUL

to law school but was laughed out of consideration because of
e qualifications. Not long after that humiliating ordeal, he started
iness using money he borrowed from a close friend. Before the
however, that business faded and failed. Lincoln claimed bank-
spent the next seventeen years paying off debt.
e fell deeply in love with Ann Rutledge, only to have his heart
n she died soon after their engagement. The following year he
lete nervous breakdown and spent the next six months in bed

he sought to become speaker of the state legislature and was

two years later, he sought to become the elector of the state,
eated.
ears later he ran for Congress and lost.
e ran again for Congress and won. Only two years later he ran
n and was soundly defeated.
he sought the job of land officer in his home state but was

e ran for the Senate of the United States. Again, he lost.
he sought the vice-presidential nomination at his party's na-
ntion. He got less than one hundred votes, suffering yet another
g defeat.
e ran for the U.S. Senate and lost again. Finally in 1860 Abraham
elected to the presidency of the United States and soon after
most devastating war our country has ever experienced. His
e rewarded him with unprecedented political success, and he
d for a second term. Sadly, only five days after Lee surrendered,
teenth of April 1865, Lincoln was assassinated. He was dead
ing sixty years of age.
wing any of that, we reflect on a presidency like his and our ten-
nink, *My, what a magnificent background he must have had.* Then
er into the dark cave of his past and realize it's riddled with failure
heartache and pain. We're surprised. Even shocked.
of greatness is forged in the pit. It's true of all of us. Don't ever

CHAPTER

May I Introduce to You Sa

E ach time we engage in a serious stu
brace ourselves for surprises. Interes
more shocking the surprises. You can
and events that led to greatness in that pers
years when few were looking and no one care

That's certainly true of America's sixteentl
dent, Abraham Lincoln. Most would assume
United States would be a fitting climax to an
all, anyone who becomes president surely gr
spoon background, emerging naturally into th
an easy slide into the role of president. Hardl

Lincoln was born in 1809 in a primitive
known as Hardin County, Kentucky. His fath
ing laborer, his mother a frail sickly woman. T
home when he was only seven. His poor motl
He had virtually no formal schooling.

He first attempted a career in business in 1831
later he ran for state legislature unsuccessfully. T

and applie
his miseral
another b
year closec
ruptcy anc

In 1839
broken wl
had a con
recovering

In 183
defeated.

In 184
and was

Thre

In 184
for reelec

In 18
rejected.

In 18

In 18
tional co
embarra

In 18
Lincoln
endurec
persever
was reel
on the
before

Not
dency i
we pee
and tra

Th

forget that, especially when you're in the pit and you're convinced there's no way anything of value will come of it.

We must not forget that as we study the life of the man they called Paul. We must also brace ourselves for some rather gruesome surprises.

A BRUTAL PORTRAIT

The first pen portrait of Paul (whom we first meet as Saul of Tarsus) is both brutal and bloody. If an artist were to render it with brush and oils, not one of us would want it hung framed in our living room. The man looks more like a terrorist than a devout follower of Judaism. To our horror, the blood of the first martyr splattered across Saul's clothes while he stood nodding in agreement, an accomplice to a vicious crime. Who was this martyr?

Stephen. A young Christian living in Jerusalem, described in Acts 6 as "full of grace and power" (v. 8), who spoke with Spirit-anointed wisdom (v. 10), and whose countenance shone "like the face of an angel" (v. 15). Still, they stoned him. Murdered him in cold blood.

The Sanhedrin, called *the Council* in the Book of Acts, despised Stephen because of the strong stand he took for Christ. They refused to sit any longer listening to his passionate diatribe. In a rage they drove him into the street through the northern gate to the outskirts of the city. There they pummeled him with large, jagged stones until he fell flat and died. Saul, observing the entire episode, stood among the howling mob, holding the robes of Stephen's murderers. No doubt, he grinned with sadistic delight.

Eugene Peterson in his work *The Message* paraphrases the scene:

> Yelling and hissing, the mob drowned him out. Now in full stampede, they dragged Stephen out of town, pelted him with rocks. The ringleaders took off their coats and asked a young man named Saul to watch them.
>
> As the rocks rained down, Stephen prayed, "Master Jesus, take my life." Then he knelt down praying loud enough for everyone to hear, "Master, don't blame them for this sin"—his last words. Then he died. Saul was right there, congratulating the killers.[1]

Throughout our lives we've naturally adopted a Christianized mental image of the apostle Paul. After all, he's the one who gave us both letters to the Corinthians. He wrote Romans, the *Magna Carta* of the Christian life. He penned that liberating letter to the Galatians exhorting them and us to live in the freedom God's grace provides. And the "Prison Epistles" . . . and the Pastoral letters so full of wisdom, so rich with relevance. Based on all that you'd think the man loved the Savior from birth. Not even close.

He hated the name of Jesus. So much so, he became a self-avowed, violent aggressor, persecuting and killing Christians in allegiance to the God of heaven. Shocking though it may seem, we must never forget the pit from which he came. The better we understand the darkness of his past, the more we will understand his gratitude for grace.

The first portrait of Paul's life painted in Holy Scripture is not of a little baby being lovingly cradled in his mother's arms. Nor does it depict a Jewish lad leaping and bounding with neighborhood buddies through the narrow streets of Tarsus. The original portrait is not even of a brilliant, young law student sitting faithfully at the feet of Gamaliel. Those images would only mislead us into thinking he enjoyed a storybook past. Instead, we first meet him as simply a "young man named Saul," party to Stephen's brutal murder, standing "in hearty agreement with putting him to death" (Acts 7:58; 8:1).

That's the Saul we need to see to appreciate the glorious truths of the New Testament letters he wrote. No wonder he later came to be known as the "apostle of grace." Admittedly, when we return to his birthplace and childhood, the setting was not marked by anger and violence. Life for Paul actually began quite peacefully.

NO INSIGNIFICANT PLACE

"I am a Jew of Tarsus in Cilicia, a citizen of no insignificant city," Paul once announced in a masterful display of understatement. A close study of the ancient city of Tarsus reveals that Paul's hometown was no backwoods bump in the road, but a busy metropolis of diverse culture and international commerce. Its strategic location explains its significance and success.

To find Tarsus, use the map printed on page 353 and first locate the large body of water in the center; that's the Mediterranean. Next, scan your finger to the easternmost boundary of the sea, running north along its shore, up past Syria. Turn slightly west (That's to the left for you who are geographically challenged!) until you find Cilicia, a province in the southeastern corner of what was then called Asia Minor. Today it's part of modern Turkey.

There you'll find Tarsus located in the heart of the Cilician province—birthplace of Saul. Located a dozen miles or so from the glistening beaches of the Mediterranean, Tarsus sits cradled by the towering Taurus range—a line of rugged mountains running from the seacoast toward the north, providing a sweeping protective shield around the city. Because the city was near a seaport, Tarsus became a popular trade route for caravans carrying their goods from the Orient in the east all the way to Rome in the west. The journey required their passing through the Cilician Gates, an impressive span of narrow passages chiseled through the Taurus Mountains above Tarsus.

The cream of all this rich cultural and commercial diversity poured into Saul's cup as he grew up in the mesmerizing city of his birth. Though motherless from the age of nine, as the son of a prominent tentmaker, Saul became the beneficiary of an equally rich religious and intellectual heritage. John Pollock, author of *The Apostle: A Life of Paul*, skillfully describes aspects of Saul's early life and education:

> Paul's parents were Pharisees, members of the party most fervent in Jewish nationalism and strict in obedience to the Law of Moses. They sought to guard their offspring against contamination. Friendships with Gentile children were discouraged. Greek ideas were despised. Though Paul from infancy could speak Greek, the *lingua franca*, and had a working knowledge of Latin, his family at home spoke Aramaic, the language of Judea, a derivative of Hebrew.
>
> They looked to Jerusalem as Islam looks to Mecca. Their privileges as freemen of Tarsus and Roman citizens were nothing to the high honor of being Israelites, the People of Promise, to whom alone the Living God had revealed His glory and His plans ...

By his thirteenth birthday, Paul had mastered Jewish history, the poetry of the psalms, and the majestic literature of the prophets. His ear had
been trained to the very pitch of accuracy, and a swift brain like his could
retain what he heard as instantly and faithfully as a modern "photographic
mind" retains a printed page. He was ready for higher education.[2]

That's at age thirteen. Pollock continues:

A strict Pharisee would not embroil his son in pagan moral philosophy. So, probably in the year that Augustus died, A. D. 14, the adolescent
Paul was sent by sea to Palestine and climbed the hills to Jerusalem.

During the next five or six years, he sat at the feet of Gamaliel,
grandson of Hillel, the supreme teacher who, a few years before, had
died at the age of more than a hundred. Under the fragile, gentle
Gamaliel, a contrast with the leaders of the rival School of Shammai,
Paul learned to dissect a text until scores of possible meanings were
disclosed according to the considered opinion of generations of rabbis
... Paul learned to debate in question-and-answer style known in the
ancient world as the "diatribe," and to expound, for a rabbi was not
only part preacher but part lawyer, who prosecuted or defended those
who broke the sacred Law. Paul outstripped his contemporaries. He
had a powerful mind which could lead to a seat on the Sanhedrin in
the Hall of Polished Stones, and make him a "ruler of the Jews."[3]

Saul lived for the day he would become a member of the Jewish Supreme Court, called then, the Sanhedrin. Together, those seventy-one men
ruled over Jewish life and religion, seated on curved benches in a courtroom—precisely the place where they heard Stephen deliver his brave yet
fateful confession of faith.

Saul, now a successful lawyer in the bustling courts of Jerusalem, was
most likely part of the larger audience who heard Stephen's defense. Little
did he realize then how God would use the events leading up to and following the young disciple's death, to change his life dramatically and impact
the story of religious history.

A FUTILE CONFRONTATION

Since the day of Pentecost, recorded in Acts 2, Jerusalem had been astir with unprecedented religious activity. The more the now-bold apostles preached the good news of Christ, the more the people were converted. Everything was changing, even long-standing traditions. Jews living in Jerusalem and pilgrims visiting from around the region were embracing Christ literally by the thousands. Dyed-in-the-wool religious leaders were incensed by what they were witnessing. Enough was enough. As a result, according to Acts 5:18, "They laid hands on the apostles, and put them in a public jail."

These Spirit-filled apostles were giving the religious establishment fits. Let's not look at these scenes through lenses that are *too* Christian. Better to view them from the perspective of the citizenry of Jerusalem. These were maddening times for the Sanhedrin. Their attempt to silence the followers of Jesus by crucifying their Master had backfired. And so, incarcerating the religious fanatics seemed the best strategy to prevent further proselytizing of Jews. But not even that worked. To make matters worse for the religious officials, something miraculous happened: "An angel of the Lord during the night opened the gates of the prison, and taking them out he said, 'Go your way, stand and speak to the people in the temple the whole message of this Life.' And upon hearing this, they entered into the temple about daybreak, and began to teach" (Acts 5:19–21).

Talk about a backfire! The religious leaders thought they had dealt with these rebels, when, in fact, they had only motivated them to return to their preaching, more emboldened than ever. It was similar to what happened following the scene at Golgatha. The Jewish leaders felt certain that crucifying Christ would end everything. They couldn't have been more wrong. Christianity flourished following His Resurrection. Now, ablaze with the power of the Spirit, the apostles were setting Jerusalem aflame through their preaching. Their zeal was contagious and their message, convincing. It wasn't long before the religious officials found themselves among a quickly shrinking minority. That prompted them to call an emergency meeting to determine their next move.

Now when the high priest and his associates had come, they called the Council together, even all the Senate of the sons of Israel, and sent orders to the prison house for them to be brought. But the officers who came did not find them in the prison; and they returned, and reported back, saying, "We found the prison house locked quite securely and the guards standing at the doors; but when we had opened up, we found no one inside."

Acts 5:21–23

Is that great, or what? The angel of the Lord had unlocked the prison, liberated the apostles, and then locked the place up again. When they came to the jail they found the guards asleep, the gates secured, and no prisoners.

Quite likely, Saul was numbered among the group who heard that troubling report. This would have been the full body of the Sanhedrin, including those who accompanied them, such as junior lawyers, advisors, and perhaps even servants. Not wanting to miss any of the action, Saul absorbed every detail as the events unfolded. Things were getting out of control.

Understand also, a growing frustration swept through the ranks of religious officials. We read, "When the captain of the temple guard and the chief priests heard these words, they were greatly perplexed about them as to what would come of this" (Acts 5:24).

Don't you love the way that reads? In today's terms, "greatly perplexed" would come out, "WHAT DO YOU MEAN YOU DIDN'T FIND THOSE PEOPLE?" These prejudiced judges are out of their minds trying to figure out what happened. To make matters worse, another messenger came running with an even more startling report:

"Behold, the men whom you put in prison are standing in the temple and teaching the people!"

Then the captain went along with the officers and proceeded to bring them back without violence (for they were afraid of the people, lest they should be stoned).

Acts 5:25–26

Don't miss the significance of that added detail. These pious leaders now feared for their lives as they sensed the tide turning against them. More and more people in the streets were saying, "Don't touch these men. They're telling us things we need to hear . . . things which you never told us." The blind confidence the people of Jerusalem had placed in their leaders was now eroding as their eyes were being opened to the Truth of the Gospel. Because the masses were believing it, the Council proceeded with caution: "So when they brought them in, they stood them before the Council" (v. 27).

Now watch closely: "And the high priest questioned them, saying, 'We gave you strict orders not to continue teaching in this name, and behold, you have filled Jerusalem with your teaching, and intend to bring this man's blood upon us'" (Acts 5:27–28).

In other words, "You're telling people that we are the reason that that false Messiah was crucified. I want you to know that the Romans did that. We merely followed along with the plan. But you're making us look bad." Notice how the apostles and particularly Peter responded: "But Peter and the apostles answered and said, 'We must obey God rather than men. The God of our fathers raised up Jesus, whom you had put to death by hanging Him on a cross. He is the one whom God exalted to His right hand as a Prince and a Savior, to grant repentance to Israel, and forgiveness of sins. And we are witnesses of these things; and so is the Holy Spirit, whom God has given to those who obey Him'" (Acts 5:29–32).

Saul heard that speech. Ever thought of that before? While standing in the shadows listening to Peter speak, the hair on the back of his neck bristled. This young, pious Pharisee, a Hebrew of Hebrews, listened angrily as the ignorant fisherman named Peter spoke of the now-dead Jesus who claimed to be God. It was almost more than he could bear. Passion boiled within him as Saul began formulating plans, thinking, *If I could just get my hands on him, I'd kill him like all the rest.* Little did he know this "ignorant fisherman" would be his co-laborer in the work of establishing Christian churches throughout the known world. Before Saul could organize an assault on this man and his companions, God intervened in another surprising turn of events as Saul's mentor stood to his feet.

AN UNEXPECTED ALLY

> But when they heard this, they were cut to the quick and were intending to slay them. But a certain Pharisee named Gamaliel, a teacher of the Law, respected by all the people, stood up in the Council and gave orders to put the men outside for a short time.
>
> Acts 5:33–34

Wait a minute. Who's Gamaliel? Saul studied under this man during his schooling in Jerusalem; he testified that he was "educated under Gamaliel" (Acts 22:3). He sat at Gamaliel's feet during his formal training in Jewish law. He stared breathlessly as he watched his mentor in action. It's like a law student, who after graduation visits a courtroom to observe his admired professor practice law. What a great moment for Saul. He may have anticipated strong words of condemnation against Peter. Quite the contrary.

> And he said to them, "Men of Israel, take care what you propose to do with these men. For some time ago Theudas rose up, claiming to be somebody; and a group of about four hundred men joined up with him. And he was slain; and all who followed him were dispersed and came to nothing. After this man Judas of Galilee rose up in the days of the census, and drew away some people after him, he too perished, and all those who followed him were scattered. And so in this present case, I say to you, stay away from these men and let them alone."
>
> Acts 5:35–38

William Barclay calls Gamaliel an "unexpected ally." In the midst of flaring tempers and irrational thinking, this wise, seasoned teacher calmly rose to his feet and warned, "Take care here. Don't rush to judgment." In his words: ". . . stay away from these men and let them alone, for if this plan or action should be of men, it will be overthrown; but if it is of God, you will not be able to overthrow them; or else you may even be found fighting against God" (Acts 5:38–39).

The young Pharisee shook his head in disbelief. "This man was supposed to be a spokesman for Judaism. He taught me much of what I know about Judaism and the Law. He schooled me in how to do precisely what I'm doing. Master Gamaliel, you've lost your mind!"

Saul, of course, had no way of knowing that it would be this sort of calm reasoning that would hold him together when he later carried the torch for Christ. He would remind himself that those who fight against him were really fighting God. But at this moment he knew none of that. All he saw was red. Blood red. He couldn't believe the Sanhedrin would heed such calm counsel and consider going soft on these infidels. But that's exactly what they did.

If you would allow me a moment of digression here, I think Peter remained alive then and in the years that followed because of Gamaliel's wise intervention. I think the "unexpected ally" saved his life. Saul and the rest of them would have stoned the whole bunch. But God graciously intervened. He used the words of a wise professor to preserve the lives of those who would later play strategic roles in the formation of the Christian church. Keep that in mind when you feel your circumstances have become hopeless. No matter what you face, God is still in control, silently and sovereignly working all things out according to His perfect plan. He has His Gamaliels waiting in the wings. At the precise moment when their words will have the greatest impact, they will step out of the shadows.

Wisely, the religious leaders took Gamaliel's advice. The Scriptures tell us, "After calling the apostles in, they flogged them and ordered them to speak no more in the name of Jesus, and then released them" (v. 40).

Wait a minute! That's not fair. What right did they have to flog these men if they were only planning to release them? It was the Council's effort to deliver a painful warning: "When you get the skin stripped off your back, maybe you won't forget, we mean business. Back off!"

By the way, how would you have responded in that setting? When your group was lined up and stripped for the beating, would you have hidden in the back hallway? Would you have searched for a way to slip out the door when no one was looking? Flogging was a terribly painful and humiliating torture. Who wouldn't try to escape?

Here's where our respect for these men intensifies. Look how *they* responded: "So they went on their way from the presence of the Council rejoicing that they had been considered worthy to suffer shame for His name. And every day, in the temple and from house to house, they kept right on teaching and preaching Jesus as the Christ" (vv. 41–42).

Remarkable courage! The blood on their wounds had hardly dried before they were back at it, preaching Christ to the people. While we respect them, Saul hated them for that. It's what drove him to take even more aggressive action against them, which he later admitted in his defense before Agrippa: "And this is just what I did in Jerusalem; not only did I lock up many of the saints in prisons, having received authority from the chief priests, but also when they were being put to death I cast my vote against them. And as I punished them often in all the synagogues, I tried to force them to blaspheme; and being furiously enraged at them, I kept pursuing them even to foreign cities" (Acts 26:10–11).

Look again. That's no meek and mild-mannered intellectual speaking. He had become a passionate, determined Pharisee—a man on a mission. Later he would write a similar confession to his son in the faith, Timothy: "I thank Christ Jesus our Lord, who has strengthened me, because He considered me faithful, putting me into service; even though I was formerly a *blasphemer* and a *persecutor* and a *violent aggressor*. And yet I was shown mercy, because I acted ignorantly in unbelief" (1 Timothy 1:12–13, emphasis added).

How's that for a two-sentence autobiography of Saul?

This is the same man who would write of God's grace and mercy. This is one would live to see the day when Peter's penetrating words would stick in his throat, and become for him the motivating force behind his commitment to Christ. "You cannot fight against God," he would preach to his opponents. But until the grace of Christ laid hold of him, he violently opposed everyone and everything related to the Way. And don't miss this: He did it in the name of God. That's why there's nothing more frightening, more vicious than a religious terrorist. What they do, they justify in the name of God.

Saul was no exception. The man, "blameless according to the Law" by his own testimony, blindly believed his bloody deeds honored God by ridding the earth of this cult. And so according to the Scriptures, Saul "began ravaging the church, entering house after house; and dragging off men and women, he would put them in prison" (Acts 8:3). That was no sight for the squeamish. It's difficult to imagine such deep hatred.

That's where we must leave Saul for now. But not before making a few more observations about this shocking period in the man's story.

NO INSIGNIFICANT GRACE

In every great life, there are surprises, often jolting surprises. Who would have guessed that the one writer of the New Testament who has probably had the most significant impact on your Christian growth came from a world of such spiritual blindness and physical brutality? But he did. That's why he claimed the title "chief of sinners." Though you may be tempted to soften that, let it be. Leave him alone in that description. Saul wasn't attempting to sound modest. In his mind, he *was* the chief of sinners. He may very well have been.

As I analyze these early scenes that emerge from our first glimpses of Saul of Tarsus, three observations seem worth mentioning.

First, no matter how you appear to others today, everyone has a dark side. You would be amazed if you knew the darkness lurking in the pasts of those people who have made a difference in your life. Seems unreal, doesn't it? We're all sinful by birth, by nature, and by choice. We remain totally and completely depraved deep within. We grope in darkness because of our spiritual blindness.

Regardless of how we look, we all have a past that is neither pleasant nor encouraging. It's the life we lived before turning to the Savior. We're just not as vulnerable and open as Paul was in sharing with others what our life was like before we embraced the Cross. Nor do we need to be.

I appreciate that great old word in the hymn we sing, "Amazing Grace." The word is "wretch." "Amazing grace how sweet the sound, that saved a *wretch* like me." Leave that word in there, don't replace it. Our existence before Christ was among the wretched. Let's never forget what life was like outside the boundaries of grace. Saul was there . . . and so were we.

Second, regardless of what you have done, no one is beyond hope. That's the great hope of the Christian message. No amount or depth of sin in your past can trump the grace of God. If you question that, remember the brash Pharisee of Tarsus. When the Lord saved him, He didn't put him on probation. The other disciples did that. No, God gave Saul a new name, and in the process, made him a new creation. That's what makes grace so amazing.

Third, even though your past is soiled, anyone can find a new beginning with God. I've made the same statement throughout my ministry: It's never too late to start doing what is right. When Saul knelt before the living God, he finally faced the reality of his sin. Deep within the man, Christ transformed his life and he started doing what was right. Grace provides that sort of new beginning.

Don't get stuck on where you *were*. Don't waste your time focusing on *what you used to be.* Remember, the hope we have in Christ means there's a brighter tomorrow. The sins are forgiven. The shame is cancelled out. We're no longer chained to a deep, dark pit of the past. Grace gives us wings to soar beyond it.

SOME FINAL THOUGHTS

Could it be that you are stuck because of something from your past? Perhaps it has pinned you to the ground with embarrassment, shame, and fear. You're crippled by it. The best you can do is to limp through each day, hoping for a painless end. That way of thinking is the Enemy, Satan. He loves to push your nose in the dirt, hoping to make you miss the marvelous claims of grace.

Don't allow him that power in your life today. Around you are people who have no greater claim on grace than you do, and the Lord mercifully brought them out of their pit of sin. If He could turn a Saul of Tarsus engaged in a murderous rampage into a Paul the apostle who preached and lived the message of grace, He can change your life too.

Read once again the words from John Newton's pen, "Amazing Grace." Read them slowly and aloud. Believe them!

Amazing grace!
How sweet the sound that saved a wretch like me!
I once was lost but now am found;
Was blind, but now I see.

'Twas grace that taught my heart to fear,
And grace my fears relieved.
How precious did that grace appear
The hour I first believed.

Thro' many dangers, toils, and snares
I have already come.
'Tis grace hath bro't me safe thus far,
And grace will lead me home.[4]

It's all there, isn't it? Our wretchedness. Our deliverance from fear. Our claim of grace to see us through . . . to lead us home. Go back and read the words again. Do you know the hymn? Go ahead, sing it to yourself. If you listen closely, you'll hear Paul harmonizing with you.

CHAPTER TWO

The Violent Capture of a Rebel Will

Notorious conversions always grab public attention. Take young Martin, for example. While studying theology the man wrestled deeply with the menacing thought that all his noble intellectual pursuits amounted to little more than empty academic exercises. Though he was, himself, opposed to many of the teachings of the Roman Catholic religion, he had gained a respected position as theological scholar, professor, and spokesman for the Church. Despite all that and his pious attempts at living a pure life, he knew no peace.

The nights were most tortuous. He would lay on his narrow, hard bed in his tiny room, tossing and turning, night after night, crying, "Oh, my sin, my sin, my sin!" Graciously the Lord led Luther to study a passage of Scripture from the Book of Romans. In the dancing glow of his bedside lamp, he read the words, "The just shall live by faith." He read them again and again, aloud . . . passionately.

They shot like flaming arrows off the page piercing deep into his heart, melting hardened layers of guilt and fear. Martin Luther was reborn. The result, as we say, is history.

Luther, along with several notable colleagues, led what came to be known as the great Protestant Reformation—a springtide of religious freedom flowing to the whole world. Remarkably, until that happened, the brilliant theologian lived in his misery as a revered expert in the Scriptures, yet at enmity with the God who spoke to him through them.

Jim's story is entirely different. He was busy, secretly working both sides against the middle. Part of the underground crime network in the 1940s, Jim Vaus, alongside his boss Mickey Cohen, was hired by the Los Angeles Police Department to help search out members of the growing crime network tunneling its way across the U.S. After years of being under the constant stress of living a double life, Vaus faced his own misery and emptiness. For reasons we may never know, he decided to attend a Billy Graham tent crusade being held by the young evangelist and his team on the corner of Washington and Hill streets in downtown Los Angeles. Amidst a crowd of over six thousand people, Jim Vaus grasped a message of grace and forgiveness he'd never understood before. According to an article printed in *The Los Angeles Times*, the notorious mobster stumbled to his feet and "walked the sawdust trail." Literally in the shadow of young Graham, Vaus knelt weeping in the dust before surrendering his life to Christ. Like Luther, he was gloriously born again.

And then there was Chuck. Known by many in the political world of the late 1960s and early 1970s as Nixon's hatchet man, Chuck Colson performed the behind-the-scenes dirty work for his friend and boss, Richard Nixon. Someone said in an unguarded moment, "Chuck's the kind of guy who would run over his grandmother if necessary to get the job done." After an unbelievably rapid assent to political power and stature, and reeling from the pain of a failed marriage, Colson reached a crisis point in his life where, he too, was enduring only misery and emptiness. As the Watergate tangle intensified, Colson descended deep into despair. He began to search for peace in his heart.

A *Christianity Today* article featuring the famed politician, summarized Colson's own recollection of his dramatic conversion, which he describes in his book *Born Again*. A rather extensive quotation from that article is necessary for his dramatic story to unfold correctly.

By late 1972 even the indomitable Chuck Colson began to buckle. He was tired. Nixon was forever calling him at odd hours, summoning him to the Oval Office to talk over this or go over that. When Nixon was reelected in November of that year, Colson resigned as Special Counsel to the President and longed to retreat into private life. But the web of Watergate only tightened its hold. In *Born Again* he recounted the story of his dramatic conversion. He had been visiting the home of friend and colleague Tom Phillips, who had been converted at a Billy Graham crusade. Phillips had confronted Colson with the gospel and read him a portion from C. S. Lewis's *Mere Christianity* that stuck with him: "A proud man is always looking down on things and people: and of course, as long as you are looking down, you cannot see something that is above you." That summer evening in August 1973, Tom Phillips asked Chuck Colson if he would like to pray with him. Colson, aching inside but hard on the outside, awkwardly agreed. ("Sure—I guess I would—fine.") He felt the inner movement of the Spirit but did not cough up the words of surrender. Later that night, "outside in the dark [sitting in the car], the iron grip I'd kept on my emotions began to relax. Tears welled up in my eyes. . . . and suddenly I knew I had to go back into the house and pray with Tom." Only Tom had already gone to bed. Colson parked along the roadside and hoped his friend couldn't hear him sobbing.

Phillips connected Colson with Doug Coe, National Prayer Breakfast organizer and a Christian networker inside the Beltway. Coe tried to convince the believers in Colson's political camp of the authenticity of his conversion, to no avail. As a last resort, Coe contacted Harold Hughes, the well-known Democratic Senator and outspoken Christian. Coe recounted at the Founder's Dinner, "I called Senator Harold Hughes and said, 'Senator, I have a friend who is in tremendous need and needs a friend. I was wondering if you could meet with him and maybe help him along with the Lord.'" When Hughes learned this friend was Colson, he uttered a stream of curses and hung up on Coe.

An hour later, the phone rang. The senator was on the other end. "I'm sorry. I know that's not what Jesus would want me to do. If you'll forgive me, I'll meet him. But it has to be after 11 o'clock at night. And it has to be out in the countryside." At this stage of his Christian life, Colson had never prayed aloud and had not finessed the art of Christian testimonials. Hughes was understandably skeptical. He asked Colson to tell him about his newfound faith. In halting gestures, Nixon's onetime hatchet man made his confession. After 20 minutes, Coe said, Hughes got up, walked across the room, and embraced Colson. "We are brothers for life," he said.[1]

Another glorious conversion of a notorious sinner.

It happens all the time. To dogmatic atheists and determined agnostics. To bright young physicians and brilliant scientists. To popular coaches and gifted athletes. To famous musicians and renowned artists. To former criminals and current pastors. One by one, these unique individuals get to the end of life's rope and, when faced with the claims of the gospel, they believe. Their lives, in a matter of moments, are transformed.

Amazingly, when well known individuals convert to Christ, the public responds with either amazement or skepticism. Did Jim Vaus really come to Christ that day in Los Angeles? Was Martin Luther's life truly transformed? What about Colson? I mean, come on—no one with that checkered a past, that deeply involved in political cover-up could change that much, that quickly.

You know our problem? We confuse conversion with maturity. We'd rather these new converts clean up their act straight away before we grant them our genuine seal of *Christian* approval. How sad. Somewhere along the way we've forgotten the details of our own miserable pasts and the grace of God at work in us.

The late Alan Redpath, longtime pastor and Bible teacher at the historic Moody Church in Chicago, put it best: "The conversion of a soul is the miracle of a moment, the manufacture of a saint is the task of a lifetime."[2] We should never forget that statement. No person, no matter how bright or how sincere or how submissive, comes to Christ and enters a world of instantaneous spiritual maturity. Becoming mature is a lifelong process. The process only begins at the moment of salvation. Conversion to Christ is the initial downbeat to an entire *magnum opus,* which God composes of our lives.

If we're going to think about remarkable conversions, though, there's been none more notorious than Saul of Tarsus. Few conversions in the history of Christianity can even be compared to what transpired on that road outside Damascus. That is true because few opponents of Christianity ever reached such a degree of despicable notoriety as Saul.

FROM A VIOLENT REBEL TO A CAPTURED WILL

Descriptions of Paul's violent past make us uncomfortable. After all, he remains the one man who, apart from Christ Himself, continues to feed our souls with life-changing truth like no other spiritual mentor in history. We don't like focusing on his lost estate. We much prefer studying and admiring portraits of him as the apostle of grace. But we can't ignore the biblical record.

The Scriptures attest to the depth of Paul's sinful past before his conversion. In fact, in many passages which tell his story, Paul disclosed himself. Witness again the repeated testimony of our hero as he confesses to his life as chief of sinners.

> And I persecuted this Way to the death, binding and putting both men and women into prisons.
>
> Acts 22:4

> As also the high priest and all the Council of the elders can testify. From them I also received letters to the brethren, and started off for Damascus in order to bring even those who were there to Jerusalem as prisoners to be punished.
>
> Acts 22:5

> So then, I thought to myself that I had to do many things hostile to the name of Jesus of Nazareth. And this is what I did in Jerusalem; not only did I lock up saints in prisons, having received authority from the chief priests, but also when they were being put to death I cast my vote against them.
>
> Acts 26:9–10

> For you have heard of my former manner of life in Judaism, how I used to persecute the church of God beyond measure, and tried to destroy it; and I was advancing in Judaism beyond many of my contemporaries among my countrymen, being more extremely zealous for my ancestral traditions.
>
> Galatians 1:13–14

You get the picture. The stories of Martin Luther, Jim Vaus, and Chuck Colson pale compared to Saul's aggressive and notorious past.

Augustine called Paul's conversion "the violent capture of a rebel will." He pictured it as being like changing the nature of a wild wolf into the spirit of a lamb. Only God could do that in a depraved soul like Saul. How did it happen? In Paul's own words, "I was shown mercy" (1 Timothy 1:13). One day, Mercy met the rebel Saul as he pressed toward Damascus.

A ROADSIDE CONVERSION OF AN ANGRY MAN

The ninth chapter of Acts begins abruptly. Saul's blood is boiling. He's on a murderous rampage toward Damascus. He charged north out of Jerusalem with the fury of Alexander the Great sweeping across Persia, and the determined resolve of William Tecumseh Sherman in his scorching march across Georgia. Saul was borderline out of control. His fury had intensified almost to the point of no return. Such bloodthirsty determination and blind hatred for the followers of Christ, drove him hard toward his distant destination: Damascus. If you were a follower of Jesus living anywhere near Jerusalem, you wouldn't want to hear Saul's knock at your door.

Eventually, God's grace laid hold of, conquered, and captured that rebel will. In the meantime, grace remained a stranger. The scene opens as "Saul, still breathing threats and murder against the disciples of the Lord, went to the high priest, and asked for letters from him to the synagogues at Damascus, so that if he found any belonging to the Way, both men and women, he might bring them bound to Jerusalem" (Acts 9:1–2).

Why Damascus? Saul had determined to go to the farthest extreme in his mission to apprehend followers of the Way. Over one hundred miles north of Jerusalem, the journey to Damascus was no small undertaking. To Saul the trip would pay off in spades.

According to Josephus, at one point in history ten thousand Jews were massacred in Damascus—hard evidence that at certain times a significant number of Jewish people lived in the city. Saul had the census figures too. He knew many Jewish turncoats had fled Israel's capitol to seek refuge in far-away Damascus. He devised an aggressive plan to storm the city, capture the infidels, and drag them into court. Thankfully, God had a different plan.

We read this: "And it came about that as he journeyed, he was approaching Damascus, and suddenly a light from heaven flashed around him; and he fell to the ground, and he heard a voice saying to him, "Saul, Saul, why are you persecuting Me?" (Acts 9:3–4). You can almost hear the screeching of brakes. At that moment, Saul's murderous journey was brought to a divine halt.

Suddenly. Isn't that just like the Lord? No announcement ahead of time. No heavenly calligraphy scrolled across the skies with the warning, "Watch out tomorrow, Saul, God's gonna getcha." God remained silent and re-strained as Saul proceeded with his murderous plan to invade Damascus. Surely, he discussed the details with his companions. God didn't interrupt . . . until. At the hour it would have its greatest impact, God stepped in. Without warning, the course of Saul's life changed dramatically.

That still happens, even in our day. Without warning, life takes its sudden turns. Maybe it's a tragic auto accident that claims the life of your mate. Suddenly, God steps onto the scene and arrests your attention. Or it may come through the death of a child. In the hour of deepest grief, your life and the life of your family are impacted forever. Occasionally life's unexpected turns come in the horrible crash of an airplane, causing a ca-lamity that wipes out half the neighborhood. Or in the halting words of your physician as she admits, "Your biopsy isn't good. Looks like malig-nancy." Like a rogue wave adversity crashes onto the peaceful shores of our lives and knocks us flat. Amazingly, the jolt awakens our senses and we suddenly remember that God is in control.

For more than three decades Saul controlled his own life. His record in Judaism ranked second to none. On his way to make an even greater name for himself, the laser of God's presence stopped him in his tracks, striking him blind. Like that group of shepherds faithfully watching their sheep years earlier on another significant night outside Jerusalem, Saul and his companions fell to the ground, stunned.

That's what still happens today when calamity strikes. You get the news in the middle of the night on the telephone, and you can't move. As the policeman describes the head-on collision, you stand frozen in disbelief. After hearing the word "cancer," you're so shocked you can hardly walk out the doctor's office doors. A friend once admitted to me that, after hearing his dreaded diagnosis, he stumbled to the men's room, vomited, dropped to his knees and sobbed uncontrollably. Life's unexpected jolts grip us with such fear we can scarcely go on.

For the first time in his proud, self-sustained life, Saul found himself a desperate dependent. Not only was he pinned to the ground, he was blind. His other senses were on alert, and to his amazement, he heard a voice from heaven say, "Saul, Saul, why are you persecuting Me?" (Acts 9:4). Saul was convinced he had been persecuting people—cultic followers of a false Messiah. Instead, he discovered that the true object of his vile brutality was Christ Himself.

Warren Wiersbe provides an excellent imaginary answer Saul might have given to some brave soul who would dare to ask why he did what he did:

> Jesus of Nazareth is dead. Do you expect me to believe that a crucified nobody is the promised Messiah? According to our Law, anybody who is hung on a tree is cursed. Would God take a cursed false prophet and make him the Messiah? No! His followers are preaching that Jesus is both alive and doing miracles through them. But their power comes from Satan, not God. This is a dangerous sect, and I intend to eliminate it before it destroys our historic Jewish faith.[3]

All such boldness vanished at the moment he heard, "Saul, Saul, why are you persecuting Me?"

I find it interesting the Lord knew his name. Not only that, He knew every hair on his head, every vicious thought he'd conjured in his mind, every poisonous motive that drove him toward Damascus. The Lord knew everything from start to finish; make no mistake about it.

We live in a culture that regularly confuses humanity with deity. The lines get blurred. It's the kind of sloppy theology that suggests God sits on the edge of heaven thinking, *Wonder what they'll do next?* How absurd! God is omniscient. This implies, clearly, God never learns anything, our sinful decisions and evil deeds notwithstanding. Nothing ever surprises Him. From the moment we're conceived to the moment we die, we remain safely within the frame of His watchful gaze as well as His sovereign plan.

All this brings us back to the dramatic scene on the Damascus Road. "Saul, Saul, why are you persecuting Me?" Saul, who had never been under such a blazing light or heard such a magnificent voice, answered meekly and with respect, "Who are You, Lord?" Some believe that marked the moment of his conversion. But he used the Greek word *kurios*, which means "lord" or "master." It was a title of respect. "Sir" would be our term today. "Who are You, Sir?" Saul was not only blind, he was confused. The authoritative voice was one he had not heard before.

The answer hit him like the blow of a stun gun: "I am Jesus whom you are persecuting." There must have been several seconds of deafening silence as Saul let in the wonder. Once that happened, he stopped believing Jesus was dead. His rebel will was captured. His journey reversed directions. His mind did a turnaround that would ultimately transform him from the inside out.

That's the essence of genuine repentance—the mind does a turnaround. The Greek word is *metanoia* from the verb *metanoeo*, meaning, literally, "to change one's mind." That's precisely what happened to the once-proud Pharisee on the road to Damascus. So many things within Saul's thinking changed—and changed completely. He changed his mind about God, about Jesus, about the Resurrection, about those who followed Christ. He must have shaken his head for days. He thought Christ was dead. Now he was convinced Jesus was alive. This One who knew his name also knew what he'd been doing. The raging rebel had finally met his match and there was no place or way to hide.

As a kid I recall being afraid of the dark. Bedtime especially scared me. I'd grab the covers and pull 'em up over my head to hide from the "boogey man," lest he appear in my room and begin to look for me. Scary! Deep down I knew I couldn't hide from this frightening presence. If he was in that room, he'd find me for certain!

God's certainly no "boogey man," but the same is true of Him. We cannot hide from or escape His presence. Psalm 139:12 says, "The darkness and light are both alike to You." We can't hide from the all-knowing, all-seeing, all-encompassing God. Saul learned that great lesson in theology on the road to Damascus. His life was forever transformed when Jesus interrupted his plans. Mark it down—Saul, at this magnificent moment, was born anew.

Now let me pause to clarify something important. Some Christians try to impose their rigid system of dos and don'ts to the issue of conversion. I want to caution against that sort of exercise. It's impossible to find any single place in Scripture that reveals the one-and-only way every sinner comes to Christ. While the message of the Gospel is the same, methods differ. We are so conditioned by denominational backgrounds, religious traditionalism, and narrow-thinking prejudice, we miss the point of God's grace. We tend to require more than God does! Be careful about exacting requirements on someone who genuinely turns to the Savior.

Lost people are saved while listening to a great song about Christ or while hearing a preacher or Bible teacher explaining God's Word from a pulpit or over television or on the radio. Others are saved during a small group Bible study. Many come to Him all on their own, while praying in the privacy of their homes. Day or night a sinner can call on the Lord Jesus Christ in faith and be saved. Let's stop making it so complicated. As it happened with Saul, grace abounds.

Regardless of exactly *when* Saul was converted, he realized that the living Jesus, whom he had hated and denied his entire life, was now his Savior and Lord. It was in the dialog that followed where he also learned the Lord had been there all along.

KICKING AGAINST GOD'S GOADS

Acts 26 provides an intriguing reflection on Saul's blinding encounter with Christ. While standing before Agrippa, Paul recalled the words Jesus spoke: "Saul, Saul, why are persecuting Me? It is hard for you to kick against the goads" (Acts 26:14). That unusual word picture fascinates me. Let me explain the meaning.

Apparently, "to kick against the goads" was a common expression found in both Greek and Latin literature—a rural image, which rose from the practice of farmers goading their oxen in the fields. Though unfamiliar to us, everyone in that day understood.

Goads were typically made from slender pieces of timber, blunt on one end and pointed on the other. Farmers used the pointed end to urge a stubborn ox into motion. Occasionally, the beast would kick at the goad. The more the ox kicked, the more likely it would stab into the flesh of its leg, causing greater pain.

Saul's conversion could appear to us as having been a sudden encounter with Christ. But based on the Lord's expression regarding his kicking back, I believe He'd been working on him for years, prodding and goading him. Let me suggest several "goads" the Lord used to bring Saul to this place of repentance. Three come to mind.

The Goad of Jesus' Life and Words

I believe the words and works of Jesus haunted the zealous Pharisee. Quite likely, Saul had heard Jesus teach and preach in public places. Similar in age, they would be contemporaries in a city Saul knew well and Jesus frequently visited.

Imagine Saul (the name *Paul* means "small" suggesting he may have been shorter than average), standing on tiptoe, straining to watch Jesus, all the while grudgingly wondering how this false prophet could be gaining popularity. *Nonsense . . . has to be of Satan!* Pharisees loved to think that. Nevertheless, Jesus' ministry stuck in Saul's mind. The more it goaded him, the more he resisted God's proddings.

Once you've seriously encountered Jesus there's no escaping Him. His words and works follow you deep within your conscience. That's why I regularly encourage people who are intensifying their efforts to resist the Gospel's claims to study the life of Christ—to examine carefully His captivating words. Most who sincerely pursue them, can't leave Him without at least reevaluating their lives.

The Goad of Stephen's Peaceful Death

Saul probably never fully recovered from the mental image of Stephen's death. He may have kept one of the robes he held, now stained with the martyr's blood. It wasn't the fact that Stephen died that troubled Saul. It was the way he died that haunted him. No screaming. No pitiful pleading for mercy. No cursing. No recanting of his faith as he faced the threat of execution. Instead, his face shone like one "who had the face of an angel." And he prayed! With compassion for his executioners, he petitioned, "Don't hold this charge against them, Father. They don't know what they're doing."

I wonder if in some unguarded moment when Saul walked alone, or perhaps while on that arduous, long trek to Damascus, he relived in his mind how peacefully Stephen died. If so, it goaded him.

The Goad of Christians' Courageous Faith

Saul surely could not have escaped noticing the courage of his prisoners. The believers he illegally and viciously apprehended rarely resisted the torture. Though some shrank in their faith, the vast majority stood firm in allegiance to their Master, Christ. Their undaunted courage in the face of certain death must have goaded Saul. He simply could not put all this out of his mind.

GOD WINS IN THE END

God goaded and prodded the stubborn pride of that Pharisaic ox. Day after day he kicked against those goads, until finally he got the message. There would be no more running. No more hiding. The fight was over. As always, God won.

C. S. Lewis likened God's conquering work of Saul's rebel will to a divine chess player systematically, patiently maneuvering his opponent into a corner until finally he concedes. "Checkmate."

Like Saul, we're no match for God. Checkmate is inevitable. It's no game either. God will do whatever it takes to bring us to a point of absolute dependence on Him. He will relentlessly, patiently, faithfully goad until we finally and willingly submit to Him.

You're probably not a notorious criminal. I know that. More importantly, God knows that. Your life may be morally clean. Let's face it, you may qualify as the finest person on your block. You don't cheat on your taxes or deliberately lie to your partner. You may have never committed what we would call a scandalous act, to say nothing of seriously hurting someone you love. You're living a life that's impressive to others, but you are light years from being righteous before God. Until you've surrendered your life to Christ alone, by faith alone, you're as lost as Saul was on the Damascus road.

If you've never made that decision, what a great moment this would be if you'd set this book aside, bow your heart before the living Christ at this tender moment, and receive Him as your Savior.

You may have been a Christian for some time, but you're clinging to the reigns of your own rebel will. You need to know . . . God will goad you, too. Sooner or later He'll get your attention. No matter what it takes. He'll bring you to a place in your life where you realize there's no point in continuing to kick against the goads.

Don't wait for a storm. By then it may be too late. Settle it today on your knees. Give Him complete control. Stop your own Damascus Road journey today. Like Saul, surrender. And like Saul, you'll never regret it.

CHAPTER THREE

The Memorable Faith of a Forgotten Hero

Let's pretend it's 1940. You have moved to the outskirts of Vienna, Austria. The Nazis have occupied the beloved city you once called home. Now the entire country has fallen under Nazi occupation. You are Jewish. Most of your relatives have vanished—arrested secretly in the cover of darkness by armed soldiers. You've made the painful decision to gather your family and flee your comfortable home near the city of your birth and take refuge in a remote cottage far away in the mountains.

The night before the planned escape, you're awakened by a strange presence in your bedroom. Rubbing your eyes, you apprehensively sit up in bed and try to focus your thoughts. *Am I dreaming?* Fear grips you. Then, out of the darkness comes an unrecognizable voice saying, "Arise, go to a street named Wickenburg, just to the west of the campus of the University of Vienna. There you will find a home owned by Franz Kaiser. When you enter there, you'll find a man from Braunau, Upper Austria. His name is Adolf Hitler. I have appeared to him, and he is now praying. He is blind and I've revealed myself to him. Go and touch him, and he will regain his eyesight, and he will save your people."

You sit stunned, desperately trying to make sense of what you just heard. You can scarcely believe the command. Vienna is crawling with grim-faced Nazis carrying loaded weapons. Their orders are to seek out and capture Jews. Perhaps it's a set-up or a tasteless practical joke. No. The voice was real. The command clear.

Here's the question: Would you go? Would you believe that what you heard was true? Can you imagine yourself coming out of hiding and risking life and limb to find your way down a dark Vienna street and knock on the door of a home you've never visited? Don't answer that just yet.

ANANIAS: A REAL MAN WITH A SURPRISING COMMISSION

No more pretending. Instead, journey with me back through time to a *real* place in a *real* point in history. Damascus. Shortly after Stephen's death, during a period of intense persecution of Christians. Situated well over one hundred miles northeast of Jerusalem, the city, known for its fragrant gardens and fruited meadows, has been targeted by Saul and his fanatical band of extremists. There the Lord spoke to a disciple of the Way and commanded him to go to a house he had never visited, owned by a man named Judas he had never met. In that house, the Lord said he would find a man, blind and praying. Not just any man, however. Of all things, he would encounter Saul of Tarsus, the dreaded enemy of Christians. As the messenger touched him and talked with him, the blind Pharisee would regain his sight, recover from his condition, and ultimately become God's chosen vessel. How's that for a surprising commission?

Remarkably, that is precisely the order Ananias received from the Lord in a vision. It was one of those once-in-a-lifetime assignments. Watch how the scene unfolds:

> Now there was a certain disciple living in Damascus, named Ananias; and the Lord said to him in a vision, "Ananias." And he said, "Behold, here am I, Lord." And the Lord said to him, "Arise and go to the street called Straight, and inquire at the house of Judas for a man from Tarsus named Saul, for behold, he is praying, and he has seen in a

vision a man named Ananias come in and lay his hands on him, so
that he might regain his sight."

Acts 9:10–12

Ananias knew about Saul. Like a raging bull charging loose in the streets, Saul had been viciously pursuing Christians with a furious, Hitler-like determination. The safety Damascus once afforded Ananias and other followers of the Way had long since vanished in the intense heat of persecution. Now the unsuspecting Christian faced yet another unsettling change in his life as the result of a vision he received from the Lord.

Without some degree of imagination some stories of the Bible can become antiseptic, too remote. So let's allow the original scene to unfold with the help of some sanctified creativity. Imagine sitting in the very comfortable sanctuary where you and your family worship regularly. Suddenly, the cracking sound of a door flying open interrupts the stillness of the meeting. Armed men stream into the room carrying automatic weapons. The frowning leader barks, "Everybody! Up on your feet . . . now! Form a line in the rear of the building. Family by family, walk quickly outside into the parking lot for interrogation. Following that, you'll be ushered to vans waiting to take all of you downtown, where you will be forced either to deny your belief in Jesus or die for your faith." Try to imagine. Most Christians living in the Western world would never expect that to occur. Not in their lifetime. That happened regularly in Jerusalem, as well as in numerous villages outside its limits. And it was Saul who led the attacks, barking orders and breathing insulting threats.

We need to resist the temptation to come to a passage like this with a laid-back yawn, viewing it as simply a quaint story. On the contrary, nothing about this scene is anywhere near business as usual.

The Command

Though tradition identifies Ananias as possibly one of the bishops of Damascus, little is known of the man. He slips into the Saul narrative in the Book of Acts out of thin air. Besides his name, all the Bible tells us is that he was a disciple living in Damascus. No great religious figure here. No profound reputation preceding him into this moment in history. Nothing. What plucked this ordinary individual out of certain obscurity and into the immortal record of sacred Scripture was a vision. Not just your run-of-the-mill kind of vision. A vision with a surprising punch in the form of a divine command.

> "Ananias." And he said, "Behold, here am I, Lord." And the Lord said to him, "Arise and go to a street called Straight, and inquire at the house of Judas for a man from Tarsus named Saul, for behold, he is praying, and he has seen in a vision a man named Ananias come in and lay his hands on him, so that he might regain his sight."
>
> Acts 9:10–12

Eeeeeeeeeek! (Those are brakes screeching in Ananias' head.) SAUL! That would have sounded like the name HITLER to a Jew living outside Nazi-controlled Vienna. "You're kidding, right?" But having heard the authenticity of the voice and sensing the power of the Lord's presence, Ananias realized the strange command was no joke. He could not escape the Source of the message.

I don't believe God speaks to His children through visions today. He could, but I don't believe He does. However, back in the days before the Scriptures were completed, He certainly did. The writer of the Book of Hebrews wrote, "God, after He spoke long ago to the fathers in the prophets in many portions and in many ways, in these last days has spoken to us in His Son" (Hebrews 1:1–2). One of the *many ways* in which God revealed Himself in the Old Testament was through visions. He later appeared to individuals in visions during the New Testament era, even after the Incarnation. That's what happened in Ananias' case. Yet, even with that, the disciple was so bewildered that he attempted to dissuade the Lord.

The Argument

Stalling for time and trying to get matters clear in his head, Ananias respectfully pressed the issue: "Lord, I have heard from many about this man, how much harm he did to Thy saints in Jerusalem; and here he has authority from the chief priests to bind all who call upon Thy name" (Acts 9:13). (As if the Lord needed to be informed of Saul's reputation!)

We must understand Ananias' reluctance. He was a sincere disciple of Christ—born again and dedicated follower—a bona fide believer. Saul killed Christians. See the dilemma? Ananias had heard God's voice. The plan was troublesome. God had told him Saul was blind and praying somewhere in the city. "In that case, keep him blind," might have been Ananias first thought. At this point, understand, Ananias had no guarantee that Saul would be transformed (v. 12). From Ananias's chair, God's plan was filled with uncertainty and enormous risk.

Read how Eugene Peterson paraphrased the scene in *The Message:*

> Ananias protested, "Master, You can't be serious. Everybody's talking about this man and the terrible things he's been doing, his reign of terror against your people in Jerusalem! And now he's shown up here with papers from the Chief Priest that give him license to do the same to us." But the Master said, "Don't argue. Go!"[1]

The Command

I love God's response. "Go!" *He* never stutters when it comes to revealing His will. He knew exactly what was necessary. He knew that commissioning Saul required the obedience of Ananias. He also knew that it called for faith—an absolute trust in Him. Getting Ananias from Point A to Point B was the challenge. Heaven knows no reluctance. Reluctance to obey God's will is a purely human response.

Sensing Ananias's need for more information, God brought out from behind the counter a few more details about His plan. Speaking of Saul, He said, "He is a chosen instrument of Mine, to bear My name before the Gentiles and kings and the sons of Israel." Don't miss the word "chosen." Jesus chose Saul long before Saul chose Jesus. "You did not choose Me," said the Master to his twelve disciples, "but I have chosen you, and I have set you apart" (John 15:16). Ananias needed to know that God had chosen Saul as His "instrument." In what seems to us a mystery, God's sovereign plan called for the presence of Ananias in the divine equation. To put it straight, He chose to use Ananias in the initial stage of transforming a raging bull named Saul into a bleating lamb named Paul.

FROM RAGING BULL TO BLEATING LAMB

If you haven't yet done so, stand for a few moments in Ananias's sandals. Understand how difficult it would have been to see how God's plan could possibly work. How in the world could God take a man known for such vicious, merciless, and murderous treatment of innocent Christians and turn him into an ambassador for Christ? Perhaps Ananias failed to hear the answer in the Lord's Word to him: "But the Lord said to him, 'Go, for he is a chosen instrument of Mine, to bear My name before the Gentiles and kings and the sons of Israel; for I will show him how much he must suffer for My name's sake'" (Acts 9: 15–16).

God's answer to Ananias's question is clear: "I will show him how much he must suffer for My name's sake."

Suffering. Down through the centuries it has been God's taming ground for raging bulls. The crucible of pain and hardship is God's schoolroom where Christians learn humility, compassion, character, patience, and grace. It's true for you and for me . . . it would soon be true for Saul.

Years later, with scars to prove it and under the pile of heavy ministry responsibilities, he gave testimony that suffering had been his companion. If any should entertain doubts that God uses affliction to humble the proud, a review of these words is sufficient to erase them:

> Are they servants of Christ? (I speak as if insane) I more so; in far more labors, in far more imprisonments, beaten times without number, often in danger of death. Five times I received from the Jews thirty-nine lashes. Three times I was beaten with rods, once I was stoned, three times shipwrecked, a night and a day I have spent in the deep. I have been on frequent journeys, in dangers from rivers, dangers from robbers, dangers from countrymen, dangers from the Gentiles, dangers in the city, dangers in the wilderness, dangers on the sea, dangers among false brethren; I have been in labor and hard-

ship, through many sleepless nights, in hunger and thirst, often without food, in cold and exposure. Apart from such external things, there is the daily pressure upon me of concern for all the churches.

2 Corinthians 11:23–28

If Bible colleges and seminaries used those verses for their programs to recruit ministry candidates, enrollments would soon be in decline!

Incidentally, it was my privilege to be appointed the fourth president of Dallas Theological Seminary, where I served from 1994 to 2001. Though I faced many of the toughest challenges of my career while in that position, the years I spent at the seminary were some of the most rewarding of my life, mostly because of the students.

Men and women came to the campus of that great school from all corners of the globe—most entering their training convinced of God's call on their lives. I watched them change. I watched as brilliant Asian and African seminarians, endured the humbling, often humiliating, experience of fulfilling rigorous academic requirements, while struggling to think, speak, and write in English. It changed them. I witnessed others—many gifted engineers, skilled musicians, and talented college athletes—brought to their knees by the exhausting, relentless demands they faced while mastering biblical Hebrew and Greek. That too changed them.

The curriculum included physical adversity and emotional suffering for others. One young man in particular, early in his master's degree program, and ecstatic at the birth of his first child, stood stunned in disbelief as he heard his wife's diagnosis: *Leukemia*. Two years later, following a failed bone marrow transplant, after months of excruciating radiation and expensive chemotherapy, which ravaged her already frail frame, that beautiful young wife and mother slipped away. Gone forever from his side. A toddling child and a broken-hearted husband remained to pick up the shattered pieces of their lives. That young man may have entered seminary a raging bull—full of dreams, ambition, and confidence in his abilities—but he walked out a bleating lamb, convinced more than ever of his need for grace. Suffering changed him. It has changed me. It changes everyone.

I don't understand all the reasons we suffer for the Name. But I'm convinced of this: It is part of God's sovereign plan to prepare us to be His instruments of grace to a harsh and desperate world. Clearly, that was God's plan for Saul. On his body would be the enduring stripes of his suffering—imprisonment, severe beatings, stonings, shipwreck, near-drowning, ambushes, robberies, insomnia, starvation, loneliness, disease, dehydration, extreme hypothermia . . . and beyond all that, the stressful, inescapable responsibilities of church leadership. Each painful, awful ordeal brought him to his knees, turning him into a deeper man of grace, humbly committed to following his Savior's lead.

Ananias needed to know that part of God's plan. It not only gave the message authenticity, it steeled him to take a memorable step of heroic faith.

PORTRAIT OF A FORGOTTEN HERO

Luke wastes no words in describing what happened next. He writes, "So Ananias departed" (v. 17). Somewhere between fearful confusion and quiet resolve, Ananias's reluctance dissolved. He stepped out of his home into the cool night air and walked to Straight Street, one of the few straight avenues among the winding corridors of Damascus. He rapped feebly on the door of the home. "Perhaps no one's home." He knocked again, more vigorously. Judas unlocked the large wooden door, peered at the stranger and nodded. Ananias stepped into the home as Judas whispered, "We've been expecting you." Ananias swallowed hard. He blinked several times as his eyes adjusted to the dimly lit surroundings. He traced the dancing shadows caused by the flickering lamps in the hall, stooping once to clear a low-hanging archway in the hall. Glancing to the far corner of the room, he fixed his gaze on a frail figure of a man, bent low on his knees, praying. It was his first-ever glimpse of Saul of Tarsus. He walked over to him in halting steps. As he laid his trembling hands on him he said, "B-B-B-B-B-Brother S-S-S-S-Saul." (That's how the *Swindoll Revised Standard Paraphrase* reads!) Don't you love the way he started? "Brother Saul, the Lord Jesus, who appeared to you on the road by which you were coming, has sent me so that you may regain your sight, and be filled with the Holy Spirit."

What a moment of courageous faith for Ananias. He not only touched the notorious killer of Christians, he immediately accepted him, calling him his brother. That's what I call trusting God's plan! This was Saul's initial touch of grace from a fellow believer. John Stott in his book *The Spirit, the Church and the World* summarizes the tender scene:

> So Ananias went to *Straight Street*, which is still Damascus's main east-west thoroughfare, and to the house of Judas, indeed to the very room where Saul was. There he placed his hands on him, perhaps to identify with him as he prayed for the healing of his blindness and for the fullness of the Spirit to empower him for his ministry. Even more, I suspect that this laying-on of hands was a gesture of love to a blind man, who could not see the smile on Ananias's face, but could feel the pressure of his hands. At the same time, Ananias addressed him as "Brother Saul" or "Saul, my brother." I never fail to be moved by these words. They may well have been the first words which Saul heard from Christian lips after his conversion, and they were words of fraternal welcome.[2]

Ananias has been called one of the forgotten heroes of the faith. Indeed he is. There are countless numbers of them serving Christ behind the scenes the world over. Most we will never meet, we'll never know by name. They are content to remain in the shadows, oblivious to the lure of lights and applause. Nevertheless, they are heroes—giants of the faith because of their selfless, understated acts of obedience to God. Faithfully carrying on. Faithfully administering. Faithfully delivering sermons. Faithfully showing mercy to the sick in the hospitals. Faithfully counseling and giving hope to the discouraged.

A rare few in God's family enjoy fame and renown, position and influence. The great majority, however, are the Ananiases of the world—the errand runners, if you will, doing precisely what God has asked them to do in precisely the place He's called them to go. They keep the Body functioning in good health. None will ever know, until eternity dawns, the enormity of their investment in the cause of Christ.

When he finally got the picture, Ananias must have been thrilled to deliver the message God had placed in his care: "Brother Saul, the Lord

Jesus, who appeared to you on the road by which you were coming, has sent me so that you may regain your sight, and be filled with the Holy Spirit." What a moment—the single instrument of healing and encouragement for the apostle of grace to the world. All because he ignored his fears and stepped out in faith, in full obedience to God's surprising command.

Now, with your imagination still in gear, let your mind portray what happened next.

"And immediately there fell from his eyes something like scales, and he regained his sight, and he arose and was baptized. And he took food and was strengthened" (v. 18). The change was instantaneous. He regained his sight. When God performs a miracle there are two undeniable effects. It is *immediate*. And it is *permanent*.

Once Saul regained his sight, it was probably Ananias who baptized him. Would that have been a great scene to witness, or what? Standing waist-deep in a nearby river he could have said, "I now baptize you, my brother, in the name of the Father, and the Son, and the Holy Spirit. You have been buried with Christ in baptism, rise to walk in newness of life." What an unforgettable moment as the two men embraced, weeping with great joy.

But Saul's healing and baptism were only the beginning of God's plan. Luke writes, "Now for several days he was with the disciples who were in Damascus. And immediately he began to proclaim Jesus in the synagogues, saying, 'He is the Son of God.'" Like a racehorse, Saul broke out of the gate and boldly proclaimed Christ as Lord in the synagogues. The response was electrifying: "And all those hearing continued to be amazed, and were saying, "Is this not he who in Jerusalem destroyed those who called on this name, and who had come here for the purpose of bringing them bound before the chief priests?'" (Acts 9:21).

The transformation is stunning. Saul, no doubt with blood stains still on his garment from Christians he had tortured, now stood with arms outstretched announcing, "I'm here to testify to you that Jesus is the Messiah, God's Son." And the people who heard it were amazed. The Greek text uses the term from which we get the word "ecstatic." They responded with nothing short of ecstatic astonishment at the swift reversal in the man's life.

Imagine sitting in the synagogue. In front of you, preaching Jesus as the

Messiah, is the very man responsible for condemning innocent Christians to death. Others he had taken into prisons, perhaps, some of them relatives and friends. The room was full of jaw-dropped stares. The next statement assures us he didn't slow down: "But Saul kept increasing in strength and confounding the Jews who lived at Damascus by proving that this Jesus is the Christ" (Acts 9:22).

It gets better. Not only did Saul preach about Christ, he preached with remarkable skill. The word translated "proving" comes from a Greek verb, which means, "to knit together from several different strands." Saul's sermons were skillfully woven together, seamlessly delivered with compelling logic—all signs of a gifted expositor.

Word by word, sentence by sentence, point by point, Saul walked his listeners through the powerful passages of the Old Testament Scriptures, including the writings of the prophets, presenting an air-tight case for believing in Christ as their promised Messiah. Until Saul made his case, most had never made that connection. What a convincing communicator!

Before we go on, let's pause and remind ourselves, none of these remarkable events could have been witnessed, or even recorded for that matter, had it not been for Ananias's courageous faith. You may have never thought of that until now. Saul would have remained blind and trembling had the disciple of Damascus refused to obey and go to Straight Street. All this was set in motion because God used the memorable faith of a little-known but faithful hero. His obedience changed the destiny of millions.

SOME SURPRISING ELEMENTS OF GOD'S WILL

Let me tie these observations together by pointing out some of the inevitable elements of God's leading. I'll mention only four.

Surprises are always part of God's leading. In Saul's case the surprise came in the form of a light from heaven, marking a life-changing transformation. For Ananias, it was a seemingly unreasonable and illogical command from the Lord, delivered in a vision.

There is a statement in Hebrews chapter eleven that seldom fails to make me shake my head. "By faith Abraham, when he was called, obeyed by going out to a place which he was to receive for an inheritance; and he went out, *not knowing where he was going"* (v. 8, emphasis added). All Abraham knew was that God wanted him to move. He didn't have a clue about the final destination. Nothing about the weather or the crime rate in the area. No information about the neighborhood he'd live in or the problems he would have to face. Nothing. He knew only that God had told him to go. The details would follow. Plain and simple, he went, just like Ananias.

If you're waiting on God to fill in all the shading in your picture, you will never take the first step in obeying His will. You must be prepared to trust His plan, knowing it will be full of surprises. Surprises are always a part of God's leading.

Surprises always intensify our need for faith. When you encounter the surprising element of God's will, your faith must engage full throttle. Otherwise, you'll turn and run the opposite direction. At times God's plan will frighten you. Or you'll be intimidated by its demands. Other times you'll be disappointed. For instance, when God tells you no, to wait, or to sit tight, you'll want to argue. You may decide to fight. You might attempt to negotiate. You may become angry. But when your faith kicks in gear, none of those impulses will control you. Faith says, "I can do this. I trust you, Lord. I don't understand everything, but I trust you completely. Let's do it."

Let me make an observation you may need to consider. Quite possibly God has a major move in store for you in the near future. After well over sixty years on this earth, and having spent forty of those years studying and learning more about the ways of God, I can tell you His will for our lives is full of surprises. He has more moves in mind for us than we could possibly anticipate. And they're not all geographical.

Many are attitude adjustments. Some mean moving us out of our comfort zones to touch the lives of people we've never met. Or we might be in for a cross-country or cross-cultural journey that requires a level of faith we've not exercised in the past. Be careful about feeling too settled where you are—physically, emotionally, spiritually, *or* geographically. If the Lord wants you to move, I strongly suggest you cooperate, regardless of the risks. If He leads you to change, then change. Surprises from God always intensify our need for faith.

Stepping out in faith always brings clarification of God's plan. When Ananias went, he received additional information. As Saul submitted himself to the ministry of Ananias, he found out more about God's plan for his life. "You're a chosen vessel of Mine. I'm going to use you to bear My name." Saul hadn't known that before. (He had never read the Book of Acts!) He knew nothing of what was in store for him until Ananias took that initial step of faith. Both men discovered that God Himself chose Saul to be His instrument and that intense suffering would mark his ministry. That's the way God operates.

When Cynthia and I first sensed God's directing us to leave California and relocate our ministry, we could hardly believe it. We had planned on staying in the same place for the rest of our lives—serving Christ at the First Evangelical Free Church in Fullerton and continuing to lead the ministry of Insight for Living. Space nor time allow me to describe the things God has shown us since we made the decision to move. Initially, very few people could grasp God's plan for us. It came as a surprise to everyone. In fact, some firmly rejected it. But now as God continues to put the finishing touches on His magnificent portrait, what we see is absolutely beautiful. Until we took that initial step of obedience, all we had was, "It's time to go." It's amazing to me even as I write these words! Surprises always bring about clarification of God's plan.

Obedience always stimulates growth. By the way, the Swindolls have grown deeper in our relationship with the Lord, having trusted Him without first knowing all the details. Obeying God drives the roots of your faith much deeper. And that obedience stimulates growth in every area of life. We're stretched emotionally, often physically, but most importantly, spiritually.

Ananias's compliance with God's surprising plan allowed him to witness supernatural power. No one else in Scripture witnessed the scales miraculously falling from the contrite Pharisees' eyes. Only Ananias. As a result, his own eyes were opened to the amazing power of God to transform a life. Obedience always stimulates growth.

LET'S GET REAL

We started by pretending we were in Nazi-controlled Europe. Now let's get real. This is about life today. It's not about Austria or Damascus. This is about here. This is about now. This is about you. Could it be that something in your life has blinded you to God's power? Perhaps fear of the unknown or the uncertainty of the future hinders you from obeying God's clear leading. Don't allow the day to end without deciding to trust Him, no matter how surprising His plan.

Only eternity will reveal the impact of your memorable step of faith. Go ahead, take that step. The world needs more heroes.

CHAPTER FOUR

The Necessity of Solitude, Quietness, and Obscurity

In his splendid book *Celebration of Discipline,* Richard Foster writes words that penetrate: "Superficiality is the curse of our age. The doctrine of instant satisfaction is a primary spiritual problem. The desperate need today is not for a greater number of intelligent people, or gifted people, but for deep people."[1]

The deeper life is a subject greatly admired but rarely experienced. In fact, it is seldom discussed, even though all of us would consider it of highest importance. We sing of its virtues, but we don't embrace them. We long for its quenching water, but rarely dip into its well. We love the benefits it affords, but our frenzied lifestyles crowd out their significance. Unless we're compelled by the Lord Himself to accept the ingredients of the hidden life, either through a lengthy period of illness or some cataclysmic event, depth of character remains a distant dream.

A life marked by depth can only be cultivated in protracted periods of time spent in solitude, quietness, and obscurity—concepts foreign to those who live their lives at the speed of light. The mere fact that you've picked up this book shows that you, along with other well-intended believers, desire to go deeper in your relationship to Christ. Yet, a major obstacle that prevents us from getting there is our lifestyle. We're simply too busy.

I'm not talking about a sabbatical every six or seven years. I'm not even talking about disengaging from normal activities for months at a time. That's not only impractical, it's impossible for folks who have to earn a living. What I have in mind is brief periods of time when we deliberately slow down and meet, alone, with our God.

Stop and think for a moment. When was the last time you carved out time to be absolutely alone with God? You made arrangements for it. You set aside responsibilities and said no to things that would have filled your schedule, robbing you of any remaining time for quietness before the Lord. Can you remember? If you're like most, you'll have difficulty stating the last time you did that. Quite possibly, you've never considered taking time away to rearrange your private world, rethink your priorities, and simplify your life.

It's time for an honest confession. Cynthia and I did our own evaluating recently and discovered it had been years since we had done what I'm recommending to you. Neither one of us could recall the last time we took a weekend off, all by ourselves, let alone an extended spiritual retreat (when I wasn't the speaker). Most of our time spent traveling as a couple has been connected to our ministry responsibilities. So, lest you think I'm some sort of super-spiritual saint, let me assure you, the message is as much for me as it is for you.

BIBLICAL RETREATS AT A GLANCE

A survey of the Scriptures reveals that those God used greatly were often prepared for those exploits during periods of solitude, quietness, and obscurity. Let's sample only a few.

Moses. Having grown up in the prestigious environment of Pharaoh's lavish courts, Moses had positioned himself to embrace a remarkable political future. After murdering an Egyptian citizen, however, Moses fled to the plains of Midian, where he married the daughter of a local priest. He spent the next forty years tending his father-in-law's sheep. It wasn't until he was eighty years old that God finally plucked the once-Egyptian prince-turned-shepherd, out of obscurity and into the annals of greatness. You read correctly: *He was eighty!*

David. Anointed king over Israel as a teen, he didn't assume the throne until age thirty. After his heroic victory over Goliath, he spent the next thirteen years as a fugitive, hiding out in the caves of Engedi from King Saul, who had grown nearly insane with jealously. A few of David's beloved psalms were born out of this crucible of solitude, but mostly he lived in obscurity, surviving in the Judean wilderness, one of the most rugged, harsh territories of the world.

Joseph. Thrown in jail because of the deceitful rant of Potiphar's seductive wife, whose wild advances he had repeatedly scorned, the man must have felt abused and abandoned. He spent two years in the prisons of Egypt, wondering if he'd ever see the light of day again. Though his sentence was unfair, Joseph learned much in that cell of confinement.

Elijah. Standing toe-to-toe with Ahab the king, he boldly delivered his oracle of judgment. No rain or dew would fall on the kingdom for as long as it would take for them to repent. To protect His faithful prophet from the expected backlash, the Lord hid Elijah by a brook called Cherith. He remained camped there east of the Jordan River in the company of only ravens, which God used to deliver food to the weary prophet. To Elijah's dismay, the fresh-water brook dried up, much like his own spiritual and emotional vitality. But God had custom-designed this brookside retreat as a place of renewal for the weary prophet.

John the Baptist. The locust-eating prophet in the New Testament spent most of his adult life preaching to stones in the desert. I mean, what kind of assignment was that? No distinction, no prominent place of ministry, no compelling message that appealed to the masses. Only years of solitude, silence, and obscurity, which ended when he was beheaded at the request of a silly dancing girl. Yet, God called him to the desert. He had His reasons and John submitted to the plan.

I'm convinced those sustained periods of preparation fueled the future effectiveness of each choice servant. They learned the value of growing deep, of spurning the shallow life so they could minister out of the overflow of the inner life. That is precisely why superficiality is the curse of our age. Our shallow lives offer no promise for lasting impact.

Why didn't David assume the throne of Israel at age seventeen? Wasn't he more qualified than bumbling, self-willed Saul? Actually, he wasn't. The Lord knew that only a man seasoned by years of life's lessons and protracted times of solitude and obscurity was fit to be the next king.

God could have allowed Elijah to face Jezebel one on one. But he wasn't ready. Later God used him mightily, primarily because of time spent at Cherith. He had grown deeper, wiser, and more dependent on God's provision.

Our problem is that we are blinded in our perspective. We see ourselves as resourceful, talented, articulate, responsible, efficient. So why pause? Why take a break? We have important matters to attend to, meetings to hold, numbers to crunch, programs to launch, and children to rear and on and on and on it goes. It's downright remarkable what we are able to accomplish drawing from our own well of human ingenuity.

Everything's fine . . . until the well runs dry. At that point, we start to "gut it out." We continue to run on empty until finally our lives fracture deep within. At that point we begin to sputter, clog and chunk, and finally grind to a complete stop. That's when the truth comes out: Ministries fold, marriages crumble, children wander from the Lord unattended, and our character weakens to the point of blowout. Those painful experiences demonstrate that the dangers are real. We're not nearly as resourceful as we think. The recently converted Saul learned that crucial lesson in the silence and obscurity of his desert sabbatical.

SAUL'S DESERT RETREAT

Roy Jenkins, in his book on Winston Churchill titled *Churchill: A Biography*, quotes Lady Lytton as she described her experience in meeting the great British leader: "The first time you meet Winston, you see all his faults, and the rest of your life you spend in discovering his virtues."[2]

That is equally true of Saul of Tarsus. We first meet him as a raging bull, standing proudly, fighting battles, and persecuting followers of Christ in the name of God. On his Hitlerian march out to Damascus, God interrupted his journey by striking him blind. For the first time in his adult life he was knocked flat. For the first time, he found himself dependent. He had to be led into Damascus. While there, in the home of Judas, he encountered Ananias, a messenger sent from God.

In less than a week, God transformed Saul from a vicious, Christian-hating murderer into a passionate preacher. Not until then do we begin to see the Christ-born virtues that made this man truly great. But God had only begun. His ongoing process of preparing Saul was time away, all alone, to think through the implications of his newfound faith, to begin to know his Savior much more intimately, to come to terms with what it meant to be a messenger of grace.

In Galatians chapter one, Paul writes of that experience in solitude. Let's look at the extended passage and use it as a backdrop for where we go from here.

> For am I now seeking the favor of men, or of God? Or am I striving to please men? If I were *still* trying to please men, I would not be a bond-servant of Christ.
>
> For I would have you know, brethren, that the gospel which was preached by me is not according to man. For I neither received it from man, nor was I taught it, but I received it through a revelation of Jesus Christ. For you have heard of my former manner of life in Judaism, how I used to persecute the church of God beyond measure, and tried to destroy it; and I was advancing in Judaism beyond many contemporaries among my countrymen, being more zealous for ancestral traditions. But when He who had set me apart, even from my mother's womb, and called me through His grace, was pleased to reveal His Son in me, that I might preach Him among the Gentiles, I did not immediately consult with flesh and blood, nor did I go up to Jerusalem to those who were apostles before me; *but I went away to Arabia*, and returned once more to Damascus.
>
> Galatians 1: 10–17 (Italics mine)

Notice the phrase "still trying to please men" in verse 10. Saul of Tarsus lived with the ever-imposing drive to please people. A large part of what motivated him was the affirming nod of the Sanhedrin. They were impressed with his fierce efforts to eradicate the region of infidels. He lived for their approval. Their smiles and affirming gestures fed his pride. The Damascus road experience began a process that would change all of that.

The ladder of religious success is his to climb. Don't get in his way! He's going. He's moving up. He's fighting. He's assertive. He's striving. He's determined. He's intense. He's passionate. Saul marches straight ahead with his impressive resumé firmly clutched between his fingers. If you had been a member of the Sanhedrin looking for a blue-chip leader to head the assault on Christians, Saul's name would have quickly come to mind. He's your man. He confessed, "That's what I was doing, day after day, month after month. I was pursuing these members of the Jesus sect to get rid of them."

During Saul's furious climb up the religious ladder, God stopped Saul, brought him to his knees, made him new, set him apart, and (of all things!) called him to preach the very Gospel he had tried to silence. Saul's emphasis changes from what *he* had been doing to what *God* had done.

> But when He who had *set me apart*, even from my mother's womb, and *called me* through His grace, was pleased to reveal His Son in me, that I might preach Him among the Gentiles, I did not immediately consult with flesh and blood, nor did I go up to Jerusalem to those who were apostles before me; but I went away to Arabia, and returned once more to Damascus.
>
> Galatians 1: 15–17

I find it fascinating that Paul deliberately mentions two things he did *not* do. First, he didn't immediately consult with flesh and blood, that is other people. He didn't go searching around Damascus, seeking others to shape his theology by consensus.

Second, he didn't rush to Jerusalem to present himself to the apostles— the very men who had walked with and served alongside Jesus. But Paul had his reasons for emphasizing this point as commentator Leon Morris explains:

> This emphatic disclaimer of any contact with earlier believers and their leaders makes it clear that Paul did not derive his understanding

of the Christian message from any who were Christians before him. Specifically, he did not learn from, nor was he commissioned by, those who had been apostles before him. It could not be said that he had had instruction and had misunderstood what earlier teachers were trying to convey to him. It is of primary importance for Paul that he had been directly commissioned by Jesus.[3]

If he didn't consult with other Christians or their leaders in Jerusalem, where did he gain all his insight into the nature of God's call, the reality of the Gospel, and his direct commission from Christ? I'm convinced he received all that and much more during his period of solitude, silence, and obscurity when he "went away" to a place he calls Arabia.

The Place of Arabia

Though we are hard-pressed to identify the precise location of Saul's Arabian retreat, he most likely went to a vast expanse of desert. It stretches from as far south as Sinai near Egypt all the way north to the lower boundaries of Syria. It may not have been that far from Damascus. Since the northernmost part of Arabia is only a hundred miles from Damascus, Saul may have gone just over the border.

But, make no mistake, it was a barren wilderness. For the most part, it was deserted, except for a few Bedouins. Perhaps Paul lived among these desert dwellers—people whose lifestyle would have been welcome contrast to the frantic pace of his former Pharisaic lifestyle.

But that's the *where* of Arabia. Far more important is the *why* of Arabia.

The Purpose of Arabia

Whenever the Bible remains silent on a subject, scholars and theologians love to fill in the holes with theories. Since Paul doesn't describe any details explaining the reason for his exodus to Arabia, various suggestions abound.

Early church fathers believed Saul traveled there as a missionary, bringing the Gospel to a savage group of desert dwellers. That's an interesting idea. The problem is, flipping through the Scriptures, I don't see any mention of savages.

One scholar proposes that Saul fled to Arabia to protect himself from the

Jewish leaders who, having heard of his newfound faith, wanted to nip it in the bud. That too is a compelling thought, but one Paul never mentioned.

Someone else suggested that he needed the same amount of time (three years) that the disciples enjoyed while traveling with and learning from the Lord Jesus. Now, that's better yet! Makes sense, doesn't it? Same problem, however: I can't find it anywhere in the Scriptures. Truth is, we don't know. The only thing Paul reveals is, "three years later I went up to Jerusalem to become acquainted with Cephas, and stayed with him fifteen days" (v. 18).

For three years, Saul lived somewhere in the desert, cut-off from his former manner of life—in solitude, quietness, and obscurity.

Do the math and you come up with well over one thousand days unaccounted for in Saul's life. A thousand plus days he most likely spent alone. All alone. Thinking. Praying. Wrestling within. Listening to the Lord. If he had ever been addicted to popularity, he lost the urge to pursue it during those years in the desert. If at one time he had become enamored with his own spiritual significance, that self-inflated pride melted away in the warmth of God's presence.

I'm convinced it was there, in that barren place of obscurity, that Paul developed his theology. He met God, intimately and deeply. Silently and alone, he plumbed the unfathomable mysteries of sovereignty, election, depravity, the deity of Christ, the miraculous power of the Resurrection, the Church, and future things. It became a three-year crash course in sound doctrine from which would flow a lifetime of preaching, teaching, and writing. More than that, it's where Paul tossed aside his polished trophies and traded his resumé of religious credentials for a vibrant relationship with the risen Christ. Everything changed.

It was there, no doubt, he concluded "whatever things were gain to me, I counted as loss for the sake of Christ. More than that, I count all things to be loss in view of the surpassing value of knowing Christ Jesus my Lord, for whom I have suffered the loss of all things, and count them but rubbish in order that I may gain Christ" (Philippians 3: 7–8).

He had been so busy, active, engaged, advancing, and zealous. The same words describe many Christians sitting in churches today. And therein lies our problem. We're not busy doing all the wrong things or even a few terrible things. We're certainly not persecutors or destroyers. But if the truth were known, we'll go for miles on fumes, all the while choking the life-giving spirit within.

Not long ago academy-award-winning actor, Tom Hanks, starred in *Castaway*. It was one of those films with few words but an enormous amount of emotion. He plays the part of an executive with FedEx, whose fast-paced work took him on flights all over the world. While flying aboard a freight-heavy 747, he experiences the worst of his fears. The plane crashes in the Pacific Ocean not far from a tiny, uninhabited island. He is the lone survivor, and he washes ashore, bruised and shaken, but thankfully, alive. He will live—totally alone—on that remote piece of land *for four years.* The changes that occur within him are slow, but ultimately, extensive. He goes through great bouts within himself, struggles too deep for words, and finally learns to live on the bare essentials of island existence. Back home in the States, there's a burial in his honor and life speeds on without him.

How he escapes is fascinating, but the good news is he is picked up by a ship and is, at last, returned safely to the now-unfamiliar world of life as it used to be. And he doesn't fit in at all. The changes that transpired within him are so radical, so all-consuming, he finds himself a different man—much deeper, much more observing, much less demanding—all because of the lessons learned in solitude, quietness, and obscurity.

And so it was with Saul. He changed. How greatly he changed!

HIDDEN LIFE REVISITED

Let's revisit the necessity of cultivating the hidden life—of putting into place those disciplines of solitude, silence, and obscurity, which became for Saul the key to his monumental effectiveness. Several notable scholars speak to that point.

> In Arabia, he was alone with God, thinking through the implications of his encounter with the risen Christ on the Damascus Road.[4]
> —Charles Ryrie

The replacement of his Jewish world and life view by a Christian theology would have been the work of more than a long weekend. Paul went into Arabia to think and study rather than to preach.[5]

—James Montgomery Boice

He went into Arabia for quiet and solitude. He seems to have stayed there for three years. In this period of withdrawal, as he meditated on the Old Testament Scriptures, on the facts of the life and the death of Jesus that he already knew and on his experience of conversion, the gospel of the grace of God was revealed to him in its fullness. Now he had Jesus to himself, as it were, for three years of solitude in the wilderness.[6]

—John R. W. Stott

Month after month he wandered to and fro, sharing the rough fare of some Essene community, or the lot of a family of Bedouins; now swept upwards in heavenly fellowship, and again plunged into profound meditation. Deeper than all was God's work in his soul. Grain by grain his profound self-reliance and impetuosity were worn away. No longer confident in himself, he was henceforth more than content to be the slave of Jesus Christ. We all need to go to Arabia to learn lessons like these.[7]

—F. B. Meyer

Let's not take that last statement literally. God doesn't always require geographical isolation to teach us the lessons learned through solitude. So don't feel obligated to book a flight to Arabia just yet. I believe we can grow deep during protracted times we deliberately set aside for quietness, soul searching, confession, and meditation. Personally, I long for more of that in my own life. Such times are essential for our spiritual depth and emotional survival.

During one of my trips to Israel, our tour guide drove us from that ancient oasis town of Jericho, via the winding road leading up to Jerusalem. The road is treacherous and narrow, and most of us held our breath as the driver skillfully maneuvered the large air conditioned coach through an endless series of spine-tingling turns. All that lay between us and a one-thousand-foot drop-off was a narrow, gravel shoulder. At a certain point on the road, the driver stopped and allowed us to get off the bus. The guide directed our attention to a magnificent monastery, literally carved into the side of the rock, across the gaping valley now beneath us. From where we stood, the place looked miniature, and the people moving about its grounds looked less than an inch tall. I overheard several folks in our group wondering to themselves how anyone could maintain that lifestyle without going crazy. It occurred to me, the monks who lived in that breathtaking place were probably looking back across the rocky expanse wondering the same thing about us!

Saul was there, not with others on a brief tour, but in remote, obscure places . . . for three years. Try to imagine! In that interlude, while his public ministry was put on hold, he gained the immeasurable benefits of what Raymond Edman calls "the discipline of delay."

> Paul came to know the patience of hindered purpose. Stopped at the gate of Damascus, penitent in the street called Straight, seeing under the touch of Ananias and filled with the Spirit he was a chosen vessel to bear the gospel to great and small . . . Then came the discipline of delay in the desert of Arabia, where he learned by revelation of God, not by precept of man, the glorious gospel of the grace of God. From Arabia he could go to Antioch and its world-wide missionary program, to Athens and its proud Areopagus, to Achaia and its wicked Corinth, to the arena of Ephesus, and if necessary, Rome. The delay that instructs and prepares saves time, never loses it. From it one can walk with a step of assurance and a heart of flame.[8]

In that period of delay he learned about the *real* Saul—the Saul God had uniquely called and chosen for a ministry of grace to the world. It was also there he saw the darker side of himself—the ugliness of his depravity. But against that bleak backdrop shined the greatness of God's mercy and love. Arabia became a temple where he worshiped the Lord in a way he had never experienced in his life. Solitude helped. The scales of spiritual blindness fell from his heart as he gained a fresh glimpse into the marvelous mystery of God's plan. As the desert winds howled across rocky gorges, God revealed Himself to His servant. As the stars lit the sky, like silver-headed nails across the heavens, Saul became enraptured by the glory of his Master.

Now stop and think about this for a moment. Chances are good your life has grown more complicated than it was ten years ago, or for that matter, even five years ago. Over time you've collected more and more stuff, engaged in more and more activities, taken on more and more debt, accepted more and more responsibilities. Now your well is dry. Bone dry. You're not necessarily unhappy, but you're empty! The deeper life has eluded you. Like an illness that threatens your physical life if ignored, living life on empty eventually siphons your spiritual vitality. If we hope to grow deeper, we must find a solution to this maddening pace. The tyranny of the urgent cannot continue.

PRESCRIPTION FOR GROWING DEEP

I believe part of the solution is to pursue the benefits of solitude and silence found in times of obscurity. For the first time in seven years, I took six weeks off this past summer. No preaching, no writing, no counseling, no speaking engagements . . . no nothing. I focused on slowing down and refilling my soul with the deep things of the Lord. I prayed, I sang, I studied, I walked, I fished, I stayed quiet, and I sat thinking about and reevaluating my life. It was magnificent.

You may not have that much time available. You may have only three days, or perhaps two weeks. If you're not careful, you'll quickly fill those days with things to do, places to go, and people to see. Resist that temptation to crowd out the Lord. What a perfect opportunity to carve out time to be alone, just you, the family, and the Lord. Computer off. Fax unplugged. Cell phone tossed in the ocean.

So your voicemail fills up. You know what? People will survive. Believe this: They don't need you or me to make it through their day. They don't need you nearly as much as you need the relief. You say, "That's pretty radical stuff." Radical? Perhaps. Unreasonable? Absolutely not. Radical change is essential if we're going to become deeper, more effective servants. Let me get even more specific. I'd like to suggest three strategies that will help you make some of those radical, but essential adjustments.

First, instead of speeding up, slow down and rethink. I don't want you to miss any of these words. I've thought about them for years. Instead of speeding up, let's find ways to slow down and rethink. Taking time to discover what really matters is essential if we're going to lift the curse of superficiality that shadows our lives. Don't wait for the doctor to tell you that you have six months to live. Long before anything that tragic becomes a reality, you should be growing roots deep into the soil of those things that truly matter.

Once Saul left Damascus and slipped into Arabia, he began taking inventory. There was no "To Do Before Sundown" lists. No "Six Fast Steps to Success" or other self-help scrolls clumped under his arms. He was alone. He walked slower. He watched sand swirl over the stones. He thought deeply about his past. He relived what he had done. He returned to what he had experienced on the road to Damascus. He considered each new dawn a gift from the Lord, the perfect opportunity to rework his priorities and rethink his motives. It takes time, of course . . . lots of time. But time spent in solitude prepares us for the inevitable challenges that come at us from the splintered age in which we live.

Second, instead of talking more, be quiet and reflect. Words, words, words, words, words. They're everywhere. Words blare at us from the radio, the television, the answering machine. Others lunge at us from billboards and web banners, magazines, journals, and newspapers. Silence is rarely tolerated in our culture. There's even music in *elevators!* Do you ever hum in an elevator? Me neither! Who needs that nonsense! Still there's music in that moving cubicle to fill the silence.

As soon as you get in your car, you turn on the radio. Most times its already on as soon as you crank the engine. If it isn't Rush Limbaugh, it's Dr. Laura. If not her, it's a blaring ad with a bad jingle. Or a talk-show host. Or a news commentator. Or a sports enthusiast. How desperately we need to punch the mute button on all this noise. Some have made truly radical decisions to find solitude and silence.

Cynthia and I have a friend who every year takes time, usually a week (sometimes more) to spend in a monastery. He's a fine Christian friend of ours who has discovered that a monastery is one of the last remaining places on earth where you are *expected* to be silent. He thinks. He prays. He reflects. He eats lightly. Walks slowly. That busy attorney from Vancouver admits that without those times he would lose all perspective on life. He confessed, "When I'm alone and the solitude is so quiet it's deafening, it's amazing how I rediscover who I am, and how things become clear that I'd never been able to unravel before." That's what happened to Saul in Arabia. He met with God, who helped him figure life out.

Some of us talk so much we can't even remember what we've said. We've formulated answers to questions nobody asks. We put words on parade, few of them worth anyone's attention. So on and on we talk, talk, talk, talk, talk, talk, talk.

Third, instead of seeking a place of power, be still and release. This is particularly applicable to the life of people in vocational Christian service, especially pastors. I've hung around the training of ministers long enough to know that there can be an enormous amount of envy among individuals in our line of work. Insecurity surfaces as competition abounds. The push for power is so evident it's sickening. No doubt the same sort of silly battles with pride and prestige exist in other professions as well.

What is it going to take for us to give up this idea that we've got to *be somebody*? Everyone joins the race to the top. Sadly, I can report that the loneliest, most unfulfilled people I've ever met are people at the top. They've arrived, but most are lonely, living on empty, desperate to find a meaning for their existence. Sadly, Christians aren't immune. We spot some gifted individual and push them into action. With little thought for their lack of depth, we find new ways to keep them busy. Their popularity outgrows their maturity, which means image must be substituted for integrity. Rootless, insecure, superficial, and unaccountable, they fall. And we're surprised? Richard Foster addressed this dilemma:

Today we have forgotten the importance of this hidden work of God.
As a result (and remember this), we immediately thrust people into

notoriety, bestowing on them unbelievable power, and then we wonder why they are corrupted. Unless we are ready for it, power will destroy us. This is no small matter in the Church today. Because of our whole-sale ignorance of the importance of hidden preparation, we have thrust untold numbers of workers into the limelight before they were ready.[9]

The professional athletes are classic examples. Often they are recruited fresh out of high school, many more off the college playing fields, with virtually no life training under their belts. They sign contracts worth mil-lions of dollars a year. They've never been prepared for what they are facing. Soon, the world watches in shock as many of them turn to drugs and alcohol to ease the disillusionment and pain that results. They simply can-not handle the power or the prestige. The applause intoxicates them. They know nothing of the value of living a simpler, deeper life. The shallow layers of their young, fragile souls rupture, and their lives are fractured by the rush and the race to the top.

Odds are you've never been offered a million-dollar deal. On the con-trary, you may be one of those individuals desperately seeking a way off the treadmill. My advice to you is to stop trying to be the tops in your field. Be an excellent *whatever*. Do the very best you can with what God has given to you. If His plan includes bringing you to higher levels of success, He'll do that, in His time, according to His master plan. Your part is to get out of the traffic and set your mind on kingdom priorities—stuff that *really* matters. Got it? Good.

Now let's bring this closer to home for both of us.

BRINGING TRUTH HOME

Much of what you've just read has been my message to our flock at Stonebriar Community Church. That's what impelled me as a shepherd to promise our congregation that I would not run on empty—I'd not fake it. The call to solitude and silence is as much a call to me as it is to anyone who reads this book. Since we're all in a fallen world, all of us face the need to make a difference. That starts by *being* different.

May God begin with you and me. May He cultivate within us a greater hunger for authenticity as He grows us into deep people, who keep a lot more behind the counter than we ever have on display. May He forge in us the character of men and women like Moses and Joseph, David and Elijah, Ruth and Esther, John who baptized in the river Jordan, and yes, Saul, who grew deep in the desert of Arabia.

I'm ready to go deep. Will you join me?

⁓

Lord God,

You are very patient and gracious with us. You allow us so much of the rope, until finally we come to an end and realize this must be addressed. Thank You for Your understanding. Thank You for the wooing of Your Spirit, who has a way of finally getting our attention.

I pray for all those on some kind of maddening pursuit to make a name or somehow feeling indispensable in the equation. Stop that kind of nonsense in us! Remind all of us, Father, that only One is truly indispensable, and that is Yourself, You who dwells in absolute silence and beauty and purity. No wonder You are so deep and profound.

Give us, our Father, a holy hatred for activity for activity's sake. Force us to reevaluate why we do what we do when we do it. And may we become Your chosen vessels, fitted and prepared for the tasks You have for us. Keep the flesh away from our involvements, Lord, and give us a holy discipline to address the things that lead to the death of authenticity. Whether we're single or married, younger or older, give us a dissatisfaction for the energy of the flesh, and show us the value of the hidden life as You prepare ours for whatever You have planned for the future.

I ask it through Jesus Christ our Lord. Amen.

CHAPTER FIVE

Mission Underway . . . Thanks to the Lesser-Known

G od is never pleased with an independent spirit. That comes as shocking information to people who live and work in America. After all, every year we observe what we call *Independence Day,* celebrating our nation's independence from England. But I'm not talking about national independence; I'm talking about a spirit of independence that pervades our culture. And though all of us were raised to value it, an independent spirit doesn't please God.

That truth cuts cross-grain against the way we were taught to cultivate an independent attitude. I was raised to be my own man, to pull myself up by my own bootstraps, to lean on no one, to take care of myself and my family, to do what I believed to be right, to ignore others in the process, and never depend on anyone. Never! So much of that is bad counsel. You won't find that type of philosophy supported anywhere in the Scriptures. In fact, much of it is a blatant declaration and exaltation of humanism. Taken to the extreme, it can have a devastating impact on an individual and a society.

A TRAGIC END TO AN INDEPENDENT SPIRIT

There is perhaps no more chilling example of the independent spirit taken to the extreme than in the tragic, criminal life of Timothy McVeigh. He lived most of his life outside the boundaries of dependence on others. He lived as an outcast, an extremist, refusing to place himself under any authority, let alone the United States government, which he despised. Free to do completely as he pleased, he did the unthinkable. He took the lives of 168 innocent Americans, many of them children, when he bombed the federal office building in Oklahoma City. After a long manhunt, and months of legal meandering, Timothy McVeigh was sentenced to death by lethal injection for that vicious crime. Throughout the entire ordeal, he maintained an eerie, calm composure, not once showing even a shred of remorse or regret. Defiant and proud, he accepted his fate as a martyr for his demented cause.

When asked how he could face death with such stoic resolve, he said he was unafraid. When asked why, he said he controlled his own fate. He then cited the following poem, written over a century ago, by William Ernest Henley:

Invictus

Out of the night that covers me,
Black as the Pit from pole to pole,
I thank whatever gods may be
For my unconquerable soul.

In the fell clutch of circumstance
I have not winced nor cried aloud.
Under the bludgeonings of chance
My head is bloody, but unbowed.

Beyond this place of wrath and tears
Looms but the Horror of the shade,
And yet the menace of the years
Finds and shall find me unafraid.

> It matters not how strait the gate,
> How charged with punishments the scroll,
> I am the master of my fate:
> *I am the captain of my soul.*[1]

Chilling words, aren't they? But they were treasured by a man who believed his soul was unconquerable—that he was, in fact, in charge of his own destiny.

Thankfully, most people will never take an independent spirit to such hostile extremes. We're not dangerous people, most of us. Yet the subtle influences of that sort of thinking counteract our ability to depend on the Lord and each other.

"We'll make it on our own!" Or in Texas we say, "Don't mess with Texas! We're our own people." Whether they know it or not, those who dogmatically champion that mentality are as dependent on God for life as those who would never utter the words.

THE VIRTUES OF A DEPENDENT SPIRIT

Inevitably, when we stand strong and alone like a steer in a blizzard, looking like we can make it on our own, we easily forget that each life-sustaining beat of our hearts is a gift from God—we're really not that independent after all.

We not only need the Lord, we need each other. Desperately. That need for others only intensifies when the barometer of life drops to the bottom of the gauge—when the winds of adversity blow hard against our souls. We cannot make it on our own. We were created for dependence, not independence. We cannot direct our own steps in the right way without the Lord and without each other.

I've heard people justify their independence by saying, "Well, you know, the Bible says God helps those who help themselves." In no part of the Bible does that line appear. In fact, the Bible teaches the opposite truth. God waits to assist those who finally come to the point in their lives where they *cannot* help themselves. In fact, He brings each of us to that place where we'll willingly surrender and say, "You take over. You give me strength. My way hasn't worked. You teach me to lean and to trust and to wait. I need You, Lord and I need Your people."

When was the last time you told the Lord that? You're no Timothy McVeigh, but you may be living your life secretly thinking you too are the captain of your soul. You are more like Saul than you realize. You need to learn some lessons in humility—lessons he learned by depending on others when the odds turned hard against him.

Before I proceed, I want to make an observation. Quite likely, you too were raised to embrace and nurture the independent spirit within. Over the years, you have grown stubbornly independent, convinced that you need no one but yourself to see life through to the end. You may be in your second, third, or fourth marriage—still trying to prove you can make it. Truth be told, you've been a miserable marriage partner. You've neglected your responsibilities as a wife or husband, as a mother or father. You've bulldozed your way through life determined to make it on your own. You're a proud, card-carrying member of the society of Self-Willed Individualists. If any part of the above is true of you, then you need to keep reading. You'll soon discover that the trail you're blazing actually leads to a dead end.

Several years ago I followed with interest the life of a certain athlete, who was still in high school at the time. The father and mother of the athlete had divorced, and the boy was living with his father. The father had one plan in mind—that his boy would become a professional football player. He showed all the signs of athletic coordination and greatness. As a matter of fact, the first gift the boy received as an infant from his dad was a full-sized football. Imagine. By the time the young champion was out of high school, he had eleven trainers. Eleven! He had numerous scholarship offers and chose the school he liked best. He became an instant star. In a few years he entered the ranks of the NFL.

His dad strictly monitored everything the boy ate. In fact, the young man said on one occasion that he'd never eaten one Oreo cookie. (That kid missed a lot in life. Talk about sacrifice!) All the while he grew increasingly independent . . . and arrogant, I should add.

Not surprisingly, he fizzled out as a professional player, and in less than five years he vanished from the scene. Few people today even know where he is.

Same song, thirty-fourth verse. Whether it's a young actor or actress or athlete or artist, as I said earlier, we promote them too fast. We get them quickly on the pedestal, so that by the time they turn twenty they're suing their parents for all the money they've earned.

What's wrong with that picture? We love to promote an independent spirit without ever considering the value of time-forged character. God never promotes like that. God takes His time. When God plans to use us, He puts us through the paces. He allows a certain amount of suffering. God may use the strong, stubborn, independent individualists in the world, but not long-term. He much prefers the humble, the broken, the bruised, the humble, even the crushed. He works much more effectively in the lives of people who've learned they can't make it on their own, especially those who acknowledge they desperately need God and others. More than anyone in his day, Saul needed to learn those lessons. And so God made sure he did. Let's return to his story in Acts 9 and watch how the drama unfolds.

THE LESSER-KNOWN IN DAMASCUS

By the time Saul left the solitude of Arabia, the Lord had already begun to work on his stubborn will, reversing the effects of a life lived independently of God and others. Unlike his conversion, such a transformation would not be instantaneous. Instead, Saul learned dependence through a series of circumstances where, without the assistance of lesser-known individuals, he wouldn't have been able to continue.

> Now for several days he was with the disciples who were at Damascus, and immediately he began to proclaim Jesus in the synagogues, saying, "He is the Son of God." And all those hearing him continued to be amazed, and were saying, "Is this not he who in Jerusalem destroyed those who called on this name, and who had come here for

the purpose of bringing them bound before the chief priests?" But Saul kept increasing in strength and confounding the Jews who lived at Damascus by proving that that this Jesus is the Christ. And when many days had elapsed, the Jews plotted together to do away with him, but their plot became known to Saul. And they were also watching the gates day and night so that they might put him to death; but his disciples took him by night, and let him down through an opening in the wall, lowering him in a large basket.

Acts 9: 19–25

The scene opens with Saul preaching in the synagogues of Damascus. He's amazing the people with his remarkable preaching. You wonder where he learned to preach so effectively. After all, he's like a recent seminary graduate. He knew just enough to be dangerous—a new believer straight out of the chute. He was gifted and intelligent, to be sure. But he was woefully unprepared to meet the challenges ahead. Preparing for a life of that degree of significance would take *years* of training in places where suffering and hardship were common. The Bible teaches that fundamental principle consistently from beginning to end. And I repeat, it cuts directly across the grain of our American soul.

Saul's intellect no doubt focused on a new theology. As he put it together, I'm sure those new and fresh insights came as a welcome balm to verbally abused people, stinging from the whip of legalism. He may have been smart and gifted, but not everyone in Damascus appreciated Saul's words. By now his ministry was taking off. His growing popularity was viewed as a threat by the Jewish leaders. So they devised a plan to rid their city of this gospel-preaching menace.

It's difficult for you and me to imagine what it would be like to have a contract out on us. But that's what Saul experienced fresh out of the gate. As we often say, "What goes around comes around." The mighty hunter became the hunted. His enemies wanted him so badly they posted guards at every gate around Damascus. The fear and humiliation of that alone must have humbled the blazing preacher. Yet, it was all part of God's plan to break an independent spirit.

For as soon as the tables turned for Saul, people came to his rescue. They're called simply "his disciples" (v. 25). They're in the ranks of the lesser-known in the Bible. In this case *the unknown*. You won't find their names anywhere in the Scriptures. Even in the letters Paul later wrote to the churches where he mentions these incidents, he never identifies his rescuers by name. All we're told is that, "His disciples took him by night, and let him down through an opening in the wall, lowering him in a large basket." How's that for a special operations rescue!

Imagine the great Saul of Tarsus five years earlier stooping over and saying, "Sure, I'll get in a basket." That sort of capitulation would have been miles beneath him. But that was then. This is now. His need forced the once-independent Saul to depend on a nameless group of faithful disciples to rescue him from certain death, by means of a basket hanging from a rope.

Just picture this remarkable man hunched up in a fish basket (probably made out of rope), dangling from a stone wall. What a way to begin a public ministry!

Let me pause to ask you a question. Have you had your own net let down lately? They all look differently. Have you ever known a time in your life when you depended on other people like that? Have you been in such need that your only hope for going on was being rescued by some caring, faithful friends? There is nothing like a basket rescue to teach a little humility.

R. C. H. Lenski writes, "Paul's career began, like that of Moses, with flight and with a long period of waiting, waiting, nothing but waiting. This makes the flight from Damascus so significant. It forced Paul into the long wait in which he fully learned he was nothing, that his mightiest asset was utter weakness, weakness which enabled God to do everything with him and through him."[2]

This story makes for great writing, but it makes for *hard* living. In the middle of his first ministry opportunity, a threat on his life forced him to escape under the cover of night. He came in with such pomp and pride. Then he was blinded. Starved. Met by an unknown disciple named Ananias. Brought to a group of disciples. Escaped to Arabia. Came back to Damascus. Only to be rescued from death by the hands of a few nameless friends. Now where would he go? The plot thickens as the curtain rises in Jerusalem.

MORE ENCOURAGEMENT FROM A LESSER KNOWN

Act two of the drama opens with, "And when he had come to Jerusalem . . ." (v. 26). *Jerusalem!* Saul owned Jerusalem. He went to graduate school in that great town. I mean, the man knew that old city like the back of his hand—every alleyway, every narrow passage, every escape route. He knew virtually everyone of any significance. What a venue to restart his public ministry. "Get the microphones. Turn the lights up bright. Pharisee-turned-evangelist now appearing at the central Jerusalem Auditorium. Come and hear! Come listen to this man preach!" Forget it. It was nothing like that.

Instead, we read this: "He was trying to associate with the disciples; and they were all afraid of him, not believing that he was a disciple" (v. 26). Rejected again, only this time by those he most wanted to meet. Fear stood between them and the zealous, gifted preacher.

That's understandable; who wouldn't be afraid of him? He killed their fellow Christians, some of whom may have been relatives. They thought Saul was a spy—part of an elaborate hoax designed to trap them and drag them to trial. "Saul? No way. Don't let him in our ranks!"

Ever felt the sting of that kind of rejection? Have you ever had such a bad track record that people didn't want to associate with you or welcome you into their fellowship? (Or welcome you back?) It happens all the time. People are rejected because of their pasts. The load of baggage they drag behind them as they enter the Christian life keep them from enjoying what should be instant acceptance. The rejection at times is unbearable. You may say, "Yes. I've been there. And I'm trying to forget those memories, thank you very much." No, don't forget those times. Those painful memories are part of God's gracious plan to break your strong spirit of independence. They've become an essential segment of your story—your testimony of God's grace.

Thankfully, in the midst of those times, God faithfully provides lesser-known individuals who come alongside and say, "Hey, I'm on your team. Let me walk through this with you." That's exactly what happened to Saul in Jerusalem. Someone stepped up, voluntarily. He didn't have to, he wanted to. His name . . . Barnabas.

> But Barnabas took hold of him and brought him to the apostles and
> described to them how he had seen the Lord on the road, and that He
> had talked with him, and how at Damascus he had spoken out boldly
> in the name of Jesus. And he was with them moving about freely in
> Jerusalem, speaking boldly in the name of the Lord.
>
> Acts 9: 27–28

The disciples feared Saul. They couldn't bring themselves to believe he
was a disciple. "*But Barnabas . . .*" Isn't that a great opening? Out of nowhere
comes Barnabas to encourage Saul and be his personal advocate. How did
Barnabas know Saul needed his help? We don't know. Yet we do know that
God is sovereign and has his Barnabases in every town, every church, on
every college and seminary campus, and even on the mission field. Each
Barnabas stands ready at a moment's notice to come to the aid of someone in
need of encouragement. In fact, that's what the name Barnabas means—
"son of encouragement." What a label! (You might consider naming your
next boy Barnabas. He won't appreciate it at first, but after a while he'll see
the significance of it.) Every time we see Barnabas in the story he's offering
encouragement to someone—to the underdog, the one with the bad track
record; to the scrawny one standing at the end of the line waiting to be
chosen for the team; to the one who's fallen and is full of shame and humiliation. People like that need a Baranabas.

So rather than operating out of fear and prejudice, Barnabas stepped
up and "took hold of Saul." Saul was willing to accept his assistance. That's
a healthy dependence. He took Saul under his wing and said, "Come with
me, I'll set this thing straight with these men. They trust me." So off they
went, and the sacred narrative says that Barnabas "brought him to the
disciples and described to them how he had seen the Lord on the road, and
that He had talked to him, and how at Damascus he had spoken out boldly
in the name of Jesus." That's what I call divine intervention through a
lesser-known saint! Barnabas basically said, "I've checked this guy out—
he's the genuine item. He saw the risen Christ, just like all of you. The man
is on our team. Make room . . . relax!"

The next statement describes the result of Barnabas's action on behalf of Saul: "And he was with them moving about freely in Jerusalem, speaking boldly in the name of Jesus." For the first time in his ministry, Saul spoke freely about Christ in Jerusalem, in the company of respected disciples—set free to be himself for the glory of God. What made the difference? *Barnabas!* You may be a Barnabas today. Do you know someone who has been kicked in the teeth because he has a bad track record? Someone who can't get a hearing, yet she's turned her life around and nobody wants to believe it? I urge you to step up like Barnabas did for Saul. Look for those individuals who need a second chance—a large dose of grace to help them start over in the Christian life. Everybody needs a Barnabas at one time or another. And for Saul there would be others.

Some Lesser-Known Brethren

As successful as Saul had become in Jerusalem, God wasn't finished preparing him. The stubborn patterns of fierce independence take a long time to break. And he was in for yet another humbling lesson on his need for others to help him survive. "And he was talking and arguing with the Hellenistic Jews; but they were attempting to put him to death. But when the brethren learned of it, they brought him down to Caesarea and sent him away to Tarsus" (Acts 9: 29–30).

Wait a minute. Who were "the brethren?" No one knows for certain. Our best guess is that they were probably a group of believers living in Jerusalem who had grown fond of the fledgling apostle. It isn't important who they are. For that matter, Saul isn't all that important either. Only *God* is important. His plan is to build His church, no matter how relentless the opposition or how clever the enemy. When He's got a man He's preparing to be used for a little while, He brings along some lesser-known folks to help him down a wall or gain an audience with some prejudiced disciples or, in this case, help him escape. As the heat started rising again, along came *the brethren* who said, in effect, "You know what, Saul? You're history. Those guys will slice your throat so fast you won't know it until you sneeze! You're going on a trip—a cruise, in fact—to Tarsus. So, pack light. You sail tonight."

A bunch of unknowns help him escape Jerusalem—the city he once owned. Now he fled her gates to preserve his life. How things have changed! Following that, he boarded a ship bound for his hometown of all places—Tarsus. What in the world was God up to now?

A LESSON IN HOMETOWN HUMILITY

Can you imagine going back to your hometown with a track record like Saul's? They know you well—at least, they know how you used to be, and they're not impressed. Talk about learning humility!

Whenever I return to Houston I give serious thought to hiding out from my high school English teacher. In my senior year Lupe Lopez and I rode that motorcycle right down the middle of her English literature class. Broooommmmm! Our dear teacher grabbed for her heart pills and popped them like candy under her tongue. We rode that bad boy down the stairway, straight into the principal, who promptly ran us right out of the school for the next several days. (He never could take a joke.) I'll never forget that scene. I think about that every time I drive to Houston. And there are a dozen other memories I could mention. Our past haunts us for more serious reasons than that though, doesn't it? Saul's probably did, too.

Maybe he had some folks with whom he had to set matters right. Perhaps he needed to mend a broken relationship with some close friends. No doubt, his bullish ways in his youth left some painful marks on individuals who were lesser-known than he. I don't know all the reasons he returned to Tarsus, but I do know God doesn't make mistakes when He leads us to specific places. This is especially true when it's to places we would not have chosen on our own. It's all part of His plan to teach us lessons in humility as we learn the value of dependence.

F. B. Meyer writes, "So the disciples brought the hunted preacher down to Caesarea, and sent him forth to Tarsus; not improbably he resumed tent-making there, content to await the Lord's will and bidding. Years passed slowly. Possibly four or five were spent in comparative obscurity and neglect."[3]

Wait a minute. Wasn't this man commissioned by the Lord Jesus to reach the kings and rulers of the world? Isn't he the one who was to open the door of the Gospel to the Gentiles? Now he's back in Tarsus and being asked to wait. What gives? That goes against all the rules of success, right?

We don't like to wait, even for red lights that take forever to turn green. If you're gifted and the need is great, waiting makes no sense at all. We want progress now, before we get older, or before people decide to go somewhere else to find truth. I mean, "C'mon, Lord . . . the people need us now!"

No they don't. Notice the very next sentence in the biblical narrative: "So the church throughout all Judea and Galilee and Samaria enjoyed peace, being built up; and, going on in the fear of the Lord and in the comfort of the Holy Spirit, it continued to increase" (Acts 9:31). You mean, without Saul? Yes, without Saul. The church not only went on, it flourished without his help. That's hard for most folks to accept, especially those who are called and gifted, starting out in the work of the ministry. But, accept it we must. The secret of the church then and now is not a remarkably gifted individual like Saul (or someone as uniquely gifted and talented as you). The secret to the blessing and health of *any* church is Almighty God. Period. It's not you, it's certainly not me, or anyone else we may be tempted to think is indispensable to the cause.

That's tough talk, but it's true. We love to put people on pedestals. If they're singing great at age thirteen, we want to promote 'em so they're going for a Grammy at fourteen. If he handles a ball pretty well at age fifteen, we want him out there where the college and university scouts can get a good look at him by sixteen. If he shows any promise for preaching or teaching the Bible when he's in Bible college, let's offer him a pastorate as soon as possible. Mistake. Mistake. Mistake. Mistake. That's *not* God's way. Only on the rarest of occasions does He choose to use someone mightily while that person is young, immature, and new in the faith. Not even for a leadership position in a local church should a new convert be considered (I Timothy 3:6).

But wasn't it a waste of great talent for God to put Saul on hold? Not at all. Wasn't Tarsus a strange assignment? Not if He wanted him to be prepared to write the letter to the Romans. Not if he would have any lasting impact on the back-sliding believers at Corinth. Not if He wanted Saul to mentor Timothy for a lifetime of strategic ministry in Ephesus. Those projects (and dozens of others) called for a depth of character, forged through the lessons that taught him dependence—both on God and on others.

The Message, Eugene Peterson's paraphrase, wraps up this part of the narrative nicely: "Things calmed down after that and the church had smooth sailing for a while. All over the country—Judaea, Samaria, Galilee—the church grew. They were permeated with a deep sense of reverence for God. The Holy Spirit was with them, strengthening them. They prospered wonderfully."[4]

They didn't need Saul. In Tarsus he had the time to learn that *he* needed *them.* It wasn't about independence. It was about his discovering the value of dependence. Tragically, some never learn.

LINGERING LESSONS FROM THE LESSER-KNOWN

This is a good time to pause and make a twenty-century jump to today. I don't want us to miss three timeless lessons from this story of lesser-known players in Saul's life.

First, value others. Learn to appreciate and embrace the value of other people. Don't try to go out there on your own. Rather than viewing others around you as hindrances, become aware of their value. Remind yourself that they play a strategic role in your survival and your success. God rarely asks us to fly solo. When He leads us to soar the heights, there is safety in others soaring with us.

Part of my training in the Marine Corps included some tips for surviving in combat. One was: Always dig a hole big enough for two, preferably three. Inevitably, the strain of battle will cause you to go weak in the knees. You get scared and can lose heart. You need somebody near you, to keep you steady and help you stay strong. God has designed His family to be that sort of support network for all of us. Nobody can handle all the pressure over the long haul. Companionship and accountability are essential!

You may be resisting becoming an active member of a church or enrolling in a small-group fellowship at your church. You think you can go it alone—and so far, your plan has worked. But it's only a matter of time before a gust of adversity knocks you off your feet, and you'll need someone to pick you up. Don't let a stubborn spirit of independence rob you of the joy of sharing your life, your weaknesses, your failures, and your dreams with others. You and I are not indispensable. You and I are not irreplaceable. God is both. It's His church. He's looking for broken vessels, wounded hearts, and humble servants, even those with bad track records who have some scars, who have learned not to hide them or deny them—people who understand and appreciate the value of others.

Second, humble yourself. Rather than racing into the limelight, we need to accept our role in the shadows. I'm serious here. Don't promote yourself. Don't push yourself to the front. Don't drop hints. Let someone else do that. Better yet, let God do that.

If you're great, trust me, the word will get out. You'll be found . . . in God's time. If you're necessary for the plan, God will put you in the right place at just the precise time. God's work is not about us; it's His production, start to finish. So back off. Let Him pull the curtains and turn on the stage lights. He'll lay hold of an Ananias or Barnabas, who'll come and find you at your most vulnerable point and lift you over the wall. Or He may choose you to be one of the nameless, lesser-known individuals who make the difference for someone else. Your part, pure and simple: Humble yourself.

This would be a good time for you to resist going through life trying to live according to your own understanding—thinking if you can just climb up one or two more rungs on the ladder, you'll be there. You'll have what you need. Your family will be (what's that word we like to use?) . . . "comfortable." You know what your family needs more than extra money in the bank or a more impressive address or a TV in each room? *They need you to be right with the Lord.* That means that you walk humbly with Him. They need your gentle touch, acknowledging that He's the Lord of your home, not you. That takes humility. Go there, my friend, go there.

Third, trust God. Rather than considering yourself (even secretly) indispensable, remind yourself often, it's *the Lord's work* to be done *the Lord's way.* I first heard that principle from Francis Schaeffer while attending one of his lectures. There he stood in knickers and a turtleneck sweater, delivering this very message to a group of young, idealistic listeners—many of us struggling to find our way. I heard him say this again and again: "The

Lord's work must be done the Lord's way. The Lord's work must be done the Lord's way. The Lord's work must be done the Lord's way."

If you're in a hurry, you can make it work your way. Your stuff may even get big. It'll have all the marks of promotion, but it won't be the Lord's way. Stop and realize that. It may be time for you to be let down off your wall in a basket to learn that in your life.

John Pollock, in his splendid book *The Apostle*, states, "The irony was not lost on him that the mighty Paul, who had originally approached Damascus with all the panoply of the high priest's representative, should make his last exit in a fish basket, helped by the very people he had come to hurt."[5]

That about says it all, doesn't it?

ONE FINAL THOUGHT

Just to set the record straight. William Ernest Henley was absolutely wrong. So was Tim McVeigh. Our lives are not caught "in the fell clutch of circumstance." Our heads are not to be "bloodied, but unbowed." You and I are neither the "masters of our fate" nor are we the "captains of our souls." We are to be wholly, continually, and completely dependent on the mercy of God, if we want to do the Lord's work the Lord's way. Paul had to learn that. My question is: Are you learning that? If not, today would be a good day to start. Now is the time to humble yourself under His mighty hand. If you don't, eventually, He will do it for you. And it will hurt. In His time, in His way, He will conquer your stubborn independence.

God is never pleased with an independent spirit.

Chapter Six

Out of the Shadows

I want to dispense a fresh supply of hope in this chapter. Some of you who read these words today could use a little extra, especially you who find yourself in a waiting mode. You were once engaged in the action, doing top-priority work on the front lines. No longer. All that has changed. Now, for some reason, you're on the shelf. It's tough to stay encouraged perched on a shelf. Your mind starts playing tricks on you.

Though you are well educated, experienced, and fairly gifted in your particular field, you are now waiting. You're wondering, and maybe you're getting worried, that this waiting period might be permanent. Admittedly, your response may not be all that great. You can't see any light at the end of the tunnel. It just doesn't seem fair. After all, you've trained hard, you've jumped through hoops, and you've even made the necessary sacrifices. Discouragement crouches at the door, ready to pounce on any thought or hope, so you sit wondering why God has chosen to pass you by.

I want to offer you some encouragement in the next several pages, but I need to start with a realistic comment: It may be a long time before God moves you into a place of significant impact. He may choose not to reveal

His plan for weeks, maybe months. Are you ready for this? *It could be years.* I have found that one of God's favorite methods of preparing us for something great is to send us into the shadows to wait.

But that doesn't mean you're doomed to terminal darkness. Take heart from the words of British author James Stalker who wrote, "Waiting is a common instrument of providential discipline for those to whom exceptional work has been appointed."[1] Pause and let that sink in. Read the statement again, slower this time.

Waiting is one of God's preferred methods of preparing special people for significant projects. The Bible makes that principle plain from cover to cover.

THE BIBLICAL PRINCIPLE OF WAITING

The exceptional work for the point man of the Exodus was to deliver the children of Israel out of the chains of Egypt and into the freedom of Canaan. What a significant project! And it was Moses' privilege to carry that out. Yet, while watching this "friend of God" perform astounding miracles in the desert and demonstrating his unusual leadership skills, it's easy to forget he waited forty years to become leader of the Hebrews. Think of it! Four decades dragged by as the aging Moses tended sheep on the plains of Midian, waiting in the shadows of Sinai. He didn't encounter that burning bush until he turned eighty. That's e-i-g-h-t-y.

The exceptional work for David was that he would lead the nation of Israel for forty years—in fact, for forty of their greatest years. He received that remarkable appointment by divine decree. However, we forget he waited thirteen years before he actually became king, living as a fugitive, hunted and haunted by Saul.

Elijah's exceptional appointment was to confront the evil empire of Ahab and Jezebel. He did that in the strength of God's power but not before spending an extended period of time in God's waiting room at the brook called Cherith. It wasn't easy, especially when that brook dried up, and he was forced to move to the obscure Zarephath. During those years there were no headlines, no significant ministry accomplishments, no souls for the kingdom. Nothing. He simply waited.

The exceptional work of Joseph was to be the Prime Minister of Egypt and to hold that nation together during the long years of deadly drought. He was called to fill that role at a critical time in Egyptian and Jewish history. But long before he reached those galactic heights of prominence, he spent an enormous amount of time in the shadows—sold as a slave by his own brothers, bought like a piece of property by a wealthy Egyptian ruler, forced to learn a completely different culture and a foreign tongue, serving as a house-boy to Potiphar. While there, his master's wife attempted to seduce him into an adulterous affair. Young Joseph wisely ran for his life. Falsely accused of rape, the man was dumped into prison where he spent over two more years doing what? Waiting.

Esther stepped out of the shadows and courageously faced her husband the king with the truth of a secret conspiracy. God used her, literally, to save the Jews from extermination. It's easy to forget, though, that the other years of her life were spent in the shadows—waiting. There must have been days (months) wondering what her purpose in life would be.

Here is a principle that can stir a glimmer of new hope, if you remind yourself of it: *Exceptional work is preceded by extended waiting.* Very few individuals jump into exceptional work, though most would prefer doing just that. As soon as we walk across that stage and receive that diploma, we're ready for the big time. Our slick resumé makes us look like a combination of Joan of Arc, Winston Churchill, Mother Theresa, Bill Gates, Michael J. Fox, and Billy Graham—all wrapped into one, magnificent piece of work. And oh my, only twenty-three years old! We're ready to orchestrate the next Great Awakening. Watch out world, here we come!

There's only one minor problem; that's not God's way. He prepares His servants most often through extended periods of waiting, designed to hone skills and break wills, to shape character and give depth. While He works, we wait.

Let's sample a few biblical passages on the value of waiting. Take the time to read each one slowly, preferably aloud.

> Wait for the Lord; be strong, and let your heart take courage; yes, wait for the Lord.
>
> Psalm 27:14

Rest in the Lord and wait patiently for Him.

Psalm 37:7

Wait for the Lord, and keep His way, and He will exalt you. . . .

Psalm 37:34

My soul, wait in silence for God only, for my hope is from Him.

Psalm 62:5

He who dwells in the shelter of the Most High will abide in the shadow of the Almighty.

Psalm 91:1

If the Lord had not been my help, my soul would soon have dwelt in the abode of silence. If I should say, "My foot has slipped," Thy lovingkindness, O LORD, will hold me up. When my anxious thoughts multiply within me, Thy consolations delight my soul.

Psalm 94:17–19

Those who wait for the Lord will gain new strength; they will mount up with wings like eagles, they will run and not get tired, they will walk and not faint.

Isaiah 40:31

Those who hopefully wait for Me will not be put to shame.

Isaiah 49:23

Wait for your God continually.

Hosea 12: 6

The Bible is packed with verses like that. The concordance I consulted to find those verses, includes column after column listing every verse in the Bible containing the word "wait" or "rest." Wait. Rest. Wait. Rest. I rarely found the word "hurry" in the Scriptures.

That reminds me of a creative piece by Ruth Harms Calkin I came across on the subject.

Could You Hurry A Little?

Lord, I know there are countless times
When I must wait patiently for You.
Waiting develops endurance.
It strengthens my faith
And deepens my dependence on You.

I know that You are Sovereign God—
Not an errand boy
Responding to the snap of my finger.
I know Your timing is neatly wrapped
In Your incomparable wisdom.

But, Lord
You have appointed prayer
To obtain answers!
Even David the Psalmist cried
With confident boldness:
"It is time, O Lord, for you to act."

God, on this silent sunless morning
When I am hedged in on every side
I too cry boldly.
You are my Father, and I am Your child.
So, Lord, could You hurry a little?[2]

The word "hurry" shows up far more in our vocabulary than it does in God's plan. Waiting goes against human nature. We like to hurry, and so we want God to hurry, too. But He doesn't. Not even for someone as gifted and strong as Saul. As he would learn, God prepares us during times when the whole world seems to be going on without us. He patiently, deliberately, steadily, molds us in the shadows, so that we might be properly prepared for later years when He chooses to use us in the spotlight. That's precisely where we find our man, Saul. The eleventh chapter of Acts opens with him still hidden in the shadows as God faithfully continues to prepare him for something great.

FINDING SAUL IN THE SHADOWS

Doubts may have begun to creep into Saul's mind as he waited on God during his years on the shelf in Tarsus—he'd been living there now for a period of five, perhaps six, years or more. If I'm figuring correctly, he was in his mid-forties before God finally called him back onto the scene to use him effectively for the next twenty years.

John Pollock writes, "The best years of Paul's life were slipping away between the Taurus Mountains and the sea. It was harder to bear because he cared so deeply that all men everywhere should hear and believe, yet during his later thirties and into the early forties when a man approaches his prime, Paul drops out of history."[3]

When was the last time someone encouraged you to wait? Not to be ambitious. Remember what we learned in the previous chapter: If you're gifted, they'll find you. Self-promotion is neither necessary or attractive. That's especially true in God's work. I find few things more distasteful than assertive ambition among the young whom God has called. God will raise up whomever He wishes at His appointed time. So, relax. Be patient.

Occasionally, I encourage folks to memorize a particular verse of Scripture. On this subject one comes to mind, which I believe all of us would be wise to keep lodged in our brains. It is Romans 8:25. "If we hope for what we do not see, with perseverance we wait eagerly for it." Let's make that our verse of the year. Put it on a card and slide it under the glass at your desk or tape it on your mirror in the bathroom. Best of all, apply it to your own situation. It will give you hope during the time you spend in the shadows.

By the time the apostle wrote his letter to those believers at Rome, he had learned the value of waiting for things which he could not see. I think he learned that lesson during the years he spent in the shadows in Tarsus, waiting for the Lord to move.

So whatever it is you are waiting for but cannot see, my advice for you is to "wait eagerly for it with perseverance." As the psalmist writes, "Be still." As my grandkids say to me on occasion, "Cool your jets, Bubba. Chill." So, let's all chill! (I don't find that in the Scriptures, but maybe it is somewhere hidden in the Greek text).

Our culture says just the opposite. "If you've got it, flaunt it. Go for it! You deserve it!" Like odorless gas we inhale that all-pervasive message, which says, "name recognition is everything." I mean everything! Don't worry about the depth of your character or the motive of your actions. Worry mainly about your *image*. Making sure you look presentable on television is more important than substance—that's the message of today. After all, image sells. Nonsense! Neither name recognition nor image matters to God. Substance and character are His concerns. Saul learned the truth of all that in Tarsus. And while he waited, God began to move mightily in a city called Antioch, down southeast of Tarsus.

NO SMALL REVIVAL GOING ON

The eleventh chapter of Acts opens with a bang. This is no sleepy hamlet we happen upon here. Revival fires are sweeping the region, and Antioch is the nerve center. The spotlight has turned from Saul to Peter (Acts 10). Peter received a vision confirming God's plan to offer the Gospel to the Gentile people. In that vision, a sheet was let down holding all kinds of foods for him to eat. Since it wasn't kosher food, Peter resisted partaking of the meal. He wrestled with his understanding of what the Law clearly prohibited—how could God now be making it lawful? The Lord insisted that he open his eyes to a new outpouring of His grace to the Gentiles. What a turning point this was for the big Jewish fisherman! Ultimately, Peter got the message. The result? Many believed, including a Gentile named Cornelius. Even the people of Cyprus and the people of Cyrene responded to the Gospel. Revival continued to move across the islands of the eastern Mediterranean. By the time this sweeping demonstration of grace reached Antioch, it was downright electric. The work of God's Spirit was abundantly evident to all.

So then those who were scattered because of the persecution that arose in connection with Stephen made their way to Phoenicia and Cyprus and Antioch, speaking the word to no one except to Jews alone. But there were some, men of Cyprus and Cyrene, who came to Antioch and began speaking to the Greeks also, preaching the Lord Jesus. And the hand of the Lord Jesus was with them, and a large number who believed turned to the Lord.

Acts 11:19–21

This must have been remarkable to witness at that time, as the Spirit of God used various evangelists to proclaim with fiery boldness the message of Christ to the Gentiles. Even Greeks in Antioch were being saved through the preaching of certain men from Cyprus and Cyrene. News of that reached the believers in Jerusalem, the Scripture says, and "they sent Barnabas off to Antioch" (v. 22).

Why send Barnabas to Antioch? Because he was from Cyprus (Acts 4:36). Since there were people in Antioch from Cyprus, Barnabas could minister effectively. He knew that culture. He knew the language. He understood the mindset. Also, remember, he was an encourager—he understood and embraced grace. So the church at Jerusalem held a quick commissioning service and dispatched Barnabas to Antioch. What he experienced when he arrived was more than he could possibly have imagined. I would have loved to watch the expression on his face as he stepped into that scene in Antioch. Talk about excitement! Barnabas fit right in. "Then when he had come and witnessed the grace of God, he rejoiced and began to encourage them all with resolute heart to remain true to the Lord; for he was a good man, and full of the Holy Spirit and of faith. And considerable numbers were brought to the Lord" (vv. 23–24).

People were coming to Christ by the droves. It must have been breathtaking for Barnabas to be a part of all that. By the way, I want to point out that these people weren't "brought to the Church." They were "brought to *the Lord.*" Revival isn't about enlarging the membership rolls of a church. It's about adding names to the Book of Life. Admittedly, a local church does grow and take shape in Antioch. In fact, it becomes one of the more significant churches in the first century. But observe, a "considerable number were brought to the Lord." That's the mark of genuine revival. Transformed lives.

Scholar A. T. Robertson, in his outstanding work *Word Pictures in the New Testament*, writes, "These people were added to the Lord Jesus before they were added to the church. If that were always true, what a difference it would make in our churches."[4]

Revival is not so much about what happens in a church; it is about what happens when people repent of their sins and turn by faith alone to Christ alone. The unbelievers in Antioch and in surrounding towns were doing that in ever-increasing numbers.

Incidentally, I've been in settings where such a movement of God's Spirit was evident. I can testify, it is absolutely phenomenal to witness and to be a part of. You can't stop it, because you didn't start it. You can't explain it, because you didn't manufacture it. You can't duplicate it, because you didn't create it. What you are witnessing is the Lord's hand as He moves through His Spirit in and among His people. The lost are saved, and the saved are revived. Plain and simple, that is what "revival" means—a renewing of spiritual life to those who are spiritually dead and spiritually dull. All of that is happening at Antioch. Knowing what we now know of Saul, that momentous occasion has got to have his name all over it, right? Wrong. He may not have known anything about the Antioch Revival.

A CONSPICUOUS ABSENCE

Have you forgotten? The man is living many miles away. Most likely, he was hunkered down in some cave near Tarsus, far removed from the celebration going on in Antioch. By now his immediate family had probably thrown him out of their home. The leaders of the synagogue had flogged him repeatedly, excommunicating him from Judaism. He probably found refuge in some Gentile homes, learning to appreciate and enjoy their food and lifestyle. In many respects, he lived as an alien in his hometown for years. He's in the shadows. He is growing and learning as God is preparing him for exceptional ministry in the future.

Don't miss the big picture. While in Tarsus, Saul lost confidence in the flesh. In fact, it was most likely during that time in the shadows that he received from the Lord the thorn in the flesh, which he writes about in his second letter to the Corinthians. Due to the remarkable nature of the truths—the divine revelations he received from the Lord Jesus—he needed an affliction to keep him humble. He sheds light on one of those mysterious revelations in 2 Corinthians 12. Allow me to quote that passage so you get the force of his feeling:

> I know a man in Christ who fourteen years ago—whether in the body I do not know, or out of the body I do not know, God knows—such a man was caught up to the third heaven. And I know how such a man—whether in body or apart from the body I do not know, God knows—was caught up into Paradise, and heard inexpressible words, which a man is not permitted to speak.
>
> 2 Corinthians 12:2–4

Paul continues:

> And because of the surpassing greatness of the revelations, for this reason, to keep me from exalting myself, there was given me a thorn in the flesh, a messenger of Satan to buffet me—to keep me from exalting myself!
>
> 2 Corinthians 12:7

Let's pause for a moment. If you go back fourteen years, from the time Paul wrote the second letter to the believers at Corinth, that places him at the time he was waiting in Tarsus. Quite possibly, during one of his numerous floggings he received in Tarsus, or in an agonizing battle to survive being stoned, he lapsed into a semi-conscious state—something of a trance. Possibly, while in that state of mind, the Lord transported him to Paradise and revealed inexpressible, profound truths to him.

The point I want to make is, even in all that, he refused to boast in his giftedness. Instead, he confessed, "I will rather boast about my weaknesses, that the power of Christ may dwell in me . . . for when I am weak, then I am strong" (vv. 9, 10). That's true humility. Incredible perspective. He learned *to boast* in nothing but his own weakness. And, remember, he learned that in the shadows. But nobody knew about it. His transformation never made the headlines.

Your time of God-ordained waiting will never be all that significant in other people's minds. All they may know is that you dropped out of sight. You're gone from the scene. It may begin with a bankruptcy. It may start with a horrible experience you go through, such as a tragic accident or a devastating illness. You may endure the pain of a torn reputation caused by someone who didn't tell the truth. All that devastation has a way of breaking you. The Lord uses the disappointment to lead you to your own Tarsus—otherwise known as His waiting room. There He begins to work deep within your soul. Until you, like Saul, gain such a renewed perspective, you can honestly confess, "When I am weak, *He* is strong." When that happens, as it did with Saul, you will be ready to come out of the shadows. Saul was now ready. Not surprisingly, God moved.

A MINISTRY EMERGING FROM THE SHADOWS

Let's return to the narrative in Acts eleven. Barnabas has a tiger by the tail in Antioch. The city walls have begun to swell with new converts. He realizes he needs help. He doesn't have the gifts required or the energy needed to handle the enormous growth. But he remembers one who does. He remembers Saul up there in Tarsus. It wasn't long before "he left for Tarsus to look for Saul" (11:25).

You want to know what impresses me? Saul had not sent Barnabas his resumé. Nor had Saul sent a messenger saying, "If Barnabas needs a hand, I've got the gifts." No, he remained in Tarsus, content to remain out of the limelight for as long as was necessary. Keep in mind, it was in Tarsus that Saul learned not to boast in his strengths, only in his weakness.

So Barnabas had to search for the man. He didn't have a current address in his Day-Timer. But the next verse says, he "found him."

Where was he? We don't know. Barnabas didn't know. But he happened on a residence where he knocked on the door.

"Yes?"

"Saul, is that you?"

"Barnabas! Come in. Have a seat on a rock over here by me. It's kind of damp in here, but it's the best I can do."

"Saul, you'll never believe it. Remember Antioch?"

"Of course, I do."

"Do you have any idea what's going on down there?"

"I haven't heard."

"Oh, let me tell you." With that the excited Barnabas unfolded to Saul the story of the Antioch revival. And the Scripture says that Barnabas "brought him to Antioch" (v. 26).

Saul heartily agreed to join Barnabas in Antioch. But there's no self-promotion in it. It took five, perhaps six difficult years to get rid of that attitude. The things he once considered great now meant nothing. He wasn't going to Antioch to prove something or to make a name for himself. He went for all the right reasons—the reasons he had learned in the shadows. In that journey with Barnabas to Antioch, the Lord lifted Saul from the shadows of obscurity and placed him back in the action. It was as if the Lord said, "Now is the time." And "it came about that for an entire year they met with the church, and taught considerable numbers; and the disciples were first called Christians in Antioch" (v. 26).

Saul's teaching made a remarkable difference because Saul was different. Under the shadow of the Almighty he had been humbled. Away from the activity and excitement, he had been given fresh revelations of the Lord's plan, new insight regarding His church and the importance of grace. Out of great weakness he ministered with even greater strength. Why? Don't hurry through this—because he waited. Patiently, willingly, he trusted God in the shadows.

FOUR PRINCIPLES FOR TRUSTING GOD IN THE SHADOWS

As I mentioned at the beginning of this chapter, I want to dispense a fresh supply of hope. To help accomplish that, let me suggest four principles I find between the lines of the events we've just considered. They may mean more to you later than now—in a time when God leads you to wait in the shadows.

First, when God prepares us for effective ministry, He includes what we would rather omit—a period of waiting. That cultivates patience. As I write these words, it occurs to me that I've never met anyone young and patient. (To be honest, I've not met many *old* and patient folks either.) We're all in a hurry. We don't like to miss one panel of a revolving door. Patience comes hard in a hurry-up society. Yet, it's an essential quality, cultivated only in extended periods of waiting.

Second, as God makes us wait, hiding us in His shadow, He shows us we're not indispensable. That makes us humble. One major reason the Lord removes us and has us wait in His shadow is to remind us we're not the star attraction. We're not indispensable. That realization cultivates genuine humility. I'm convinced Saul never once questioned God for having his hand on Peter and Barnabas, rather than on him. In a time when most gifted individuals would have been volunteering at the revival headquarters, Saul willingly remained behind the scenes. All the while waiting for his time—correction—*God's* time.

Third, while God hides us away, He reveals new dimensions of Himself and new insights regarding ministry. That makes us deep. I need to repeat something I've already written: What we need today is not smarter people or busier people. A far greater need is deeper people. Deep people will always have a ministry. Always. God deepens us through time spent waiting on Him.

Fourth, when God finally chooses to use us, it comes at a time least expected, when we feel the least qualified. That makes us effective. The perfect set-up for a long-lasting, effective ministry begins with surprise. "Me? You sure You don't want that other person? She's got great qualifications and obvious gifts. You may want to talk to her." That's the idea. It is refreshing, in this highly efficient age, to find a few who are still amazed at the way God is using them.

F. B. Meyer wrote these fitting words in his insightful biography on Paul:

At last one day, as he waited, [Saul] heard a voice saying in the doorway, "Does Saul live here?" And in another moment the familiar face of his old college friend was peering in on him, with a glad smile of recognition. . . . "And he brought him to Antioch; and . . . taught much people." Be not afraid to trust God utterly. As you go down the long corridor you may find that He has preceded you and locked many doors which you would fain have entered; but be sure that beyond these there is one which He has left unlocked. Open it and enter, and you will find yourself face to face with a bend of the river of opportunity, broader and deeper than anything you dared to imagine in your sunniest dreams. Launch forth on it; it conducts to the open sea."[5]

I love that. As always, F.B. Meyer is right on the mark.

Tragically, more often than not, we push at the doors—often with a crowbar of self-effort. We try to break the locks. We are determined *this* is His plan for me. *"This* is what I had in mind. I've waited long enough." We manipulate things and we forcefully step into the scene. Been there, haven't you? God doesn't strike you blind, but He can sure make life miserable. You enjoy no sense of satisfaction. There's also an absence of inner peace. Eventually, the pressure will get to you, and you'll end up regretting the day you forced open that closed door.

Here's fresh hope in three words: *God is able.*

I know you're weary of waiting. I know it's hard. But it's a required course in God's curriculum. Avoid being a dropout in God's School of Waiting. Stay there. Stay right there. Your time will come.

CHAPTER SEVEN

Finding Contentment in God's Sufficient Grace

Any study of the life of the apostle Paul requires a serious look at the subject of pain. Suffering is not a pleasant subject to explore, especially in our western culture. Perhaps you heard, as I did growing up, that, "Pain and suffering come from the devil. Since God wants His servants well and free of pain, healing and happiness are of the Lord." That sounds great. The problem is, it's neither true nor biblical. The devil is not always the one responsible for the pain and suffering in our lives. You may be surprised to know that there are times when pain comes as part of God's sovereign plan to prepare us as useful servants. He knows what is best *for* us in light of what He's doing *in* us.

UNDERSTANDING SUFFERING
FROM GOD'S PERSPECTIVE

Our theology gets fuzzy here in these United States because of our addiction to the creature comforts. I'm not the first to observe this. Well-known pastor and theologian, Helmut Thielicke, after an extended visit to the

States was asked what he believed was the greatest defect among American Christians. His answer: "They have an inadequate view of suffering." How's that for insightful?

I smiled as I read John R. W. Stott's comments on the subject of suffering as he reflected on Romans 8:22–23. First, let's look at the verses before we consider Stott's observation.

> For we know that the whole creation groans and suffers the pains of childbirth together until now. And not only this, but also we ourselves, having the first fruits of the Spirit, even we ourselves groan within ourselves, waiting eagerly for our adoption as sons, the redemption of our body.
>
> Romans 8:22–23

Explaining Paul's words to the Romans, John Stott writes, "It is not only our fragile body (s_ma) which makes me groan; it is also our fallen nature (sarx), which hinders us from behaving as we should, and would altogether prevent us from it, were it not for the indwelling Spirit (7:17,20). We long, therefore, for our sarx to be destroyed and for our s_ma to be transformed. Our groans express both present pain and future longing. Some Christians, however, grin too much (they seem to have no place in their theology for pain) and groan too little.[1]

The man has grown weary of the perpetual Christian grin—frankly, so have I. If you groan and allow your countenance to reflect any measure of inner turmoil, people frown at you judgmentally, as if to suggest you're not walking in the Spirit. Don't get me wrong. I find nothing offensive about Christians laughing. I wrote an entire book affirming that God's people need to laugh more. Laughter demonstrates authenticity in our lives. I simply believe there's no need to glue a permanent Cheshire grin to our faces, lest we look like we're not living a victorious Christian life. If a fellow believer tells you he's going through a particularly tough time, I urge you not to insist he smile. (I tell the folks at the church not to ask me to listen to one of my tapes on joy when they notice I'm feeling down.) Don't urge people to sing along with you on some tune you think they should be singing. Sometimes we just don't feel like singing or smiling. Matter of fact, there are times it's hypocritical to paste a smile on your face.

Folks who know me well know I don't linger very long in the doldrums—rarely do I slip into extended periods of depression. I'm not melancholy by nature. But frankly, I find some days pretty close to tragic (September 11, 2001, comes to mind). There are days when my heart feels so heavy I dread preaching, or writing, or doing anything else related to the work of the ministry. Those are the days I don't grin. Yet regardless of how I feel, my responsibility is to communicate the truth—even when that truth is hard to deliver and even harder to receive. So I've not written these words necessarily to comfort you. That's God's work, ultimately.

My desire is to help equip you for what life will inevitably sling across your path. I understand you may be bearing a burden or heartache the likes of which I've never known. You may be living with pressures or some debilitating physical disease or emotional pain I couldn't even begin to imagine. In almost four decades of pastoral ministry, I've often seen the evidence of inner turmoil surface on the faces of God's people. It is in those times, when I feel at a loss to offer encouragement, that I am most thankful for the Scriptures. In God's Word we not only discover His will for our lives, we find words of genuine comfort for those times when life comes unglued.

All this brings us back to Saul of Tarsus. A day rarely passed in his Christian life when he didn't face intense pain, suffering, and/or pressure—almost all of which were related to the harshness of life and the hardships of ministry. Thankfully, he doesn't keep those experiences to himself. He bares his soul and lets the unedited truth flow.

AN OPEN WINDOW INTO AN APOSTLE'S SOUL

The apostle's second letter to the Corinthian Christians is the most autobiographical of all his writings. Though most of his letters are filled with passion and conviction, none other demonstrates the depth of emotion woven throughout the fabric of this letter. A glimpse at a few passages reveals a transparent and vulnerable soul.

> Blessed be the God and Father of our Lord Jesus Christ, the Father of mercies and God of all comfort; who comforts us in all our affliction so that we may be able to comfort those who are in any affliction with the comfort with which we ourselves are comforted by God.
>
> 2 Corinthians 1:3–4

You know what that means? Specific pain enables us to comfort others specifically. If you lose your child, God uses you in the life of another mother as she endures the loss of her child. If you've struggled through the dark tunnel of divorce, no one understands as you do when a friend tells you his wife just walked out on him. You are able to comfort them with the same comfort with which you were comforted by God. If you've received a bad x-ray, revealing the presence of a suspicious tumor in your body, you understand intimately the emotions and fears your sister experiences when she receives the same diagnosis. That's how God works. I've never had cancer. I could not offer the depth of comfort you could if you've had that disease.

A little later, Saul gets even more specific. He writes, "For we do not want you to be unaware, brethren, of our affliction which came to us in Asia, that we were burdened excessively, beyond our strength, so that we despaired even of life" (1:8). How about that? Saul—the man God used so mightily—despaired of life. Did you know that there was a time (possibly several times) when he suffered such a depth of depression that he no longer wanted to live? He wasn't sure he would make it through.

Still, God held him together. He confesses, "Indeed we had the sentence of death within ourselves in order that we should not trust in ourselves, but in God who raises the dead" (v. 9). "In my despairing of life," says the apostle, "I learned to trust, and God showed me His remarkable power—the same power He used to raise His Son, Jesus, from the grave." What a magnificent perspective on his own suffering!

And the somber beat goes on . . .

> We are afflicted in every way, but not crushed; perplexed, but not despairing; persecuted, but not forsaken; struck down, but not de-

stroyed; always carrying about in the body the dying of Jesus, that the
life of Jesus also may be manifested in our body. For we who live are
constantly being delivered over to death for Jesus' sake, that the life of
Jesus also may be manifested in our mortal flesh.

> 2 Corinthians 4:8–11

Leave out the triumph and here's what he faced: We are *afflicted, persecuted, crushed,* and *struck down.* That was his life in a nutshell. That was his
lot. But he isn't through.

> But in everything commending ourselves as servants of God, in
> much endurance, in afflictions, in hardships, in distresses, in beat-
> ings, in imprisonments, in tumults, in labors, in sleeplessness, in
> hunger . . .
>
> 2 Corinthians 6:4–5

And if that isn't enough . . .

> Are they servants of Christ? (I speak as if I'm insane) I more so; in far
> more labors, in far more imprisonments, beaten times without num-
> ber, often in danger of death. Five times I received from the Jews
> thirty-nine lashes. Three times I was beaten with rods, once I was
> stoned, three times I was shipwrecked, a night and a day I have spent
> in the deep. I have been on frequent journeys, in dangers from rivers,
> dangers from robbers, dangers from my countrymen, dangers from
> the Gentiles, dangers in the city, dangers in the wilderness, dangers
> on the sea, dangers among false brethren; I have been in labor and
> hardship, through many sleepless nights, in hunger and thirst, often
> without food, in cold and exposure.
>
> 2 Corinthians 11:23–27

Can you hear the groaning? If not, you read too quickly. The man is
telling us he developed his theology of pain in the awful crucible of suffering. He knew first-hand what it meant to be misunderstood, mistreated,

forsaken, forgotten, abused, maligned, shipwrecked, attacked, starving, imprisoned, and left for dead.

Remarkably, despite all of that suffering, he chose not to boast in his remarkable grit, or in his ability to face enormous odds with undaunted courage, or in his physical stamina and emotional stability. He testifies to none of that. Rather, he confesses, "If I have to boast, I will boast of what pertains to my weakness" (2 Corinthians 11:30). Boasting *in weakness?* You're not serious!

I repeat, such a testimony is not *in vogue* in the western world, especially among Christians. If you offered a report like that in some public setting, you'd likely receive anonymous letters exhorting you (in love, of course) to walk in the Spirit rather than in the flesh. Surely a Christian suffering that degree of adversity could not be walking with the Lord!

Not true. Certainly not true of Saul. He had learned to glory in suffering, without retaining in his soul an ounce of blame or bitterness toward the Lord. How could he do that? With all of the abuse, the defection of friends, the persecution from the synagogue leaders, why didn't he retaliate? I believe the answer to that lies in the meaning and circumstances surrounding a remarkable vision, which the humble apostle describes in this same letter to the Corinthians, chapter 12. Let's take a closer look at that amazing scene.

THE MAN WHO SAW SO MUCH

For a number of reasons, Paul is in the process of passionately defending his authority as an apostle. Those believers were a fickle bunch—concerned more about outward appearances and dropping the names of respected apostles, than with their responsibility to care for the poor and live holy lives. As a part of his defense, he includes a description of supernatural revelations he received from the throne room of heaven, which he identifies as Paradise. We looked at these words earlier. Let's examine them more carefully:

> Boasting is necessary, though it is not profitable; but I will go on to visions and revelations of the Lord. I know a man in Christ who fourteen

years ago—whether in the body I do not know, or out of the body I do not know, God knows—such a man was caught up to the third heaven. And I know how such a man—whether in the body or apart from the body I do not know, God knows—was caught up into Paradise, and heard inexpressible words, which a man is not permitted to speak.

2 Corinthians 12:1–4

Though mostly shrouded in mystery, that passage is one of the most remarkable in all of Scripture. Paul realizes he can't explain everything, yet he doesn't hold back the truth. Rather than trying to explain the unexplainable, he simply admits, "I don't know." Though intellectually gifted, there are some things he knows but can't describe, so he doesn't try. He merely presents the truth of what occurred. I love that kind of candor.

Let me simplify all that happened by suggesting five observations about this particularly vulnerable confession by the apostle. Hopefully, they'll help put some handles on what is one of the most mysterious passages in the Bible.

1. *He is writing about himself.* He calls himself "such a man" in verses two and three. Only the one who experienced them could know such details about the event. He describes a time. He describes a place. He, personally, went through it, so he was able to communicate the information. That reveals he must be speaking of himself.

2. *He is certain of his location, but he is uncertain of his orientation.* Follow the depth of thinking of this broken, scarred man. He calls the place "the third heaven." In verse four, Paul gets more specific when he refers to the place as "Paradise," suggesting the very presence of God. Still, he was uncertain about his orientation: "Whether in the body or out of the body I don't know." His all-consuming consciousness of the presence of God in that remarkable place must have eclipsed any awareness of the physical realm. Somehow he was transported far beyond the conscious limitations of space and matter and time, and escorted directly into the presence of the Lord.

3. *The experience happened to him suddenly.* Twice he says he was "caught up," a term which denotes a swift rapture, not a gradual assent. He didn't slowly leave earth and ease through the stellar spaces. This was no Charles Dickens-like-ghost-of –Christmas-past experience where Paul was led on a journey that eventually led to the gates of heaven. He *suddenly* found himself in God's third-heaven abode: Paradise.

4. *What he heard and witnessed, mere words could not express.* Though he struggled to put his experience into words, only he himself got it. Not only did he get it; the message he received fortified him for future service amid the most intense periods of suffering. This supernatural experience was part of God's unique plan of preparation for Saul. I've never had an experience that even comes close to what he describes. Saul was taken from earth directly into the presence of the Lord Jesus. Standing before his Master, face to face with the living Christ, he received profound, wonderful truths, too deep for human expression.

Think about all that for a moment. Now answer this question: *What would be the most natural human response to experiencing such phenomenal ecstasy?* In one word, *pride.* Enormous pride. Spiritual conceit of the worst magnitude. Did any other apostle receive that message? No. What other man or woman in the first century spoke directly to the risen Lord in His throne room? No one. Imagine bearing that sort of privileged burden. God understands the peril of such spiritual pride. And in His grace, He solved the pride problem for Saul in the form of a painful affliction, which he called a "thorn in the flesh." Read the man's own words:

> And because of the surpassing greatness of the revelations, for this reason, to keep me from exalting myself, there was given to me a thorn in the flesh.
>
> 2 Corinthians 12:7

THE THORN THAT WOULDN'T GO AWAY

Saul accepted his heaven-sent affliction with the same humility with which he received the vision from the Lord. In his words, "Because of the surpassing greatness of the revelations, for this reason, to keep me from exalting myself, there was given me a thorn in the flesh, a messenger from Satan to buffet me—to keep me from exalting myself!" He not only understood the nature of the thorn, he grasped the reason for it—to ensure a humble spirit.

The word translated "thorn" comes from the Greek term *skolops*, meaning a "sharply pointed stake." Specifically, Saul wrote, "There was given to me a *stake* in the flesh."

After the glory came the groaning. On the heels of supernatural privilege came physical throbbing pain. Following the exalted heavenly revelations came humiliating and agonizing earthly suffering. It was an agony which would accompany him the rest of his life.

Now, what was that thorn? Suggestions abound. Some say it was a series of spiritual temptations. Others point to carnal temptations. Still others suggest relentless opposition and persecution. Physical deformity. Epilepsy. Migraines. Chronic eye trouble. A hunchback. Recurring bouts with malaria and its accompanying throbbing head pain. The truth is, we don't know.

You read one biblical scholar, and he'll identify the *thorn* as definitely one thing. Another theologian may say, "Couldn't possibly be that, it's got to be this." You read another reliable New Testament authority, and he'll say, "Neither that nor this, but I believe it means this." When you're all through hearing their opinions and theories, you're tempted to toss them all out. Nobody knows for sure. And you know what that means? *It doesn't matter.* The man who endured it calls it a "messenger of Satan." The enemy hoped to use it to cause the apostle to defect or to retreat from his calling. God used it to keep the gifted servant on his knees.

Sailors on the high seas understand the importance of securing themselves to something sturdy in a fierce gale. You learn to cling to what's secure in a storm. Saul learned to cling to what he knew to be true about himself and the Lord who held him in His grip.

I see an interesting tension here. While Satan punched and pounded the apostle's resolve, the Lord's purpose was to humble him, to keep him from exalting himself. Pride doesn't reside in the hearts of the broken, the split-apart, the wounded, the anguished of soul.

Many years ago I read these words: "Pain plants the flag of reality in the fortress of a rebel heart." Mothers and fathers keeping vigil in the leukemia ward of a children's hospital do not wrestle with issues of pride. They are humbled to the point of despair.

Now, I need to point out that I'm not qualified to give you the intimate details of how Saul's thorn affected him. However, he does confess that he begged the Lord on three separate occasions to remove it from him (v. 8). And you know what? We would have done the same. You and I would have prayed and prayed and prayed and begged for relief. "Father, please take away the *thorn*. Lord, I beg of You, remove it. Take this pain away from me." That was Saul's response.

I see amazing transparency written in those lines. The world needs more followers of Christ who embrace pain and hardship rather than deny it. How helpful for us to see all this as God's plan to keep us humble. That can't be taught in Bible colleges or seminaries. Those lessons are learned in the harsh realities of life. What people of prayer we would become! How often we would turn to Him. How fully we would lean on Him. And what insights we would glean.

That is precisely what happened as Saul turned again and again to his Lord. God gave an answer he never expected.

A GRACE THAT WON'T LET GO

And what was that answer? God answered, "No." But He offered something far better than relief. Sufficient grace. "My grace is sufficient for you, for power is perfected in weakness." That's where this man of grace and grit got his remarkable perspective on human weakness. It came as an answer to his thrice-repeated plea for the Lord to remove the thorn. I suppose we could call this thorn-in-the-flesh theology. Saul didn't make that up while playing around with clever words and creative expressions. He lived it. He received that message from the Lord. "No" was God's "final answer" to his prayer for deliverance from suffering.

This is a good time to correct faulty thinking. It is not always God's will that you be healed. It is not always the Father's plan to relieve the pressure. Our happiness is not God's chief aim. He doesn't have a wonderful (meaning "comfortable") plan for everybody's life—not from a human perspective. Often His plan is nowhere near wonderful. As with Saul, His answer is not what we prayed and hoped for. But, remembering that He is forming us more and more into the image of His Son, it helps us understand His answer is based on His long-range plan, not our immediate relief.

Thankfully, in the midst of that suffering, He gently whispers, "My grace is sufficient for you." As with Saul, His grace supplies more than we need to endure whatever it is that threatens to undo us. Let me amplify that thought. His grace is more sufficient than your strength. His grace is more sufficient than the advice of any trained counselor or close friend (though God uses both). His grace is sufficient to carry you through whatever your own, unique "thorn" may be. His grace— that's the ticket.

Would you like to know why? "Because power is perfected in weakness." What an amazing statement from the Lord! And all this time we thought power was perfected in success. We've been taught all our lives that it is achievement that makes us strong. No. A thousand times, no! Those things make us proud and self-sufficient and independent. The painful thorns make us weak. But the good news is this: When we are weak, He pours His strength into us, which gives an entirely new perspective on pain and suffering, hardship and pressure. Those stresses and strains drive us to our knees. It's at *that* point our God comes through.

And so? Let's stop looking for someone or something to blame. Let's cease the incessant building of straw men only to set them on fire so we can say, "Ah ha! That's the reason my misery is so great." Don't go there, my friend. Suffering is not about identifying the cause; it's about focusing on the response. I plead with you—do not miss that! It's about willingly accepting God's plan, no matter what the circumstance. It's about finding contentment in God's grace, *regardless.*

It sounds a little too idealistic, doesn't it? We'd rather be skeptical than submissive.

Like the old saint who once prayed, "Lord, when will You cease to strew my path with trials and thorns?"

The Lord answered, "My child, that is how I prove My friends."

To which the suffering soul replied, "Lord, perhaps that's why You have so *few* of them."

I need to underscore a foundational fact: God's goal is not to make sure you're happy. No matter how hard it is for you to believe this, it's time to do so. Life is not about your being comfortable and happy and successful and pain free. It is about becoming the man or woman God has called you to be. Unfortunately, we will rarely hear that message proclaimed today. All the more reason for me to say it again: Life is not about *you!* It's about *God*.

Not long ago, following a sermon I preached at the Stonebriar Community Church on Saul's suffering, a gentleman walked up to the front of the worship center and said to me, "You know, Chuck, I've been listening very carefully to this series on Paul. Even though he is the main character, it really isn't about Paul, is it? The story is really all about God." I gave him a big hug and whispered in his ear, "You got it, now go with it!" He grasped the message of the thorn. So did Saul. He not only made the connection; he lived it in his attitude.

How can I say that with assurance? Because of Saul's response: "Most gladly, therefore, I will rather boast about my weaknesses, that the power of Christ may dwell in me. Therefore I am well content with weaknesses, with insults, with distresses, with persecutions, with difficulties, for Christ's sake; for when I am weak, then I am strong" (2 Corinthians 12:9–10). That's it! He got it, too. And he went with it for the rest of his days.

> I quit focusing on the handicap and began appreciating the gift. It was a case of Christ's strength moving in on my weakness. Now I take limitations in stride, and with good cheer, these limitations that cut me down to size . . . I just let Christ take over! And so the weaker I get, the stronger I become.
>
> [Excerpted from *The Message*, 2 Corinthians 12: 9–10]

When you and I boast of our strengths, we get the credit, and we keep going under our own head of steam. But when we boast in what He is doing in the midst of our brokenness, inability and inadequacy, Christ comes to the front. His strength comes to our rescue.

Don't miss that point. The very things we dread and run from in our lives are precisely what brought contentment to Saul. Look at the list: I am content when I lose. I am content when I am weak. I am content with insults. I am content when I'm slandered. I am content in distresses. I am content with persecutions. I am content with difficulties and pressures that are so tight I can hardly turn around. Why? "Because when I am weak then I'm strong." Knowing that brought the apostle, ablaze with the flaming oracles of heaven, to his knees. What a way to live your life—content in everything—knowing that divine strength comes when human weakness is evident.

That's what gave the man of grace true grit. It will do the same for us.

REMEMBERING, REALIZING, AND RELEASING

As we wind our way to the end of this chapter, let me suggest something to remember, something to realize, and something to release—three timeless principles to help you take the truths you've been reading and place them permanently in your heart.

First, remember that suffering is not new. In the oldest book in the Bible, the Book of Job, we read, "For man is born for trouble, as sparks fly upward" (Job 5:7). Now, there's a statement we need to teach our children and grandchildren, starting today. The message they consistently hear is that God has nothing but happiness and success in store for them if they'll entrust their lives to Him. The Bible never promises that! Amazingly, while scraping sores from his diseased and pain-racked body, Job asked, "Shall we indeed accept good from God and not adversity?" He made that statement in response to his wife's advice to "curse God and die." She too was broken from the loss of her children and the misery of watching her husband suffer so terribly. (As a young preacher, I came down too hard on Job's wife. Now I go easier on her. She was grieving, not blaming. She needed God's perspective on her pain.) It was when her husband witnessed how deep her grief was that he responded as he did. He wanted her to realize that God is not a heavenly bellboy, delivering only pleasurable and comforting things to our door. He doesn't exist to make us happy. We exist to bring Him glory.

We live in superficial, skeptical times. When hard times occur you will find scores of newly released titles questioning how a loving God could be so unfair and unjust. It is easy to be confused in one's understanding of God. But He has not changed. His ways have not been altered. As with Job and Saul, He continues to allow suffering to mold us into humble, useful servants.

In one of his earlier books, Philip Yancey writes:

> A shelf of all the religious books on this subject would cleanly divide into two groups. The older ones, by Bunyan, Donne, Luther, Calvin, Augustine, and others, are almost embarrassing in their readiness to accept pain and suffering as among God's useful agents. A sense of loyalty and faith in God's wisdom undergirds each one. God knows what He is doing in this world, and these authors do not question His actions. They merely try to "justify" the ways of God to man.
>
> More modern books on pain, beginning with some of the agnostic philosophers of the nineteenth century and continuing through to many Christians today, contrast sharply. These authors assume that the amount of evil and suffering in this world cannot be matched with the traditional view of a good and loving God. Therefore, many of them adjust their conception of God, either redefining His love or questioning His power to control evil. If you read these two categories of books side by side, the difference is quite striking. It is as if we in modern times think we have a corner on the suffering market. Do we forget that Luther and Calvin and the others lived in a world without ether and penicillin, and that Bunyan and Donne wrote their greatest works in a dungeon?[2]

Throw one of us in a dungeon, and we want to talk to our lawyer! Throw those guys in prison, and the world ends up with *Pilgrim's Progress*, or some other magnificent literary work that endures for centuries, putting our suffering back into perspective. Resist the temptation to rethink God just because hard times come. Look deeper. Cling to Him tighter. Refuse to question His motives. He's doing something great within you. Suffering is nothing new.

Second, realize that suffering plays a beneficial role. That realization will keep you from searching for someone to blame. Let me be candid. You may be consumed today with that person you feel is to blame for most of your suffering. You see him when you close your eyes. You think of him when you awaken in the morning. You get depressed when you recall the injustice of his actions. Your secret desire is to retaliate. Bitterness fills your soul, and a slow-burning rage fuels the fire of hatred.

I know what it is to hate. I hated a man once so intensely it began to consume me until I realized I was the one losing . . . and of all things, he was winning. I can tell you firsthand, that's no way to live.

Realize that, even in the injustice of it all, the suffering you endure can ultimately turn to your benefit. God is working. Only He knows the end from the beginning, and He knows you and your needs far better than even you do. Don't ask, "Why is this happening to me?" Rather, ask the question, "How should I respond?" Otherwise, you'll miss the beneficial role suffering plays in life.

Third, release the idea that contentment requires comfort. Contentment is possible no matter how dire your circumstances. Years later, while under house arrest, Paul wrote, "I have learned to be content in whatever circumstances I am. I know how to get along with humble means, and I also know how to live in prosperity; in any and every circumstance I have learned the secret of being filled and going hungry, both of having abundance and suffering need. I can do all things through Christ who strengthens me" (Philippians 4:11–13). There it is again. Did you see it? The secret to Saul's contentment was knowing Christ's strength was perfected in his weakness. He really got it . . . and what a liberating concept it became!

I have lived long enough to learn that God's best deliveries come through the back door. His gifts are best received when we need them most, and they always come in an understated manner, wrapped in mercy, framed with this tender inscription: "My grace is sufficient for you."

That penetrating message was caught in a poem written by an unknown confederate soldier, who finally learned the lesson of the thorn.

> I asked God for strength that I might achieve.
> I was made weak that I might learn humbly to obey.
> I asked God for health that I might do greater things.
> I was given infirmity that I might do better things.
> I asked for riches that I might be happy.
> I was given poverty that I might be wise.
> I asked for power that I might have the praise of men.
> I was given weakness that I might feel the need of
>   God.
> I asked for all things that I might enjoy life.
> I was given life that I might endure all things.
> I got nothing I asked for
> But everything I had hoped for . . .
> Almost despite myself my unspoken prayers were
>   answered.
> I am among all men most richly blessed.

Suffering is a delicate subject. It's not easy to address because I realize I'm writing to people who have known a depth of suffering to which I have never gone. In no way do I wish to give the impression that I am a model of how to go through it. To be honest with you, I fail in my responses to adversity, more than I succeed. It's a lot easier to write a chapter on it than it is to model those things that look good in print. Along with the occasional pity parties I throw for myself, my heart is occasionally broken and my spirit takes a tumble. So if that is your experience today, I can identify with that.

My desire is for you and me, together, to claim grace and cultivate grit in the midst of our suffering—like Job, like Saul. And in the process to wean ourselves from the rabid pursuit of happiness so prevalent in our culture. Happiness is a byproduct of contentment. Once Saul discovered that, he lived it. I'm not fully there yet. Most likely, neither are you. And so, we press on together, growing and learning, reminding ourselves that He must increase, we must decrease. Remember, it's all about Him, not us.

Next time you hear a knock at the back door, before you open it, repeat these words to yourself: "His grace is sufficient."

Chapter Eight

The Pleasure of Being in Ministry Together

The late Leonard Bernstein, composer and famed conductor of the world-renowned New York Philharmonic, was asked what he believed to be the most difficult instrument in the orchestra to play. He responded, "Second fiddle!"

When you examine the life of any great individual, you soon discover an entire section of second-fiddlers, support people, gifted in their own rights, but content to play their parts seated in the second chair.

Most folks I know could name leaders who have had a significant impact on their lives. In fact, you and I could name several, who, at a crucial juncture, stepped into our lives, fed our souls and met a particular need. Interestingly, if we were to tell those folks how we've been impacted by their lives, they'd likely react with surprise. Not only that, they'd tell us others who marked their lives in similar ways. It's funny how we view such high-profile individuals. We often think of those great souls as loners, soloists, who step onto the scene, make a huge contribution, then disappear into the sunset.

I thought that about my longtime friend and mentor, Ray Stedman. To me, he was like one of those guys out of a Zane Grey novel——you know, the grim-faced gunfighter who rides into town covered in dust, with a long-barreled six-shooter strapped to his side. And after single-handedly clearing the town of undesirables, he hops back on his horse and gallops toward the horizon.

That's how I saw Ray . . . until I got to know him. While serving as an intern at the church he pastored in Palo Alto, California, I discovered he wasn't a lone ranger at all. On the contrary, he was surrounded by numerous individuals—second-fiddlers, if you will, without whom that dear man of God couldn't have made half the impact he did on my life or the lives of so many others. I learned a valuable lesson. God's family is filled with second-fiddle players—men and women who faithfully and diligently serve as back-up to those first-chair heroes.

SOME OUTSTANDING SECOND-FIDDLERS

This is nothing new. Moses had a second-fiddler in his life——his brother, Aaron. Together they led the Hebrews out of Egypt and on a harsh wilderness journey toward Canaan.

David had Jonathan, a friend who stuck closer than a brother. He also had his mighty men whom he names right down to the last one—over twenty of them, who faithfully served their king behind the scenes, at times acting courageously (occasionally, heroically), as they flirted with death.

And then there was Elijah, whom we all admire for his heroic stand against that diabolic duo, Ahab and Jezebel. Still, we easily forget his second-fiddler, Elisha. He became an invaluable assistant to the mighty prophet, especially during his slump into deep depression, when Elijah hit bottom, despairing of life itself.

Jesus set the rule when he sent his disciples out to minister in pairs (Mark 6:7). His strategy never included sending out lone apostles to do the work of ministry. They went one with the other, and they served more effectively as a result.

Church history also includes numerous examples of great individuals accomplishing great things for the Lord, flanked by lesser-known second-fiddlers.

For instance, most everyone knows about Martin Luther. But who ever heard of Philip Melanchthon? A careful study of Martin Luther's later life reveals that Melanchthon was truly the wind beneath the wings of that soaring eagle in the Reformation era. Melancthon tempered Luther in his most uncontrollable moments. Luther wrote on one occasion, "I never preach better than when I am angry." Melanchthon stepped up and said, in effect, "Now, now, Martin. There's a better way. God's people will hear your words when they're presented with a more compassionate delivery." That was Melancthon's tune as he played second-fiddle.

The nineteenth century witnessed the power of two in the ministry of Dwight L. Moody and Ira Sankey. Moody, that powerhouse, unrefined, shoe-repairman-turned-evangelist needed the soothing, accomplished voice of Ira Sankey. Together they did a better job of bringing the Gospel of Jesus Christ to many of the largest cities in America and Europe. Using both men, God literally shook two continents for Christ.

And we all have lived long enough to appreciate the vision of the Billy Graham Evangelistic Association. You don't go and see only Billy Graham. You experience the contagious enthusiasm of Cliff Barrows, and the heart-warming melodies of George Beverly Shea, still singing now well into his nineties. They've done it *together*. For over fifty years, the team has honored Christ around the globe. Any one of them will tell you, "We couldn't do it alone."

That's the point: We're not supposed to. We're not designed to be loners. In real life, and especially in the ministry, there's no place for Rambos or 007 Agents or spiritual superstars. Not only is that unhealthy; it's simply not God's way. When He calls a man or a woman to accomplish something great, He then brings alongside other individuals who serve and assist the more public figure.

Read slowly through this fine paraphrase of Ecclesiastes chapter 4, of *The New Living Translation*. Take in the images and ponder the wisdom as you consider the meaning of these penetrating words:

> Two people can accomplish more than twice as much as one; they get a better return for their labor.

> If one person falls, the other can reach out and help. But people who are alone when they fall are in real trouble.

And on a cold night, two under the same blanket can gain warmth from each other. But how can one be warm alone?

A person standing alone can be attacked and defeated, but two can stand back-to-back and conquer. Three are even better, for a triple-braided cord is not easily broken.

Ecclesiastes 4:9–12

I hope to convince you in the following pages that God never intended anyone to sail his own boat, without assistance, through the uncharted waters of life or ministry. All of us need help. And the greater the task, the more help we need. Strange and unwholesome things happen to those who fail to stay close to others.

Consider the words of Stanford University psychologist Philip Zimbardo in a piece he wrote for *Psychology Today*, titled "The Age of Indifference: "I know of no more potent killer than isolationism. There is no more de-structive influence on physical and mental health than the isolation of you from me and us from them. It has been shown to be a central agent in the etiology of depression, paranoia, murder, schizophrenia, rape, suicide, and a mass and a wide variety of disease states."[1]

You don't have to be an expert to understand the perils of going it alone. Let's return to the action in the Book of Acts, where we left Barnabas en route to find Saul. The great encourager had realized his limitations in meeting the mounting needs in Antioch. After all, he was a faithful second-fiddler—what he needed was a virtuoso!

AN OVERWHELMING TASK AHEAD

Let's put the scene at Antioch in some perspective. Beside the sheer num-bers of converts that needed to be taught, what made Barnabas's task so daunting? There were two issues—one religious, the other cultural.

The Challenge of Religious Ignorance

Because the winds of revival had swept from as far south as Jerusalem, all

the way north into Phoenicia, an ever-increasing number of the new believers were Gentiles, with virtually no exposure to the rich religious heritage
of Judaism. In short, they were ignorant of God and untaught in the Scriptures. Barnabas, himself a native of Cyprus, had some advantages since he
knew the Greek language and understood their culture. Still the challenge
was overwhelming. That was only part of the problem.

A Culture of Moral Debauchery

Not only were these Gentiles coming into the ranks of Christianity from a
completely non-Jewish background, they were tainted by the moral decay
of first-century Antioch.

Phoenicia was no Holy Land. And Antioch was no Jerusalem. Phoenicia
was a pagan religion and Antioch, it's center, was a sprawling city of about
a half-million or more people, known for chariot racing, gambling, prosti-
tution, corrupt governmental politics, and unbridled moral debauchery. It
may have been those tempting pleasures that initially lured many of the
new converts to the city. The worship of Daphne was there; her temple five
miles out of the city was home to a number of prostitute priestesses. The
phrase "the Morals of Daphne" emerged from the openly immoral cess-
pool of Antioch.

Remarkably, the Scripture says that despite all this, "the hand of the
Lord was with them, and a large number who believed turned to the Lord"
(9:21). Try to picture it: A large metropolis in America known for its moral
looseness, being impacted by an outpouring of God's Spirit. Revival sweeps
through its neighborhoods and, before long, casinos and crack houses start
to empty, as adult bookstores and massage parlors lose their clients. Churches
in the area, which at one time wondered whether or not they should board
up their sanctuaries, now burst at the seems with new converts, most of
whom are former gamblers, prostitutes, criminals, drug addicts, and por-
nographers. Everyone needs in-depth instruction in the Scriptures, training
in righteousness, personal counseling, and mentoring.

That was the scene Barnabas stepped into in Antioch. Talk about demanding! It was like drinking out of a firehose. The place was crawling

with brand new believers, accidents waiting to happen. Only in Antioch, there were no churches. There were no seasoned pastors to help carry the load, no knowledge of the truth of God, and very little understanding of Christ. Barnabas's emotions no doubt flapped wildly between absolute joy and nail-biting frustration. And the challenge only intensified as the revival continued. Luke writes, "Considerable numbers were brought to the Lord." The more Barnabas ministered the Gospel, the greater the crowds became. Finally he realized, "I'm over my head . . . furthermore, I'm exhausted!" He desperately needed a partner in the work.

I have a friend whose eight-year-old son wanted to play soccer. His daddy hadn't played one minute of soccer. They showed up for the first day of practice, and the young father discovered, to his dismay, no one had stepped up to coach. You guessed it—my friend got the job. Facing an eager team of eight-year-old boys itching to kick the cover off the soccer ball, though a novice, he dived in headfirst.

He didn't have a clue how to organize the offense, let alone how to strategize the defense. He didn't even know the rules of the game. He said to me, "I kinda ran out of 'atta boys.' After about the third or fourth hour with these boys, I realized they needed more than 'Go out there and get 'em.' I don't know what you're supposed to do, but go out there and get 'em . . . atta boy, stay at it, you can win, you can do it." Much to his delight, one of the other fathers witnessed his futile attempts to coach, and volunteered to help. Not only had the man coached soccer in the past, he had played the game for years. My friend admitted, "Suddenly he and I became very good friends." He gladly retreated to the role of assistant coach and official encourager. Barnabas did the same thing in Antioch.

THE REMARKABLE POWER OF TWO

Barnabas knew where to find his number-one man: Tarsus. There he would find his friend Saul, humbled, willing, available. Barnabas knew he alone didn't possess all the skills or gifts required to pull together a ministry as large and diversified as Antioch. Together, by God's grace, the two of them could team up and accomplish incredible things.

Their differences would work for them, not against them. Barnabas was raised in Cyprus—a rural island setting; Saul came from Tarsus, an intellectual center, and had been schooled in Jerusalem in the disciplines of logic. Barnabas was an encourager; Saul a gifted preacher and scriptural scholar. Barnabas flowed with love and great compassion; Saul demonstrated remarkable grit and unwavering determination. Barnabas graciously reached out to the downtrodden and needy; Saul was naturally drawn to the intellectually curious.

With Barnabas at his side, Saul would deliver the theological mortar needed to cement these new believers in their faith. Together they would prove a powerful force in the establishment of the Antioch church. In fact, I believe that explains Luke's words at the end of verse 25, where he writes, "and the disciples were first called Christians in Antioch." The theology, organization, and structure these two pastors laid in place formed the foundation of the first solid ministry in Antioch.

Thinking back over the last several years in Saul's life, it isn't hard to understand why he was an excellent choice for this critical leadership role. The man had successfully completely all the initial coursework in God's schoolroom for effective ministry. God had revealed Himself and His truth to Saul. His character had been forged in the shadows. With nothing to prove, he was ready to go and willing to spend himself for the glory of God.

Let me make it even more practical. Saul was not the least bit ambitious. Even if he had heard of the revival in Antioch, he didn't rush down there to make himself known. He didn't stoop to self-promotion. Barnabas had to enlist him. I'm convinced Saul went to Antioch with a genuine spirit of reluctance. I find that kind of rare humility wonderfully attractive.

Do you recall what David did after he killed Goliath? God had already appointed the young shepherd the next king of Israel. He certainly earned his regal stripes in that courageous stand-off with the Philistine giant. Most young conquerors would have located the nearest Macy's and tried on crowns. Not David. He went right back to the Judean hills to keep his father's sheep—a true shepherd with a servant's heart.

Saul kept a similar vigil in Tarsus. He waited patiently in the shadows until Barnabas tapped him on the shoulder. Only then did he step into that critical, highly visible role of leadership.

I find nothing more attractive in a gifted and competent leader than authentic humility. Saul's giftedness was framed in the crucible of solitude where he had been honed and retooled by the living Christ.

I mentioned earlier the evangelist Dwight L. Moody. Although unschooled, this gifted man of God was preaching in Birmingham, England, far back in 1875. A noted congregational minister and well-respected theologian, Dr. R. W. Dale, cooperated in that enormously successful campaign.

After watching and listening to Moody preach and witnessing the incredible results of the ministry of that simple man, Dr. Dale wrote in his denominational magazine, "I told Mr. Moody that the work was most plainly of God, for I could see no real relation between him and what he had done. Moody laughed cheerily and said, 'I should be very sorry if it were otherwise.'"[2]

No defensiveness, no feeling of being put upon, no embarrassing uneasiness. Moody was the most surprised of anyone that God chose to use him so mightily.

That was Saul. No wonder Barnabas wanted Saul to lead the program in Antioch. What a duet they cultivated! For an entire year these two men served side by side, and God was greatly glorified.

I love Warren Wiersbe's succinct definition of ministry: "Ministry takes place when divine resources meet human needs through loving channels to the glory of God."[3]

Saul and Barnabas could have sat for that portrait. Why did Saul and Barnabas experience such pleasure in serving together? No competition. No battle of egos. No one threatened by the other's gifts. No hidden agendas. No unresolved conflicts. Their single-minded goal was to magnify Christ. It didn't matter if the crowds multiplied to thousands or shrank to only a few. All that mattered was that Christ be proclaimed and worshipped.

TIMELESS ESSENTIALS FOR MINISTERING TOGETHER

In every ministry there are at least three essentials that produce an atmosphere of joyous cooperation. They are *objectives, people,* and *places.* Each one deserves our attention before I draw this chapter to a close.

First, whatever God plans, He pursues. That has to do with the ministry essential of *objectives*. Ever since we started our church, I've repeatedly told the congregation of the Stonebriar Community Church that God's plan for our ministry together goes far beyond anything they or I could imagine. The same goes for your church or the ministry organization with which you are involved. God's work will outlive all of us. His plan, always full of surprises, is as deep as it is wide.

God's work has nothing to do with your pastor's personal agenda. It is not about a church board's five-step plan to reach the community, or the personal preferences of one outspoken deacon. It's about what God wants to accomplish through each of us working together. The secret is in that last word—*together*.

There's nothing wrong with having a clearly defined mission statement that gives direction and purpose to the vision of a ministry. In fact, there's everything right about it as long as it is the Lord who provides the direction. God's plan unfolds in ways that confounds human wisdom and sometimes defies common sense. But it is His plan. Objectives are essential when they are *His* objectives, not ours.

Second, whomever God chooses, He uses. That has to do with the ministry essential of *people*. And I must quickly add, the people God chooses are never perfect. That includes me. That includes you. In fact, we prove more useful to the Lord when we accept that reality and trust Him with our imperfections.

This does not mean we're free to operate in the flesh. Nor are we to rely on carnal plans or self-serving arrangements to meet our objectives. The Scriptures urge us over and over to walk in purity and holiness. But we are to understand that even though God chooses to use us, our imperfections don't go away.

This prompts me to offer a practical warning: If you fix your hopes and attentions on any one person you will be brokenhearted. Everyone has feet of clay. Just as that included Barnabas and Saul, it includes folks like us. Resist the temptation to put people on pedestals. We all need heroes. I have my heroes, but I can't name one who is anywhere near perfect. I admire and appreciate them, but I don't *adore* them. Like Saul and Barnabas let's keep the focus on Christ. You have every right to expect that kind of Christ-centered focus from the leaders in your church.

Third, where ever God selects, He sends. That has to do with the ministry essential of *places*. I wish He would send all of the great ones to Stonebriar Community Church. And I wish He would never let any of them leave. That's desire based on my limited human perspective. I never prayed this prayer, but I've been tempted to pray, "Lord, send us only the great ones and keep them here forever. Don't ever take them anywhere else." (Being imperfect, I'm not above a few selfish prayers!)

God's plan, however, includes removing some very gifted people among us and sending them elsewhere. We'll look at that in the next chapter. His ways are not our ways. His places are not the places we would choose to go on our own. None of that matters. What matters is this: *God sends people of His choosing to places of His choosing.* The sooner we accept and embrace that truth, the more contented we will be.

But let me remind you, going where He sends us will test our faith. And that includes adventure and risk.

> Life is not a problem to be solved; it is an adventure to be lived. That's the nature of it and has been since the beginning when God set the dangerous stage for this high-stakes drama and called the whole wild enterprise *good*. He rigged the world in such a way that it only works when we embrace *risk* as the theme of our lives, which is to say, only when we live by faith. A man just won't be happy until he's got adventure in his work, in his love and in his spiritual life.[4]

Ministering together is always an adventure. It's about embracing change. It's about maintaining flexibility. It's about walking with God through the surprising events He has designed. Barnabas needed help. The work was too much for one gifted, but limited man. Saul stepped into the gap. And together they turned Antioch upside down for Christ.

SOME CONCLUDING THOUGHTS

Ten years ago you could not have predicted where you find yourself today. Chances are good, *five* years ago you couldn't have done that. You may have thought you'd be living in the North, but now you're setting up shop in the South. Or, you thought you were safe and secure in your business. Today, you may not even have that business. So much has changed.

Instead of feeling fulfilled and encouraged, your heart may be broken today. Or you may be facing retirement, with all the anticipation and uncertainty that prospect affords. Here's my message for you in one simple statement: *Don't try to manage it all alone.* The Christian life is a team effort. God has designed it that way. Let's cooperate.

CHAPTER NINE

Released in Order to Obey

N ow there were at Antioch, in the church that was there, prophets and teachers: Barnabas, and Simeon who is called Niger, and Lucius of Cyrene, and Manaen who had been brought up with Herod the tetrarch, and Saul.

While they were ministering to the Lord and fasting, the Holy Spirit said, "Set apart for Me Barnabas and Saul for the work to which I have called them."

Then, when they had fasted and prayed and laid their hands on them, they sent them away.

So, being sent out by the Holy Spirit, they went down to Seleucia and from there they sailed to Cyprus.

Acts 13:1–4,13

For me, one word best characterizes the essence of obedience: *Change*. Just reading that word may cause you to shudder. I know very few people who enjoy change. It threatens our comfort, interrupts our routines, challenges our priorities, and introduces anxiety. Yet, I'm convinced that living a life of obedience is an impossibility if you and I are unwilling to change. That's much easier to write than it is to put into practice. Either way, I'm convinced the statement is true.

There's a strong possibility that, as you open this chapter and begin to read these words, you (or someone close to you) faces the challenge of change. It may have to do with your work setting—a change in your employment status. Or you're pulling the details together to launch a cross-country move. Perhaps, after waiting and working hard for so many years, the suddenly slower pace of retirement caught you by surprise. You aren't as prepared for the changes as you thought. I could fill two more pages with the possibilities because change is inevitable.

In our study of the life of Paul, we watched closely as that remarkable man of grace and grit handled many crucibles of change. They marked him in ways that prepared him uniquely for the task God had planned for him.

Little did he know it, but Saul was in for a few more big-time changes. No one could tell by looking, but the church at Antioch was about to lose two-fifths of its staff. Change. Change. Change. Change. Change.

CHANGE . . . THE UNFINISHED SENTENCE IN LIFE

Webster's Dictionary provides a strangely wonderful definition of the word "change": "To make different in some particular." It appears to be an unfinished sentence. You want the last word, don't you? But it stops with the word "particular." The definition goes on to include "to transform, to undergo a modification, to become different." Maybe that explains why it's so challenging; it isn't easy "to become different."

Though change is good, it's rarely easy or pleasant. We're most interested in pursuing the comfortable route. We prefer the road more frequently traveled. But change leads us down unknown paths filled with narrow passages and surprising turns. Everything within us scrambles to stay on trails already blazed.

Several years ago, a friend of mine who lived in the Santa Barbara Canyon area of California went through a frightening ordeal. One parched summer, fire swept through the region devouring thousands of acres of forest and destroying countless homes in the canyon. His home sat at the base of the long canyon. He didn't have much time to prepare his escape, but he had longer than those at the top. He could see the flames and smoke in the distance and knew he had only a short while before his home would become engulfed in fire. He hurriedly made a list of those possessions he most wanted to save. As it turned out, he didn't have time to grab any of them. When the whole ordeal was over, he stood looking at the smoldering heap that was once his home. All that remained was the list he had clutched in his hand. The impact that destructive event had on his family marked each one of them so deeply, they were never the same.

They lost everything, except of course the useless list of items they thought they couldn't do without. The fire, though unbelievably devastating, became a catalyst for changing them into a closer, more grateful family. In short, the change made them different.

No doubt the songwriter, Eddie Espinosa, understood the invaluable benefits of change when he composed these words:

> Change my heart Oh God, make it ever true.
> Change my heart Oh God, may I be like You.
> You are the potter, I am the clay;
> Mold me and make me, this is what I pray.
> Change my heart Oh God, make it ever true.
> Change my heart Oh God, may I be like you.[1]

We love to sing that song of worship at our church. Every time we do, it stays on my mind for the rest of the day. Though those words are a delight to sing, bringing them into the reality of our lives is another matter. Allowing someone to mold and make us into something different is uncomfortable and, at times, downright painful. If we were like clay—moldable and flexible and easy to reshape—changes would be a lot easier. But we're more like hard pottery—brittle and inflexible.

That tender song is based on a familiar biblical metaphor: God is portrayed as the Potter and we, His children, as the clay. Read carefully the following Scripture passages that use the image to drive home that crucial truth.

> You turn things around! Shall the potter be considered as equal to the clay, that what is made should say to its maker, "He did not make me"; or what is formed say to him who formed it, "He has no understanding"?
>
> Isaiah 29:16

> Woe to the one who quarrels with his Maker—an earthenware vessel among vessels of the earth! Will the clay say to the potter, "What are you doing?"
>
> Isaiah 45:9

> Does not the potter have a right over the clay, to make from the same lump one vessel for honorable use, and another for common use?
>
> Romans 9:21

When our wills are like clay, we understand that change is inevitable when placed in the hands of the Potter. That's why David, many centuries ago, wrote the words to his own worship chorus—poetry forged on the anvil of change:

> Be gracious to me, O God, according to Thy lovingkindness; according to the greatness of Thy compassion blot out transgressions. Wash me thoroughly from my iniquity, and cleanse me from my sin. For I know my transgressions, and my sin is ever before me. Against Thee, Thee only, I have sinned, and done what is evil in Thy sight, so that Thou are justified when Thou dost speak, and blameless when Thou dost judge.
>
> . . . Create in me a clean heart, O God, and renew a steadfast spirit within me.
>
> Psalm 51:1–4,10

In that fifty-first psalm, David called upon the Lord to change ugly habits that had held him in their grip much too long. Hypocrisy, murderous thoughts, adultery, rationalization, and a stubborn will distanced him from his Lord. Realizing the depth of his sinful condition, he acknowledged, "I need my heart changed and only You, Lord, can make it happen and cause it to last." And so he opened his heart and invited His Lord to clean it up and reshape it.

Heart surgery is God's specialty. Though the process is painful, the results are magnificent.

Turning back to the scene we left in the Book of Acts, Saul and Barnabas are having the time of their lives, ministering together amid one of the most remarkable revivals in early church history. The church is growing, lives are being transformed, and an entire culture has come under the influence of the Spirit of God. The scene is wonderfully exciting. Every day the excitement intensified. The worship, the harmony, the conversions, the growth—all so *contagious.* Suddenly God stepped in and everything changed. There's that word again—everything *changed.* Chances are good that some of the believers in Antioch might have resisted even the thought of change, at least initially. Not Saul. I don't believe he struggled with it even for a moment. He and change had gotten very well acquainted during the previous years of his life.

We need to pause and remember his remarkably pure life was directly related to his willingness to accept change. I'm convinced the main reason the man lived so cleanly before God had to do with the constant regimen of change he learned to accept.

Rewind the tape in your head. On his way to Damascus to persecute Christians, a light came from heaven, and he was converted to Christ. *A radical transformation.* He was then led to live and serve among a whole new group of people—the very Christians he once persecuted became his colleagues in ministry. *Another dramatic change.*

And then there was Arabia. Change in surroundings. Change of pace. Change of lifestyle. Though we don't know all God accomplished during that lengthy desert sabbatical, we do know this: *Saul changed.* From there he went to Damascus, then back to Jerusalem and then (of all things) back home to Tarsus, where he stayed in the shadows for years. The man changed, changed, and changed again. Doubtless rejected by his family and excommunicated from his familiar ties to Judaism, he lived cut-off from all he once held dear. A converted Jew, living in his hometown, a man no one wanted . . . friendless, homeless, directionless. For multiple years he lived as a hermit, if you will, willingly submitting to the Potter's firm, but gracious hands.

Finally, one day he hears a familiar knock at the door. To his delight it's Barnabas. He's come to enlist him back into service. Barnabas needed a point man for the enormous undertaking in Antioch. *Another complete set of changes.* Imagine the shock to Saul's system—going from the obscurity of Tarsus, where few wanted anything to do with him, to the limelight of Antioch, where throngs hung on his every word. There he and Barnabas teamed up in a teaching ministry that lasted an entire year. Who knows who may have been recruited and equipped with the truth, thanks to their mutual ministry?

And in the midst of that wonderful, fruitful, growing ministry, something totally unexpected happened. God decided to change things up again. He had plans to uproot the two of them and put them on the road. What a change! Let's zoom in for a closer look.

THE DREAM TEAM AND THE CHURCH ALIVE

The growth pattern of the church at Antioch would have made even George Barna's head spin! Talk about a model of health and effectiveness. Read again the account and try to imagine yourself in the midst of all that was happening.

> Now there were at Antioch, in the church that was there, prophets and teachers: Barnabas, and Simeon who was called Niger, and Lucius of Cyrene, and Manaen who had been brought up with Herod the Tetrarch, and Saul. And while they were ministering to the Lord and fasting, the Holy Spirit said, "Set apart for Me Barnabas and Saul for the work to which I have called them." Then, when they had fasted and prayed and laid their hands on them, they sent them away. So,

being sent out by the Holy Spirit, they went down to Seleucia and from there they sailed to Cyprus.

Acts 13:1–4

To begin with, Antioch Community Church was *the* place to be. Not only did they have incredible spiritual growth, the staff was the century-one *Dream Team*. Barnabas, Simeon, Lucius, Manaen, and Saul—how's that for your starting line-up? The believers in Antioch were under the influence of five choice prophets, preachers and teachers *par excellence*. Each was called, gifted, devoted, and set apart for the Lord's work. That's exactly what the growing new church needed—the right leaders to lay a strong foundation. How wonderful it was. The congregation loved it because they got substantive truth, incredible encouragement, and great worship. Remember that. This was no religious entertainment center that dumbed down the truth. The place thrived on the solid meat of the Word. The diet was wholesome and nourishing. The teaching was rich and deep.

Though written over a century ago, Charles Spurgeon's words have a ring of relevance for our day. Read them slowly and carefully:

> Sermons should have real teaching in them, and their doctrine should be solid, substantial, and abundant. We do not enter the pulpit to talk for talk's sake; we have instructions to convey important to the last degree, and we cannot afford to utter petty nothings. Our range of subjects is all but boundless, and we cannot, therefore, be excused if our discourses are threadbare and devoid of substance. If we speak as ambassadors for God, we need never complain of want of matter, for our message is full to overflowing. The entire gospel must be presented from the pulpit; the whole faith once delivered to the saints must be proclaimed by us. The truth as it is in Jesus must be instructively declared so that the people may not merely hear, but *know*, the joyful sound. . . Nothing can compensate for the absence of teaching.[2]

To be honest, among the most important factors in deciding where you and your family should attend church, the commitment to consistent delivery of substantive teaching should rank first. It isn't enough to attend a church simply because you have friends who go there, or because you enjoy a particular style of music. You need good food to survive! If you're like me, your soul longs for a regular diet of substantive meals to nourish, strengthen, and fortify your life.

Every great restaurant has one primary element that draws crowds night after night, week after week, and year after year. *Great food!* Most of us would sacrifice ambience, atmosphere, location, and even quality service, to savor the best food in town. Now, a few folks in other states may prefer candles and romantic music to good grub. But I can tell you, Texans like the meat—thick, choice cuts, cooked right and delivered to our table in a tasty manner. Now let me ask you: What makes the difference, no matter where you live, between a great restaurant and a mediocre restaurant? *The chef.* Though we rarely meet these talented folks, the better the chef, the better the food. And, the better the food, the more popular the place. Antioch served the best spiritual grub in Phoenicia. And it was prepared to near perfection by a group of five great chefs.

Saul fit that group like a master chef fits a great restaurant. It was a choice setting for him to exercise his gifts and deliver his best stuff. I would have loved to have been a part of that congregation. It must have been magnificent to listen to Saul of Tarsus open the ancient scrolls of the Old Testament and teach God's Word. I can only imagine how those growing babes in Christ savored and swallowed every rich morsel of truth. They learned all about grace and grit from the original man of grace and grit. Suddenly I'm envious!

I think I would have reacted as Peter did in the midst of the transfiguration (as recorded in Matthew 17:4). "Lord, let's just set up a sacred tent and stay here. Let's just make it permanent." The problem with that sort of response is that in God's work there's no permanent campsite on planet earth. Eventually, the time comes to pull up stakes.

RELEASED IN ORDER TO OBEY

While they were ministering to the Lord, fasting, singing, teaching, witnessing, and praying, the Holy Spirit said, "Okay, hitch up the wagons, fellas . . . westward ho!" (Swindoll revised paraphrase.) "I need Barnabas and Saul for the work to which I have called them."

Can you imagine how some would react today? "You can't be serious. You're gonna take two of the five chefs and send them to another joint? We'll starve! You're gonna reach down in our ranks and pull two of the best adult fellowship teachers we've got and move them to some distant mission field? That's two-fifths of our leadership. We can't let these guys slip through our fingers!"

But none of that occurred in Antioch. As soon as those folks realized it was the Spirit of God who was sending them on, they released them. And the change occurred (don't miss this!) "while they were ministering." It didn't happen in a lull, when giving was way down, or during a period of leadership transition. God lifted these men from that exciting setting while the church was at its zenith, steaming ahead full-bore. People were coming by the cartload, deep needs were being met, souls were being saved, lives were being transformed, families were getting healthy, the place was electric! Still, the Spirit said, "It's time for change." Who would've ever imagined? But God is full of surprises, since He sees the big picture while we focus mainly on the here and now.

It was God's way of telling Barnabas and Saul it was time to move. By the way, the Lord did the speaking. In those days the Lord revealed Himself in a number of ways. Today, I believe He speaks to us through His Word, through the gentle nudging of the Spirit, and through the collective witness of His people. Then it may have been in a night vision, or during a time while the disciples were praying, meditating on the Scriptures, or while fasting. A couple of the leaders sensed the Lord's leading in a new direction. Others verified the voice. The Lord said, in effect, "I have work for two of you to do elsewhere. Not all of you, only two . . . and My plan is best. Release Barnabas and Saul. They are the two I'm calling elsewhere."

There was no preliminary leading. The change of direction came without warning. No memo was sent out ahead of some meeting for prayerful consideration. The Spirit spoke and the church listened. In order for Barnabas and Saul to obey, they needed to be released. They did . . . and they were. Isn't that great?

I need to pause to make a couple of observations about the nature of ministry. The way God chooses to lead His ministry is often difficult to get our arms around. Finding direction in the corporate world comes somewhat easier. There's a clearly stated bottom line, shareholders to report to, and defined markets that guide company decisions.

Ministry matters are rarely that obvious and objective. We serve a Head we cannot see, and we listen to a voice we cannot literally hear. Often we feel as if we're being asked to follow a plan we do not understand. And I need to repeat here, during the process of discovering God's leading, we are subject to enormous changes. These are changes we must embrace in the power of the Spirit, if we are to obey our Lord's lead. Though we are accountable to the churches we serve, ultimately, each one of God's servants answers to God. Without that sort of single-minded devotion to the Lord, we run the risk of becoming people-pleasers. Christian leaders who become pawns as they focus on pleasing people are pathetic wimps.

Honestly, there have been times in my younger life when I stumbled onto that slippery slide. I look back on those few occasions with only regret. Nothing good ever comes from a ministry devoted to pleasing people.

Rather than being a warrior for the King, it is easy to become an insecure wimp, relying on human opinions and longing for human approval. By His grace I'll never go there again. I've learned so much from these biographical studies I've been writing. My responsibility is to deliver what God's people *need*, not what they *want*. As I do, that truth hits me with the same authority as it does the folks to whom I communicate. May God deliver every honest pastor, every truth-seeking board of elders, and every church leader from the bondage of pleasing people.

As in the situation at Antioch, God often reaches into a smoothly running ministry operation and says, "That person is to go, and this person is to stay. I'm calling him to leave this setting in order to go and serve elsewhere." Too often we cling to those folks too tightly. God has to pry our fingers away and give us the grace to release, so his chosen servants can obey. Selfishness wants to keep, not release.

Let's be willing to release gifted men and women without reluctance.

Think of it this way: By releasing them we enable them to obey. And when you are called by God to go to a place you would never have expected to go, there's no need to be afraid of change. Change brings adventure, and adventure stretches your faith. All that spells growth. Growth happens within us when we face risk. Head-on. Faith and risk go hand in hand. That may be a completely new concept for you.

I recently reread John Eldredge's book, *Wild at Heart.* It's a book for men and about men. But many of the author's principles transcend gender. Allow me to quote extensively one particular section of his engaging work. Picture the scene John paints, and imagine yourself in his place.

> There is a river that winds its way through southern Oregon, running down from the Cascades to the coast, which has also wound its way through my childhood, carving a path in the canyons of my memory. As a young boy I spent many summer days on the Rogue, fishing and swimming and picking blackberries; . . . I loved the name given to the river by French trappers; the river Scoundrel. It gave a mischievous benediction to my adventures there—I was a rogue on the Rogue. Those golden days of boyhood are some of my most cherished memories, and so last summer I took Stasi and the boys there, to share with them a river and a season from my own life. . . .
>
> There is a rock that juts out over that river somewhere between Morrison's lodge and the Foster Bar. The canyon narrows there and the Rogue deepens and pauses for a moment in its rush to the sea. High rock walls rise on either side, and on the north—the side only boaters can reach—is Jumping Rock. Cliff jumping is one of our family favorites, especially when it's hot and dry and the jump is high enough so that it takes your breath away as you plunge beneath the warmer water at the top, down to where it's dark and cold, so cold it sends you gasping back for the surface and the sun. Jumping Rock is perched above the river at about the height of a two-story house plus some, tall enough that you can slowly count to five before you hit the water (it's barely a two count from the high dive at your local pool). There's a faculty built into the human brain that makes every cliff seem twice

the height when you're looking down from the top and everything in you says, *Don't even think about it.*

So you don't think about it, you just hurl yourself off out into the middle of the canyon, and then you free-fall for what feels like enough time to recite the Gettysburg Address and all of your senses are on maximum alert as you plunge into the cold water down below.

. . . After that first jump you have to do it again, partly because you can't believe you did it, and partly because the fear has given way to the thrill of such freedom. We let the sun heat us up again and then . . . bombs away.

I want to live my whole life like that. I want to love with much more abandon and stop waiting for others to love me first. I want to hurl myself into a creative work worthy of God.[3]

Releasing and obeying requires that kind of fearless devotion to God's will. Learn to welcome the risk. Stop waiting for all the answers. All your ducks will never swim in a straight row. Such a guarded mentality requires very little faith, and involves absolutely no adventure. There's a word for those who take all the risk out of living . . . *boring!*

Now, back to Antioch. Pay attention to the response of the church. The Scripture says, "When they had fasted and prayed and laid their hands on them, they sent them away" (13:3). How commendable. How refreshing. No questions asked. No spirit of suspicion. No selfish clinging as if those two men belonged to them. They met with the Lord, made sure His direction was clear, and then took prompt action. They released God's men to the work the Spirit was calling them to do. And the two men, once re-leased, *jumped!* They plunged into the new calling like Eldredge and his sons hurled themselves off Jumping Rock.

Incidentally, I've left most other ministries I was involved in when there was nothing wrong. In fact, I departed at a time when everything was right. Inevitably, folks would come up to me and wonder what had gone wrong. Surely there must be a problem or I wouldn't be leaving. It was almost humorous. Some said, "Hey, Chuck. Psst! What's *really* wrong?" I smiled and told them, "Why, nothing. The Lord has called me to Dallas to be a part of the leadership team of Dallas Seminary." Some simply couldn't believe God would lead in such a way. Life was going along too well. The church was healthy and continuing to grow. People's lives were being transformed. There was a unity in the staff and among that body of believers other local churches longed to experience. Ultimately, everyone now sees how God was leading . . . and His timing was right.

Funny how human nature is put together, isn't it? Since we're often ill informed, we form false conclusions and struggle with reality. Not in Antioch. Nobody questioned God's leading. No strong-voiced leader stood up and attempted to block the board's decision. None of that. The Spirit spoke and God's people unselfishly responded. We read in verse 4, "So, being sent out by the Holy Spirit, they went down to Seleucia and from there they sailed to Cyprus" (13:4).

Talk about change! Barnabas and Saul struck out on a brand-new adventure onto foreign soil, with the Lord out front, and the Antioch church fully standing with them. But this was no pleasure cruise they had booked. Life became dicey quick. The rigors were enough to cause young John Mark (an individual we'll later examine more closely) to leave the team and return home.

While in Lystra, Saul was stoned and left for dead. Imagine, they left Antioch for this!

Serving in the center of God's will can be dangerous business. But whether in times of relative ease or abject hardship the primary principle stands: *Obedience requires change.*

RELEASING AND OBEYING, LIKE CLAY IN HIS HANDS

Keeping the clay of your will supple and flexible calls for constant attention along the way. Once you grow hard and brittle to God's leading, you're less usable to Him. I want to take the truths we've wrestled with here and make them into a softening ointment you can regularly apply when a change is on the horizon. The ingredients in the ointment you need to apply include a pinch of the negative and a smidgen of the positive.

First negative: Do not remove any possibility. Stay open to whatever it is

God may have for you by removing all the limitations. Yes, all. None of those folks back in Antioch would have expected God to lift Barnabas and Saul from the mix. (I would have chosen Lucius and Manaen. I mean, who's gonna miss those guys?) But it's so like the Lord to select the very people you and I wish would stay forever. Erase all the boundaries. Tell the Lord you're willing to cooperate. But don't forget, you may be the next Barnabas or Saul the Lord decides to move. Remember, we're dealing with change—changing so we might obey.

Second negative: Do not allow a lot of activity to dull your sensitivity. Remember, God spoke *while* they were ministering. You can be so busy in church activities you can't figure out what the Lord's saying. Those men in Antioch didn't let that happen. Howard Hendricks, one of my mentors and longtime friends, has said, "The greatest threat to your ministry may *be* your ministry." I think he's right (He usually is!). Be sure you're carving out regular time to be with the Lord, keeping an open mind, meditating on His Word, remaining devoted to prayer, and taking sufficient time to relax. Only then can you hear and discern His still, small voice amid the din of church activity. When you begin to sense He is speaking, stay sensitive, and open and ready.

First positive: Let God be God. He is selective when He moves people. He picked two and left three. That was His prerogative. He could have chosen all five or only one. It's His call. Our sovereign Lord does as He pleases, and when it's clear, our response is to obey. Or as one old preacher used to say, "Salute and charge!" And if you're not chosen to go, rather than feeling badly, rejoice! God has His plan and He has His reasons for choosing whom He chooses. Others are called to leave—you're just as called to stay. Let God be God. You'll never regret it. Don't assume anything beyond this moment.

When Cynthia and I were building our new home in Frisco, I said to a friend, "You know what? This is our last place before death." It suddenly dawned on me, that would be a *tomb!* So, I don't say that anymore.

The Lord never said Frisco, Texas, would be the last place He would use me. He's the Potter; I'm the clay. He's molding me. If it were up to me, I'd instruct Him. "Ah, don't push there. Don't make me look like a vase. I want to look like Michelangelo's *David*, ministering right here in Frisco, for crying out loud." How silly. Let's relax. Let Him do His work.

Second positive: Be ready to say yes. Don't wait for all the details to be ironed out before you agree to release and obey. Sure, there will be hardships, some uphill stretches in the road. So what? Be ready to say yes and trust Him to take care of the rest.

I need to add something here: Don't feel guilty if He doesn't include you in His list of missionaries to Africa. If He isn't leading you there, He doesn't need you in Africa. If He leads you elsewhere, go there. And if He says stay, relax, and give it all you've got right there where you've been all these years. No need to make it complicated. Grace abounds. Enjoy it.

I know that sounds crazy in our detail-conscious, bottom-line, ultra-serious, intense culture. But it takes both grace *and* grit—the stuff of men like Barnabas and Saul.

A PERSONAL HEART CHECK-UP

Only you and the Lord know the condition of your heart. Is it soft and pliable clay, ready to be molded and shaped by the Master sculptor? Or has it hardened into brittle and fragile pottery from years of faithless living? You know exactly what God is asking you to do. It may be well beyond the boundaries of logic and far outside your comfort zone. You may even have a few friends telling you that what you believe He's asking you to do is wrong, completely wrong. Still, His leading is clear. Only one thing is needed: saying yes. Oh, I almost forgot. You also must be willing to risk.

Remember the story from the Rogue River and the view from Jumping Rock? Okay, close your eyes and imagine yourself tip-toed on the edge, straining to see the water's edge below . . . it's quite a drop!

Are you there? Okay, take a deep breath . . . smile . . . now . . . *Jump!* Good for you!

Let the adventure begin . . .

CHAPTER TEN

The Jagged Edge of Authentic Ministry

Authentic ministry is not for the fainthearted or the phony. There's no promise of a life of ease and fame and all the trappings of corporate perks with open-ended expense accounts and kid-glove treatment. Most ministers of the Gospel enjoy a thirty- to forty-, sometimes fifty-year run, before it ends in little more than a cake-and-punch reception to honor their lifetime achievements. No fanfare, no striking up the band, no glamorous award galas along the way to spur weary servants on to greater works. Truth be told, it is mostly a mixture of dreams mixed with reality, joy and heartache, fresh new beginnings alongside painful transitions, loving friendships, as well as conflicts with leaders, occasional vacations plus physical exhaustion and emotional toll taking, and living on tight-budget restraints. For some who minister in many parts of the world, the drill is downright harsh. It would include persecution, imprisonment, intense mistreatment, torture, even death. Put bluntly, authentic ministry often has a jagged edge. And those edges can steal our dreams, causing us to lose heart.

God has a way of inserting periodic reality checkpoints as we journey toward the fulfillment of our dreams.

From this time on, that would certainly be true of our main character, Saul—now called Paul—along with his partner and friend, Barnabas. Young John–Mark also joined the missionary team on this initial journey. He, too, had hopes and dreams. His knees would soon go weak, however, under the pressure of it all, leaving Paul and Barnabas to continue their gospel crusade without him. More on that later.

It all began as the now-familiar sights and sounds of the Antioch revival faded into the distance, eclipsed by the sound of white-capped swells, breaking hard against the creaking, groaning hull of the Mediterranean clipper.

THE ULTIMATE FOCUS OF AN AUTHENTIC MINISTRY

Paul's first missionary journey is now underway. Armed with the call of God, the two men waste no time launching their vision to proclaim the Word of God to all who will give them a hearing. Ironically, it is their strong and healthy commitment to the Gospel that leads them into "many dangers, toils and snares." But as we shall observe, one of the marks of an authentic ministry is an unswerving commitment to the proclamation of Truth. That's why I'm focusing my writing on the record of Paul's life as revealed to us in the Scriptures, rather than on the numerous myths and legends surrounding his monumental life.

I'm convinced that there are two lasting benefits of focusing one's ministry on God's Word: *We know we are getting reliable truth, and our faith is strengthened.* Myths, legends, and fantasies promise neither. God has promised to bless His Word. A ministry that commits to communicating the truth of the Scriptures has the assurance of God's blessing.

Whenever you want to do a serious truthful analysis of any character mentioned in the Bible, that's the place to go. You turn to the Word of God for enlightenment, instruction, and encouragement.

So I regularly take the time at Stonebriar Community Church where I serve to affirm one of my strongest ministry convictions. I mention often that I am passionately committed to the expository preaching of the Bible.

In fact, it was that firm commitment which led to our starting that church back in the fall of 1998. Those who began with us then, as well as those who now comprise the congregation of the new ministry, deeply hunger for the teaching of the Word of God. Strangely, it is rare in our day.

We are living in a culture that resists the notion of absolute truth . . . absolute *anything* for that matter. The tragic results are seen all around us. This is no time for a deliberate softening of truth, to make Christianity more palatable to unbelievers. What strange thinking? That thought would have never crossed Paul's mind. Nor should it cross ours.

Pastor Steven Lawson, in a series of lectures delivered at Dallas Theological Seminary, spoke passionately about the need for churches to reaffirm their commitment to proclaim the Word of God. His words were later recorded in our school's theological journal. They are worth repeating.

> Much of evangelical preaching has become strangely impotent and, sadly, too few realize it. Like Samson, from whom the Spirit departed without his knowing it, many pastors seem to have little awareness that God's power has vanished from their once-dynamic pulpits. Rather than preaching with renewed fervor, they are preoccupied with pouring their energies into secondary strategies, such as pursuing the latest church-growth programs, alternative worship styles, and corporate marketing plans to build their churches. While some of these augmentations may have a place in the church, the crying need of the hour is for divine power to be restored to evangelical pulpits.
>
> At the heart of this crisis is a lost confidence in God's power to use His Word. While many hold to the inerrancy of Scripture, some pastors do not seem convinced of its sufficiency when preached to bring about God's desired results. They reason that biblical preaching is outdated, archaic, and irrelevant. In some churches drama, dialogue, film clips, and similar means are taking the place of solid Bible exposition. These are not necessarily bad in themselves, but expository preaching should never take a back seat to these secondary means of communication.
>
> Pastors would do well to revisit the ministries of God's servants in the Scriptures and heed their examples as proclaimers of God's Word.[1]

Lawson's conviction is commendable. Such conviction must character-ize any ministry that desires to be authentic.

Paul launched his first missionary journey with one clear, forceful objec-tive: to proclaim the Word of God. And I'm convinced it was that unswerving commitment to God's truth that brought him face to face with the jagged edges that accompany such firm convictions. This was no pleasure cruise he had booked for the holidays. Paul set his face like a flint and never looked back. His message was full of grace, but he modeled a determination that was true grit. It was his calling. It was his destiny.

When I applied to Dallas Seminary in the spring of 1959, I was fresh out of the Marine Corp, many pounds lighter, and sporting a flattop. Cynthia and I sat down in the registrar's office for our interview with Dr. Donald K. Campbell, who would many years later become the school's third president. I recall Dr. Campbell's looking over his glasses at me and asking me the following question about entering a life of ministry: "Young man (which is a great thought now for me to think about), would you be happy doing anything else with your life?" I thought about that, since I'd never been asked the question before. Finally, I said to him in all sincerity, "No sir, I would not be happy doing anything but this. I am firmly com-mitted to serving Christ for the rest of my life." A year later he told me they would never have accepted me if I had offered any other response.

Dr. Campbell knew that authentic ministry requires absolute commit-ment. Why? Because in a ministry based on God's Word, where truth is proclaimed and pleasing people is not one's objective, there are jagged edges not generally known by the public. Most believe pastors and church leaders work on Sundays and relax the rest of the week, either playing golf or fid-dling around with nonessentials and hanging out with a few friends. Those of us who've been in God's work for years, simply roll our eyes when we encounter that opinion. People say something like, "Well, all you have to do is get up on your feet and talk. Isn't that all it really is?" Few realize the intensity of pressure and enormity of responsibility connected with accu-rately presenting the Word of God, then correctly handling the fallout.

Let's get something clear before we go any further: Once you've made a commitment to serve Christ in response to His clear call on your life, the

Enemy places you directly in the crosshairs of his scope. And he is an excellent shot! It's open season on all new recruits to the ranks of gospel ministry.

Satan despises everything we love and works feverishly, diabolically against everything we attempt to accomplish in the power of the Spirit. So let me repeat the wise words of my friend and former colleague, Don Campbell: If you'd be happy doing anything else, *please do that.* If you don't, the jagged edge will take such a severe toll on you that you'll wind up disillusioned and shipwrecked.

No doubt, Paul and Barnabas determined before the Lord, "This is exactly what we want to do. We want to go where You have called us to go . . . we want to do the work You have called us to do." They didn't have a clue regarding the details of their future. That's always true. God's servants never know what's out front. (If we knew, we'd probably never go.) They packed up, said a few farewells, and headed for the coast—the first point of destination in what would become a journey of jagged-edge experiences.

> The three missionaries shipped from Seleucia in the first days of the sailing season early in March A.D. 47 for the easy run to Cyprus, an obvious preliminary choice in that Barnabas was a Cypriot and the island had a substantial Jewish minority, large enough to raise a dangerous rebellion some fifty years later. There was also a big population of pagan slaves extracting the copper which gave Cyprus its wealth. The apostles landed at Salamis, the commercial center of the eastern half (near modern Famagusta), where they "proclaimed the Word of God in the synagogues of the Jews."[2]

THE JAGGED EDGE OF PHYSICAL DEMANDS

A brief geographical tour will help orient you to Paul's first missionary journey. Barry Beitzel in his popular book, *The Moody Atlas of Bible Lands*, helps put the extent of Paul's rigorous travels in perspective. Read his words carefully, and be amazed as I was by the enormous physical demands Paul and Barnabas faced.

The distances traveled by the apostle Paul are nothing short of staggering. In point of fact, the New Testament registers the equivalent of about 13,400 airline miles that the great apostle journeyed; and if one takes into account the circuitous roads he necessarily had to employ at times, the total distance traveled would exceed that figure by a sizeable margin. Moreover, it appears that the New Testament does not document all of Paul's excursions. For example, there seems to have been an unchronicled visit to Corinth (2 Corinthians 12:14; 13:1); he refers to shipwrecks of which we have no record (2 Corinthians 11:25); and there was his desire to tour Spain (Romans 15:24,28), though it is still debated whether or not he ever succeeded in that mission. Considering the means of transportation available in the Roman world, the average distance traveled in a day, the primitive paths, and rugged, sometimes mountainous terrain over which he had to venture, the sheer expenditure of the apostle's physical energy becomes unfathomable for us. Many of those miles carried Paul through unsafe and hostile environs largely controlled by bandits who eagerly awaited a prey (cf. 2 Corinthians 11:26). Accordingly, Paul's commitment to the Lord entailed a spiritual vitality that was inextricably joined to a superlative level of physical stamina and fearless courage.[3]

What Beitzel calls commitment and vitality and stamina, I call grit. Paul had more than his share. One of the jagged edges of authentic ministry is the enormous expenditure of energy that must be sustained over long periods of time. Once Paul and Barnabas hit Cyprus, they didn't simply build a fire on the beach and wait for word to get out that they had arrived. The historical narrative states they went through the "whole island," proclaiming the gospel and teaching the Word of God.

Don't get sidetracked by the details and miss the bigger picture. There were no trams or trains, no island charter flights available. They walked for days, often through the night. And after canvassing the entire island they stopped at Paphos. Though no doubt exhausted from their traveling, it was on the heels of their island-long trek that they encountered a government official and his side-kick magician named Elymus. The latter openly opposed the apostles' teaching. Now don't miss this. Having just spent who knows how long traveling the rugged island terrain of Cyprus, spending their nights on the cold, hard ground, you'd think Paul would have had little interest or energy left to deal with a pagan magician and his stupid bag of tricks. On the contrary. He jumped on that challenge like a hen on a June bug. His calling drove him to action. Luke writes,

> But Saul, who was also known as Paul, filled with the Holy Spirit, fixed his gaze upon him, and said, "You who are full of deceit and fraud, you son of the devil, you enemy of all righteousness, will you not cease to make crooked the straight ways of the Lord? And now behold, the hand of the Lord is upon you, and you will be blind and not see the sun for a time." And immediately a mist and a darkness fell upon him, and he went about seeking those who would lead him by the hand. Then the proconsul believed when he saw what had happened, being amazed at the teaching of the Lord.
>
> Acts 13:9–12

How's that for grit? Despite his weakened physical state, Paul faced the opposition squarely by vigorously defending the truth and leading a sinner to the Savior. I love it. An uncommitted novice would have quickly drafted his resumé, fired it off to the board, and taken the next ship home. Not Paul. He didn't back off for even a moment. As we'll notice from here on, difficulties fueled his fire. The man didn't know the word "quit."

The physical challenges only intensified as the journey continued from Paphos on to Perga in Pamphylia (13:13). It was there in that rugged region several biblical scholars believe Paul contracted malaria or some dreaded coastal disease. Or, perhaps it was another illness that began here. His bad eyesight, with which he struggled throughout the rest of his ministry, may have had its roots in some exotic Pamphylian virus.

Luke also tells us that it was here in this inhospitable setting that John Mark abandoned the trip. No doubt he had been of significant help to them, assisting in practical ways, perhaps carrying the baggage for the two determined missionaries. With his sudden departure, that help was gone.

In a matter of days, they went from being a team of three down to two. They were already feeling the pressure, especially since a sickness emerged . . . now there's one less person to help carry the load.

Pamphylia is known for its rugged, rough terrain. Deserted by young John Mark, the two missionaries were left to navigate that treacherous countryside, lugging all their belongings on their backs. They're tired, they're hungry, they're sick, and they're spiritually and emotionally drained. Their muscles ache and their feet are blistered. The thirty-five-hundred-foot climb up and across that coastal range led them to Perga, then more than one hundred miles north beyond the mountains to the Roman colony of Pisidian Antioch. With dauntless determination they pressed on, alone. They refused to give in to exhaustion. What splendid models for those of us in ministry to remember! Their hardships only intensified as they continued north.

THE JAGGED EDGE OF ELUSIVE POPULARITY

The long, arduous journey eventually led them to Lystra (14:8). The men were no doubt hoping for some rest and relief, having been chased from the towns they had visited to that point. All the while, they continued to preach and teach the Scriptures. Out of the blue something amazing took place. Let's allow the Scriptures to paint the scene: "At Lystra there was sitting a certain man, without strength in his feet, lame from his mother's womb, who had never walked. This man was listening to Paul as he spoke, who, when he had fixed his gaze upon him, and had seen that he had faith to be made well, said with a loud voice, 'Stand upright on your feet.' And he leaped up and began to walk" (Acts 14:8–10).

How's that for a vivid sermon illustration? The response of the superstitious crowd was predictable: "And when the multitudes saw what Paul had done, they raised their voice, saying in the Lycaonian language, 'The gods have become like men and have come down to us.' And they began calling Barnabas, Zeus, and Paul, Hermes, because he was the chief speaker. And the priest of Zeus, whose temple was just outside the city, brought oxen and garlands to the gates, and wanted to offer sacrifice with the crowds" (Acts 14:11–13).

May I momentarily digress? What a tempting moment for a preacher! When the people are so impressed with you and moved by your message, they can make the mistake of treating you almost as if you are a god. How easy to let that go to our heads and start expecting such adoration. Not Paul and Barnabas. On the contrary, they had no intention of giving in to the perilous lure of popularity. Watch their response. This is beautiful: "But when the apostles, Barnabas and Paul, heard of it, they tore their robes and rushed out into the crowd, crying out and saying, 'Men, why are you doing these things? We are also men of the same nature as you, and preach the gospel to you that you should turn from these vain things to the living God, who made the heavens and the earth and the sea, and all that is in them' " (Acts 14:14–15).

Rather than embracing even for a moment the adulation of the crowd, Paul preached a brief sermon that pointed the people to the only true God (14:15–17). They hardly listened. They even attempted to offer sacrifices to the two men. But how short-lived was their popularity. The opposite extreme was only minutes away. Luke writes, "But Jews came from Antioch and Iconium, and having won over the multitudes, they stoned Paul and dragged him out of the city, supposing him to be dead" (14:19).

Welcome to the ministry. One moment you're taking a bow, and the next you're dodging tomatoes, or worse, stones. Been there, done that. Trust this silver-haired, old shepherd on this one: Once the honeymoon is over, the rocks begin to fly. Popularity in ministry is a perilous cliff with a jagged edge that can cut a ministry in two.

Remarkably, though laying lifeless in a pool of his own blood, Paul got right back up and walked back into the city from which he had been dragged and left for dead. I mean, is this missionary determined or what? True grit.

Let me pause right here and ask you a couple of questions: Can you imagine being so hated that people literally pick up rocks and strike you repeatedly until you're unconscious and left for dead? Here's another one: If they stone you in Abilene, are you going stay in Abilene overnight? Okay, make that Phoenix or Bakersfield. Not a chance! You're going to take as quick a flight to a place as far away from there as possible. Get serious, if you're operating strictly from a horizontal viewpoint, you don't want to be within a thousand miles of that place when the sun rises the next dawn.

That is, of course, unless you're called and fully committed to the vertical perspective. Then you stick it out. You don't quit. Neither do you retaliate or throw a pity party. You go to sleep night after night, trusting in the same God who called you to serve there—convinced that He is sovereign and in absolute control.

That's exactly what Paul did. Matter of fact, he entered that same city and spent the night there (14:20). He picked himself off the dusty ground, pushed aside the larger stones, wiped the blood from his face and hands, gathered his composure, and climbed right back into the pulpit. They could not drive him away. Welcome to an authentic ministry!

You'd think he'd demonstrate a little caution and common sense. After all, Lystra is a dangerous, unpredictable city. Paul was stoned and left for dead! They wanted him gone, but God called him to minister there.

Listen to me: *A ministry that lasts is a ministry that relentlessly perseveres through periods of enormous persecution.* It is not fickle. It does not need the applause of people. It rejects being enshrined as a god. Authentic ministry delivers the truth of God, no matter how jagged the edges or perilous the threats. Their ministry dripped with that kind of determination.

DISTINGUISHING MARKS OF AN AUTHENTIC MINISTRY

I want to give you the first two of four observations about why Paul's ministry was authentic. I'll give you two here and provide you with the final two when we get to the next chapter.

First, Paul's ministry was saturated with the Word of God. Fifteen times in chapters thirteen and fourteen the phrases "God's Word," the "word of truth," the "teaching of the Lord," the "Law and the Prophets," and the "good news" are mentioned (13:5, 13:7, 13:12, 13:15A, 13:15B, 13:32, 13:44, 13:46, 13:48, 13:49, 14:3, 14:7, 14:15, 14:21, 14:25).

On that first journey Paul took with him just enough to live on, sufficient clothing to cover his nakedness, a heart full of hope in God's truth, and a confidence in God that would keep him faithful. That's what held him together. That's what steeled him against the tightening jaws of mistreatment in the ministry.

Could it be that you've grown a little soft in the past few months in your commitment to time spent in the Scriptures? It may be happening to you just as it happens to me from time to time. Please heed this gentle warning: If you're getting ready to go off to school, or preparing to take on new ministry responsibilities, or getting ready to launch a new phase of your career, don't do it without first establishing a regular time to meet alone with the Lord, preparing yourself for the new challenge by spending time in His Word. Your spiritual future depends on it. Without that commitment to saturate your life with God's Word, you step into the unknown future at your own risk. I urge you to spend sufficient time with the Lord so you might be strengthened within. It can begin with as little as fifteen minutes each day.

Some of you are thinking, *I don't have fifteen minutes a day!* Try cutting your lunch break short so you've got time on the other end to spend reading through a Psalm or two or digesting one of the New Testament letters.

If Paul could saturate his life in the Word of God, you and I can too. You are touching some people in your sphere of influence that likely no one else will touch. Be known for your biblical commitment, your biblical counseling. Be known for your biblical advice. Be appreciated for your biblical stand on moral values. It all starts with your investment of time in the Bible. Go there. Become saturated with the Word of God. That in itself will carry you miles down the road toward establishing an authentic ministry.

Second, Paul's message emphasized the gospel to the lost and grace to the saved. That is a wonderful paradigm for any minister or ministry to adopt. As I've studied the life of Paul, particularly in his later years, I find two prominent themes woven like threads through the tapestry of his ministry.

First, to the lost he presented the gospel: "Let it be known to you, brethren, that through Him forgiveness of sins is proclaimed to you, and through Him everyone who believes is freed from all things, from which you could not be freed through the Law of Moses" (Acts 13:38–39).

Imagine the impact our churches would have on our communities if each Christian would commit to sharing the Gospel once a week with someone who expresses a need.

Recently, I had the wonderful privilege of sharing Christ with a businessman. It was not a very sophisticated presentation, but the opportunity was there, and I did my best to make the message clear. I simply grabbed a paper napkin, and on it I drew a series of islands in an open body of water. I explained to him that the choices he had made in his life were like bridges that brought him to certain islands in the sea. Unfortunately, I told him, the bridge he had chosen had led him to an island full of debris. What he longed for was to find the bridge that spanned the gulf, leading to the mainland of peace and forgiveness and hope. I then said, "You've just taken the wrong bridges all through your adult life, and they have led you to the wrong islands. This religion, that false teaching, this stack of good works, that area of self-help. You've missed the one bridge that leads to the place where all of us need to be. The bridge you have missed is Christ."

In the simplest of terms I explained to him how he could have a personal relationship with the Savior. He didn't at that moment believe. He may have in the hours that followed. Only God knows. Our responsibility is to invest the Gospel in the lives of the lost and leave the results with Him. That's what Paul did. It made his ministry authentic.

Second, his message included large doses of grace for the saved. Just as the lost don't understand the Gospel, the saved rarely understand grace. (Please read that sentence again). There are few activities more exhausting and less rewarding than Christians attempting to please the people around them by maintaining impossible legalistic demands. What a tragic trap, and thousands are caught in it. When will we ever learn? Grace has set us free! That message streamed often through the sermons and personal testimonies of the apostle Paul.

> When the meeting of the synagogue had broken up, many of the Jews and of the God-fearing proselytes followed Paul and Barnabas, who, speaking to them, were urging them to continue in the grace of God. (13:43)

Isn't that great? "Paul, Barnabas, keep telling us about grace. Keep preaching grace."

The message of grace continued to flow . . .

> They spent a long time there speaking boldly with reliance upon the Lord, who was testifying to the word of His grace, granting that signs and wonders be done by their hands. (14:3)

And it flowed some more . . .

> And from there they sailed to Antioch, from which they had been commended to the grace of God for the work that they had accomplished. (14:26)

If you and I consistently and compassionately deliver the Gospel to the lost and grace to the guilt-ridden and ashamed, we will never run of out people who long to be free.

The lost need to hear how they can go from the island of debris, filled with misery and guilt, to the land of peace and forgiveness, flowing with mercy and grace. We build those bridges when we lovingly and patiently communicate the Gospel. You don't have to have a seminary degree. You don't have to know a lot of the religious vocabulary. In your own authentic, honest, and unguarded manner, share with people what Christ has done for you. Who knows? It may not be long before you will know the joy of leading a lost sinner from the darkness of death's dungeon across the bridge to the liberating hope of new life in Christ. Once they've arrived, *release them.* Release them into the magnificent freedom that grace provides. Don't smother them with a bunch of rules and regulations that put them on probation and keep them in that holding tank until they "get their lives straightened out." Making us holy is the Spirit's work. You be faithful to dispense the Gospel to the lost and grace to the saved. Then leave the results in the Lord's hands.

It's okay to dream big. And it's fine to plan with a positive attitude. But don't forget the lessons of Paul and Barnabas: The terrain of an authentic ministry is rocky, and some of those rocks have jagged edges. And speaking of that, let me close this chapter by mentioning . . .

THE JAGGED EDGE OF DISAPPOINTING RESULTS

A sentence in the diary of James Gilmore, pioneer missionary to Mongolia, has stayed with me since the day I first read it. After years of laboring long and hard for the cause of Christ in that desperate land, he wrote, "In the shape of converts I have seen no result. I have not, as far as I am aware, seen anyone who even wanted to be a Christian."

Let me add some further reality to that statement by taking you back to an entry in Gilmore's journal made in the early days of his ministry. It expressed his dreams and burdens for the people of Mongolia. Handwritten in his journal are these dreams: "Several huts in sight. When shall I be able to speak to the people? O Lord, suggest by the Spirit how I should come among them, and in preparing myself to teach the life and love of Christ Jesus."

That was his hope. He longed to reach the lost of Mongolia with the Gospel of Jesus Christ. How different from his entry many years later, "I have not, as far as I am aware, seen anyone who even wanted to be a Christian."

What happened in between? He encountered the jagged edge of an authentic ministry. When I write about succeeding in the work of the Lord, I'm not promising success as we define it in human terms. I'm not saying because you are faithful to proclaim the Word of God your church will be packed. Some of God's most faithful servants are preaching their hearts out in places where the church is not growing. A great temptation for those in that difficult setting is to turn to some of the other *stuff* that holds out the promise of more visible results. Don't go there. Stay at it. God is at work. Some are called to minister far north of Dallas in Frisco, Texas, which is my privilege. Others are called to Lystra and Derbe, or to the outermost regions of Mongolia, where very few ever express an interest in the Savior. My respect for those people and the legion of others like them knows no bounds.

Thinking of preparing for a life of ministry? Does the thought of standing before crowds of people and delivering the Word of God with passion and conviction appeal to your sense of adventure? I need to ask you one more time: *Is there anything else in this world that would bring you greater enjoyment?* If so, go there. Don't even hesitate.

But if you know the Lord has called you into His work, and you would not be fulfilled doing anything else, then go there and never look back.

I should add, if you're sure you're called, be ready for those jagged edges. John Mark wasn't, and he quit. When those harsh edges stole his dreams, he lost his heart. He wasn't the first, and he certainly won't be the last to have that happen.

CHAPTER ELEVEN

A Game Plan for Facing Extreme Circumstances

I'm convinced there are at least three essentials for a fulfilling life: a clear sense of personal identity, a strong sense of mission, and a deep sense of purpose.

Over the years, I've observed that people who know who they are, who possess a clear sense of their mission, and who understand God's plan and purpose for their lives, are people who experience genuine fulfillment. That doesn't mean they don't face extreme obstacles. Rather, it means they have learned to face those challenges in ways that transform obstacles into opportunities. Rather than stumbling over them, they press on *through* them.

That may describe you. If so, you are pressing on through certain obstacles because you have a focus on who you are, what you're called to do, and how your particular circumstances fit into God's greater purpose.

Henry Ford said, "Obstacles are those frightful things you see when you take your eyes off the goal." That motto is framed and occupies a prominent place in my church study.

It's actually a picture of a skier who is coming down a suicide slope laden with huge mounds and steep moguls. The skier appears to be navigating that frightening descent quite effortlessly. Printed on the bottom of the photo are the words, "Obstacles are those frightful things you see when you take your eyes off the goal."

I've long dreamed of skiing with that kind of graceful style. Truth be told, I've rarely ventured off the bunny slope. And for good reason. I attempted an intermediate slope once while skiing at Keystone in Colorado a number of years ago. I thought I was making progress, until I reached a little less than halfway down the hill. To my horror, I found myself leaning sharply to the left, out of control on one ski with the other ski not where it should have been (almost over my head). About that time I whipped past a ski school class for young skiers. As I blew by, my one ski and poles flapping wildly in the wind, I heard the teacher say in a loud voice, as she was trying to protect the children from this adult missile traveling about thirty miles an hour, downhill, "That is *not* what I want you to do." Swindoll on skis with his eyes off the goal. As I recall, I wound up not too far from a herd of buffalo, grazing and staring in my direction. I lay in a hump, covered with snow, and no skies. Not a pretty sight.

THE POWER OF A REMARKABLE ATTITUDE

In his book *Man's Search for Meaning*, Viktor Frankl wrote these amazing words: "We who lived in the concentration camps can remember the men who walked through the huts comforting others, giving away their last pieces of bread. They may have been few in number, but they offer sufficient proof that everything can be taken from a man but one thing: The last of his freedoms is to choose his own attitude in any given set of circumstances—to choose one's own way."[1]

I could not be in greater agreement. We make a choice every waking moment of our lives. When we awaken in the morning, we choose the attitude that will ultimately guide our thoughts and actions through the day. I'm convinced our best attitudes emerge out of a clear understanding of our own identity, a clear sense of our divine mission, and a deep sense of God's purpose for our lives. That sort of God-honoring attitude encourages us to press on, to focus on the goal, to respond in remarkable ways to life's most extreme circumstances.

It was that kind of remarkable attitude Paul and Barnabas consistently maintained throughout their missionary journey. The two Antioch-sent servants faced and overcame countless and extreme obstacles, with a relentless determination to stay focused on the goal.

We all need a reliable game plan for facing extreme circumstances. The situation that now looms in front of you may be fixable, or it may seem impossible to overcome in your own strength. It might be the result of your own actions, or you may be an innocent victim, caught in the backlash of someone else's consequences. Whatever the case, we can easily become intimidated, even fearful, and eventually immobile when facing such obstacles. The only way to move beyond that sort of paralyzing stalemate is to learn to accept and trust God's plan. You release the controls and wait for Him to move.

Let's step back into the story as it continues to unfold in the Book of Acts. In Acts 13 and 14 we read of several extreme circumstances Paul and Barnabas faced on that initial evangelistic campaign, which proved to be a grueling marathon of tests. There was no turning back. Instead, the two companions met each roadblock with remarkable grit and fierce resolve.

MATURE RESPONSES TO MIXED REACTIONS

Though the responses were mixed, Paul's responses were mature. That's the third of four observations I want to make with regard to Paul's authentic ministry. We looked at the first two in the previous chapter. In this chapter we want to look closely at the final two.

In the pages that follow, I want to offer several examples of Paul's mature response to extreme circumstances he met along the way. I think you'll agree that seasoned maturity and determined grit marked his response to each situation.

We left Paul and Barnabas near the close of their Cyprus-island crusade. So much was riding on the success of this first missionary advance. Against all odds they forged ahead, never looking back. What kept their resolve firm? You read this earlier: their clear sense of personal identity, a firm grasp of their stated mission, and a defined purpose of building a bridge of grace to the darkened lands of Gentile hearts. That vision loomed as bright and wide as the cloudless Mediterranean sky. Storm clouds would soon roll in as cooler winds shifted their headings north toward the uncertain land of the Gentiles. Biographer John Pollock skillfully paints the scene.

> For Paul, Cyprus could be no more than a prelude; the Christian message had been known there since the arrival of refugees from his own persecution fifteen years before, whereas he was determined to go "where Christ was not named." He was confident that the Lord would unfold a strategy. He had the strongest awareness, as his actions show, that the entire operation was in the hands of the Lord Jesus, who was no passive spectator but the invisible commander, ready to seize opportunities, recover from reverses, deploy His forces as they gathered under His banner. Barnabas possibly doubted whether the Word would be received by pagans; Antioch might have been a special case. Paul had no such doubts. Both awaited a sign.[2]

That sign would be short in coming as Paul and Barnabas, along with young John Mark, rounded the turn on the last stretch of the Cyprus coast. Before weighing anchor for all points north, the missionary envoy from Antioch had a divine appointment with a false magician, who stumbles across their path, cursing and waving his opposing wand.

Responding to a Phony Prophet

When Paul needed to be firm, he stepped up. That's the first principle for responding correctly to extreme circumstances. We looked briefly at this scene in the previous chapter. Let's zoom in for a closer look. Dr. Luke succinctly recalls the event as follows:

> And when they had gone through the whole island as far as Paphos, they found a certain magician, a Jewish false prophet whose name was Bar-Jesus, who was with the proconsul, Sergius Paulus, a man of intelligence. This man summoned Barnabas and Saul and sought to hear the word of God. But Elymas the magician (for thus his name is trans-

lated) was opposing them, seeking to turn the proconsul away from the faith.

Acts 13:6–8

The word *Bar* means "son." The man had the boldness to brandish the nickname "son of Jesus." Clearly, he was a phony, absolute charlatan, or in Luke's words, "a false prophet." He accompanied a Roman official named Sergius Paulus, whom Luke describes as a "proconsul, a man of intelligence." He had officially requested a meeting with Paul and Barnabas for the purpose of hearing the Word of God.

Here's a Gentile living on Cyprus who hears about the ministry of these two missionaries from Antioch, and he summoned them into his presence. Could this be the sign they had been seeking?

He said, "I want to hear that message myself." His sidekick, Elymas, the false prophet/magician, did not share his zeal for the truth. So he opposed Paul and Barnabas and attempted to impede their progress.

I don't know what he did. Perhaps he mocked what they were saying, like a court jester would do to entertain a king. He may have mimicked them, or interrupted their teaching with pointless arguments and irritating objections. Pollock suggests a more insidious motive. He writes, "They were in full course, each adding to the other, when abruptly, in defiance of protocol, Elymas interrupted. He launched a venomous attack on them and their news, 'trying to turn the Proconsul from the faith' with all the vigor of a man who sees his influence about to be overturned."[3]

Perhaps that's what happened. Obviously, the fool would fear he'd lose his job if these zealots persuaded his benefactor to convert. He was determined to stop all progress.

This was no time for Paul to be tolerant or passive. We live in a culture that virtually deifies tolerance. One lady recently said to me with a broad grin, "I love everybody, I even love the devil." I call that "tolerance gone to seed." Make no mistake, we're not to love the devil, nor are we to love everything everybody does. Christ commands us to love people, even our enemies, but that doesn't mean we shrink from standing up for righteousness. Paul didn't back off an inch. I can see the hair stiffening on the back of his neck as he showed his spiritual teeth and growled, "'You are full of all deceit and fraud, you son of the devil, you enemy of all righteousness, will you not cease to make crooked the straight ways of the Lord? And now, behold, the hand of the Lord is upon you, and you will be blind and not see the sun for a time.' And immediately a mist and a darkness fell upon him, and he went about seeking those who would lead him by the hand" (Acts 13:10–11).

Can you imagine the shock as the mixed-up magician realized he'd just messed with the wrong guy. Only this was no sleight of hand. He was blind. I mean, the place went dark on him. Lights out!

Honestly, as dogmatic as I have been at times, I've never responded to anyone like that. I *should* have on a few occasions. But I didn't. I tend to err on the side of diplomacy. I've stood up to people, but I've never called someone a "son of the devil." Nevertheless, Paul did, and he was right on target. Grit on display. He nipped the opposition in the bud. The opportunity was simply too severe to ignore. He knew the stakes were high, and so did the devil. This was nothing short of a battle for Sergius' soul. There would be no diplomacy here.

When he had to be firm, he stepped up. The result was magnificent. Stunned by the obvious display of God's power and Paul's emboldened response, the pagan official believed, and we can almost see the door to the Gentiles opened wider.

You may face similar opportunities to confront enemies of truth. They come in a number of different forms. Some are more insidious than others. My advice, when the opposition against the truth is this severe, based on Paul's model, is that you do it. Leave the results with God. Step up and speak out in the name of the Lord. Be certain of His protection. Don't rush in. Pray for wisdom in the choice of your words before saying anything, and then speak boldly. The results may not be as dramatic as what happened in Cyprus, but the Lord will honor your faith. The few times I've had to stand this firmly against wrong, the Lord gave me a sense of near-invincible courage.

Paul handled that particular external opposition with calm confidence. Another test would soon present itself, however, and that threat would come from within.

Paul's Response to Desertion

When another defected, Paul pressed on. That's principle number two. Paul, Barnabas, and John Mark left Cyprus, and sailed to the southern coast of Turkey. A land then known as Pamphylia, whose rugged coastline ascended sharply into the towering heights of a mountain range "steeper and fiercer than the eastern Tauras near Tarsus, and more terrible than any hills known to the Cypriot Barnabas or the Judean John Mark."[4]

That sight alone may have initiated the storm surge of doubt that would eventually flood young John Mark's soul. As we learned in the previous chapter, it is in this region that Paul got gravely ill with Malaria or some other serious coastal fever. That may have been the last straw for the inexperienced traveler to endure. Without any explanation, Luke simply writes, "John left them and returned to Jerusalem."

The story begs for more information. You wish Luke would have added, "because he was homesick," or "on account of the arduous journey ahead," he left them. Nothing like that is provided, so we're left to our imagination.

Frankly, if I have to choose something, I'd say he went weak in the knees. That, coupled with a bit of homesickness, was enough to cause him to fade into the sunset. His defection troubled Paul, as we'll see in the next chapter. He defected.

But going on from Perga, they pressed on. Without even as much as a hiccup, the journey continued. Paul and Barnabas were undeterred by John Mark's desertion.

I need to make an important observation at this point: *All the way through ministry, people leave.* In every church there will be individuals, who for whatever reason, move on to other things. This includes those in leadership. They leave, but the church presses on. Regardless of the circumstances surrounding their departure, the journey continued. For Paul and Barnabas there was neither time nor need for a long, drawn-out farewell. They pressed ahead, keeping their eyes focused on the goal.

It's hard to press on when you feel abandoned. It's easy to give in to discouragement and allow that to siphon your tank dry. Paul and Barnabas had no such luxury. Emotions in check, they had a job to do. They moved forward with an even stronger determination.

One of the marks of maturity is the ability to press ahead regardless of who walks off the scene. The alternative isn't an option. Once you've said goodbye, it's time for everyone to move on. That's exactly what Paul and Barnabas did.

On they went, up the steep, jagged slopes toward the beautiful city of Pisidian Antioch, which they hoped to reach before Sabbath. If they had tarried even a day to fret over John's departure, they would have missed a remarkable opportunity the Lord had prepared for them in the next town.

Paul's Response to Unexpected Opportunities to Preach

When Paul was invited to speak, he spoke. They indeed arrived at Pisidian Antioch, weary and aching from their perilous march through the mountains. Still, they wasted no time in making their way to the synagogue early enough to find a good seat to listen to the reading of God's Word. They made their destination by the Sabbath.

> But going on from Perga, they arrived at Pisidian Antioch, and on the Sabbath day they went into the synagogue and sat down. And after the reading of the Law and the Prophets the synagogue officials sent to them, saying, "Brethren, if you have any word of exhortation for the people, say it." And Paul stood up, and motioning with his hand, he said, "Men of Israel, and you who fear God, listen . . ."
>
> Acts 13:14–16

They said to Paul, "Would you like to preach?" That was his cue! (I can read the man's mind, *I thought you'd never ask!*) Without hesitation he delivered the goods. He started in Genesis and preached all the way through to the ministry of Christ completely from memory! He had no notes. He did it extemporaneously.

Let's trace his sermon outline through the passage in Acts thirteen. In doing so, we're able to see the biblical journey on which he led his fellow worshipers.

With that he came to the end of the Old Testament. (In the Hebrew Bible, Chronicles is the last book of the Old Testament.) From there he leaps into the first century in verse 23, bringing his listeners right into the days of Christ.

By the time he reached the end of his expository sermon, he had traced the Gospel through the scrolls of Old Testament Scriptures. That's what I call seizing an opportunity!

From the Law they learned about sin and the standard of holiness. From Christ they heard about grace, forgiveness and the freedom to live under His power. It was a magnificent Sabbath sermon.

As a preacher, I must tell you, *I'm impressed.* He didn't even know he was going to preach that day. But he was prepared. He *stayed* prepared. We tell students at Dallas Seminary they "need to be ready to preach, pray, or die at any moment." Paul was ready to do all three. And the man definitely could preach!

The response was overwhelming. Luke informs us that the next Sabbath the whole town showed up to hear the message he would deliver. The same was true then as it is today: People are hungry for the Word of God. When you have hungry hearts and great food served well, there's no problem getting people to come for the spiritual meal. Finding people who long to be fed the nourishing meat of God's truth is no great challenge.

Therefore, my advice is simple: When you have the opportunity to share the good news, share it. But be careful not to dump the whole truck. If you're sitting on a plane and the opportunity presents itself, don't feel compelled to preach through the whole Old Testament before getting to the heart of the Gospel. Tell that hungry soul how to find a piece of bread. As you direct the individual to Christ, tell him of your own journey. If done courteously and interestingly, he will hang on every word. Just as they did with Paul. And the response was overwhelmingly positive.

That was until the prejudiced and hostile Jewish leaders caught wind of Paul's success. At that point, resistance replaced acceptance.

Paul's Response to Open Rejection

When Paul was rejected, he didn't quit. As my good friend and wise mentor, Howie Hendricks, often says, "Where there's light, there are bugs!" The brighter Paul's light, the more the bugs. And in that situation, those bugs had stingers filled with poison.

> But when the Jews saw the crowds, they were filled with jealousy, and began contradicting the things spoken by Paul, and were blaspheming. And Paul and Barnabas spoke out boldly and said, "It was necessary that the word of God should be spoken to you first; since you repudiate it, and judge yourselves unworthy of eternal life, we are turning to the Gentiles.
>
> Acts 13:45–46

What grit! Paul didn't back down an inch in his response to open rejection. The result? Not surprisingly, the Gentiles in the crowd rejoiced in the good news he had for them. How exciting! What started as a smoldering ember of religious curiosity, burst into flames of faith.

What made the difference? Paul did not quit when the Jews said, "Stop." Let's camp here momentarily and learn a vital lesson from this first-century situation. Good ministry will always have its critics. You can often tell who they are. They are the squint-eyed, negative folks who look for any possible reason to block the work of God. They're everywhere, even in the church. But such obstacles need not alter our course. Remember those words from the ski scene? "Obstacles are those frightful things you see when you take your eyes off the goal." If you know who you are, and if you're as convinced of your mission as you are firm in your purpose, what's the big deal? You stay focused. You respond with the same grit as Paul. You refuse to wimp out. No sniffling. No strong-armed self-defense. No changing of the message. No holding back. No apology. When the Jews rejected the message, Paul and Barnabas turned to the Gentiles. "And that's the rest of the story."

Why were Paul and Barnabas able to persevere? Neither man set his affections on temporal things. What discipline. If you want to get caught in the net of disillusionment, allow yourself to get tangled in the tangibles. You'll not only run shy of courage, you'll sink like a rock in a country pond. Why? Because others' opinions will start to mean everything. When you allow their responses to be the ballast, then their applause become essential to keep you afloat, and their assaults drag you straight to the bottom. That formula for failure can be found in all people-pleasing ministries. You're doomed to disillusionment if you don't focus on the eternal.

Lee Iacocca, not long after leaving the automobile business, said, "Here I am in the twilight years of my life still wondering what it's all about. I can tell you this: Fame and fortune is for the birds."

You may be one who lives your life pursuing fame and fortune, depending on the applause of others. Bad plan. To begin with, fortune has shallow roots. The winds of adversity can quickly blow it all away. "Riches make themselves wings" writes Solomon, "they fly away as an eagle toward heaven" (Proverbs 23:5, KJV). And fame is as fickle as the last response from the crowd. Learn a dual lesson from this fine man who had wisdom far beyond most of us. When you're praised and applauded, don't pay any attention. And when you're rejected and abused, don't quit. It wasn't human opinion that called you into the work you're doing. So don't let human responses or criticisms get you sidetracked. Keep going.

That leads to the final response . . .

Paul's Response to a Mission Accomplished

When Paul returned to places he had been before, there were no regrets. The end of Acts 14 chronicles the return trip Paul and Barnabas made back to home base, Antioch. (It would help if you took another glance at Map One, p.353). On route, they visited many of the cities where they had earlier preached the Gospel. They returned to Lystra, where Paul had been stoned, then on to Iconium. They backtracked through Pisidia and Pamphylia, then down again to Perga and Attalia. Exhausted yet exuberant, they sailed across the deep-blue waters of the northeastern Mediterranean, destination Antioch—their first missionary enterprise now in the log books.

Retracing their steps, they stopped to encourage and strengthen the disciples they had made. They planted churches and appointed elders. There's no mention of lengthy attempts to reconcile the wrongs they had suffered. There were no angry outbursts, no regrets. Their focus remained the same: pursuing an authentic ministry for the glory of God.

That leads me to the final of four observations about what made Paul's ministry authentic. *In all that Paul did, the glory went to God.* Whatever else you may remember, don't forget this. Luke writes, "And when they had arrived and gathered the church together, they began to report all things that *God had done* with them and how *He had opened a door of faith to the Gentiles*" (14:27). Is that great, or what? No big-time press conferences extolling a successful campaign. No self-serving interviews for some Christian radio station drawing attention to their hardships and successes. None of that. They reported everything that *God had done through them.* I love it.

Paul never forgot it was all about what God had done, not what he had accomplished. The work may be ours to do, but the glory belongs to God. The responsibility is ours to embrace, but the credit is the Lord's alone. There's to be no embezzling of glory. It all belongs to Him. That attitude never fails to put everything in proper perspective.

THE REMARKABLE BENEFITS OF AN EXAMINED LIFE

Let's recap what we've considered in these last two chapters.

- We need to examine ourselves to see if we are being saturated with the Word of God as a result of personal time with Him.
- We must make certain our emphasis remains on presenting the Gospel to the lost and grace to the saved.
- We should check our responses to mixed reactions, making sure they're mature responses which honor the Lord and keep the focus on His work.

- We would be wise to examine our motives for doing the work, making sure at every turn, in every achievement, with every ministry success the glory goes to Him.

Plato wrote in his *Apology,* "The life which is unexamined is not worth living." Borrowing from Plato's comment, I would offer this counsel: *The ministry which is unexamined is not worth continuing.*

My challenge to you is to live a carefully examined life in an unexamining age. That will result in your maintaining a carefully examined ministry in a day when virtually anything goes. Whatever happens, keep your eyes on the goal. However difficult, don't quit. Though the obstacles are extreme, the stakes are eternal.

CHAPTER TWELVE

The Day Two Missionaries Duked It Out

Paul and Barnabas stayed on in Antioch, teaching and preaching the Word of God. But they weren't alone. There were a number of teachers and preachers at that time in Antioch.

After a few days of this, Paul said to Barnabas, "Let's go back and visit all our friends in each of the towns where we preached the Word of God. Let's see how they're doing."

Barnabas wanted to take John along, the John nicknamed Mark. But Paul wouldn't have him; he wasn't about to take along a quitter who, as soon as the going got tough, had jumped ship on them in Pamphylia. Tempers flared, and they ended up going their separate ways: Barnabas took Mark and sailed for Cyprus; Paul chose Silas and, offered up by their friends to the grace of the Master, went to Syria and Cilicia to build up muscle and sinew in those congregations.

Acts 15:35–41, MSG

Some things sound so outrageous they're hardly believable. Several years ago I heard of a young news correspondent assigned to spend time with the late Roman Catholic nun, Mother Theresa. His assignment was to provide a snapshot of her life's work. At one point during the interview the zealous reporter asked this saintly woman if she had any other dreams in life. Was there anything else she'd ever dreamed of doing? Without a moment's hesitation, she replied, "Well, I always wanted to be a flight attendant." Now when I heard that, it seemed outrageous. Imagine Mother Theresa in uniform, serving passengers cokes and coffee and handing out little toy meals on an airplane. It just doesn't fit.

One of my all-time favorites is the true story I first told in my book, *Laugh Again*. It's what happened between a grandmother and her precocious granddaughter. The little tike was determined to find out her grandmother's age. Grandma never let on; in fact, she never told anyone. She said, "I'm not going to tell you my age; only your granddaddy knows how old I am, and you don't need to know, honey. It doesn't matter."

One evening while fixing supper, it occurred to the wise grandmother that she hadn't heard the little girl playing in her room. She wondered what she was up to since she had become much too quiet. She took off her apron and slipped upstairs to her own bedroom. When she walked in she saw the little girl rummaging through the contents of her purse, which she had spilled out on her lap on top of the bed where she was sitting. In her hot little hand she grasped her grandmother's driver's license.

"Grandma, you are 73 years old," she blurted out, with a twinkle in her eye.

"Well, yes, I am. How do you know that?" the woman asked, a little embarrassed.

"Well, I see the date of your birthday here, and I subtracted that year from this year, and you're 73."

As she continued to scrutinize the driver's license, she frowned and added, "And you also made an F in sex!"

Now you wouldn't expect a darling little granddaughter to come up with something like that. It just seems too outrageous.

Often our categories don't match reality. Without warning we encounter a situation so outrageous we're forced to rethink everything we've ever thought or believed to be true. It may be about the dreams of a servant-hearted nun, known for her sacrificial ministry on behalf of the weak and dying on the streets of Calcutta. Or it may be a shocking statement from the mouth of a seven-year-old girl reading her grandmother's driver's license.

Or it may have to do with watching two veteran missionaries engaged in a sharp disagreement, and wondering how that could possibly have happened. Missionaries duking it out? You can't be serious. Missionaries don't argue. Matter of fact, all they do is pray, live sacrificial lives, and talk about the Lord. Isn't that correct?

If you are a missionary or have spent time with those who are, you're probably smiling. You know missionaries are as human as the next person. They live with the same human tendencies toward stubbornness, selfishness, impatience, and irritability as the rest of us. Paul and Barnabas were no exceptions. In fact, I'm convinced, if Paul and Barnabas hadn't controlled themselves, they would have literally gone to the turf, slugging it out. Understand, they were not wild-eyed, carnal men who were out to get one another. They're the same men who amazed us with their remarkable responses to extreme circumstance, only a few pages before.

Nevertheless, what transpires just before the launching of Paul's second missionary journey is even more amazing than that. Some would consider it outrageous. Imagine two statesman-like men—mature, gifted, godly, sincere, and battle-scarred missionaries—standing toe to toe in a heated argument. Just doesn't fit our description of spiritual heroes, does it?

RAW TRUTH FOR REAL LIFE

One of the characteristics I find most attractive about the Bible is its raw realism. When God paints portraits of His servants in the Scriptures, He resists airbrushing away all the warts and blemishes.

Moses was a murderer. David has adultery and hypocrisy on his record. Jonah was a proud and stubborn prophet, who nearly missed an opportunity of a lifetime because of his ugly bigotry. Jacob had deceitful ways. Abraham lied, more than once. Peter waffled when the pressure was on. Even John the Baptizer struggled with doubt. So did Thomas.

So we shouldn't be shocked that Paul and Barnabas had their conflict. When the curtain closes at the end of Acts chapter 15, the two are parting company. Let's take a ringside seat for this ancient middleweight match.

MULTIPLYING THROUGH DIVISION

The powerhouse ministry team of Paul and Barnabas is almost without rival in Scripture. But to cut to the chase and give you some idea of the significance of their disagreement, this contention caused such a rift in their relationship, the two permanently separated. Their paths never crossed again.

Paul and Barnabas finished the first journey and, no doubt, were still caught up in the excitement of it all. They had co-founded numerous churches and, therefore, became known throughout Asia Minor and points beyond for their remarkable giftedness and ministry savvy. During a lengthy rest-and-recovery period in Antioch, they were summoned to Jerusalem to help settle a debate over circumcision. Acts 15 records the issues and events surrounding the Jerusalem Council, the meeting of Jewish Christian leaders to resolve the matter, once and for all, and the official decision on what the message to the Gentiles should be.

Almost the entire chapter is devoted to the hammering out of this emotionally charged theological debate. Finally, after careful consideration of the Scriptures and calm counsel from Peter, James, Silas, and Paul, the gavel came down. Gentiles would not be required to be circumcised. Grace abounded again.

Unfortunately, the next argument recorded in the same chapter, didn't end so amiably. As you read Luke's account, allow your imagination to picture the scene:

> But Paul and Barnabas stayed in Antioch, teaching and preaching with many others also, the word of the Lord. And after some days Paul said to Barnabas, "Let us return and visit the brethren in every city in which we proclaimed the word of the Lord, and see how they are." And Barnabas was desirous of taking John, called Mark, along with them also. But Paul kept insisting that they should not take him

along who had deserted them in Pamphylia and had not gone with them to the work. And there arose such a sharp disagreement that they separated one from the other.

Acts 15:35–39a

They remained a while longer in Antioch, following the Council session in Jerusalem. While in that great missions hub, they taught and preached the word of the Lord (15:35). What kind of men were these? Men of genuine character and true godliness, the kind you and I would stand in line to spend an evening with. Who would ever expect such a rift would fracture the time-tested friendship of Paul and Barnabas?

It all began with a visionary idea. Paul suggested they return to the places they had visited on their initial journey. It was a pastoral visit he had in mind—two shepherds making the rounds to visit the sheep.

Barnabas responded, "Great thought, let's do it, and let's take John Mark with us as we go the second time."

"No, John Mark won't be going."

"Oh, yes, he will," Barnabas shot back.

"Oh, no, he won't, absolutely not!" Paul retorted.

And on it went. The longer they argued, the more the heat intensified in their verbal debate. Neither party gave ground. Finally, the resolution was to divide company. They had *irreconcilable differences*. (I wish I had a ten-dollar bill for every time I have heard that excuse!)

The idea of going on the trip wasn't the problem. Both of them wanted to go. What followed the idea created the rift. In the argument that arose, the strong-hearted missionaries laid themselves bare, warts and all. In some ways, their argument brings me a measure of relief.

G. Campbell Morgan writes of this encounter, "I am greatly comforted whenever I read this. I'm thankful for the revelation of the humanity of these men. If I had never read that Paul and Barnabas had a contention, I should have been afraid. These men were not angels, they were men."[4]

The venerable expositor is correct. These were good men. Godly men. But it is essential to remember they weren't *perfect* men. It must have hit Paul across the chin to think Barnabas would include a proven defector.

And Barnabas must have been deeply disappointed that Paul (of all people!) didn't have enough grace to forgive John and allow him to travel with them. Dr. Bob Cook's words are especially fitting here: "God reserves the right to use people who disagree with me."[5]

We've made great progress in life when we realize that there are others whom, though they don't embrace our convictions, God still chooses to use.

FRESH PERSPECTIVE ON STRONG DISAGREEMENTS

I pause here to share three important elements that apply to strong disagreements. Maybe you'll never have another strong disagreement (if that's true, you need to be sainted!), but if you do, these principles might help you sort through the battle so that no one gets mortally wounded.

First, in every disagreement, there is one issue but several viewpoints. Take this argument going on between these two friends; there is an issue at stake. It's objective and clearly stated. Firm principles surround the issue. The viewpoints, on the other hand, are more subjective because they involve personalities. You look at it one way and your wife (or husband) looks at it another. You view the situation from one perspective, and your son or daughter sees it quite differently. Viewpoints are subjective. The way we look at it has a lot to do with how we're put together. That's where differing personalities play a role.

Keeping those few factors in mind will help regulate the heat and avoid a complete meltdown from occurring. Let me offer a simple definition: *A disagreement is a conflict that involves an issue seen from opposing points of view.*

"This is the issue, this is how I see it," says Paul. "I agree that's the issue, but here's how I see it," says Barnabas. That leads to the next observation.

Second, in disagreements, each side has validity. Both sides have strengths. Sure, every argument has its weaknesses, but both sides have their strengths. Neither side is what I would call a "slam-dunk." Unless, of course, *you're* doing the dunking! The point is, there are strengths on both sides of most legitimate disagreements.

Third, in heated disagreements, someone usually gets hurt. The more intense the heat, the deeper the wounds. Regardless of the level of maturity you've reached in your walk with Christ, you are not immune to hurt. Sharp words strike like shrapnel, and they get imbedded in the brain. That's especially true when character assassination occurs. Someone calls you an insulting name or attacks your character. The result is the inflicting of a wound that's slow to heal. Sometimes, regrettably, it never heals.

A friend of mine, who is in his late seventies, still recalls when his father-in-law belittled him in front of the entire family following a Thanksgiving meal. Over some silly disagreement, the patriarch snorted, "You know, I never had much use for you, anyway." Though the words hit him decades ago, the wound still breaks open and bleeds as if it happened yesterday. The words and tone of that father-in-law's verbal cut pierced permanently into my friend's soul.

I give you those three observations, not because they're original or insightful, but because I believe they are worth remembering. That is especially true as we look more closely at this verbal missionary brawl.

A NEUTRAL LOOK AT A NASTY SCENE

For the next few pages, I'm going to ask you to sit behind the bench, and in a sense, play the judge. We want to work hard at being neutral because we respect both Paul and Barnabas, not only for the kind of men they are, but on account of their remarkable achievements. Some of us are much more like Barnabas than we are like Paul. Others of us think like Paul more than like Barnabas. And so we must first get down to the issue at hand.

Allow me to present it in the form of a question: *Should a person who once walked away from a serious responsibility be given a second chance?* Worded another way, *Should someone who leaves people in the lurch later be allowed to go on a similar mission?* That's the primary issue.

Barnabas says, "Yes, by all means." Paul answers, "No, absolutely not."

Obviously, a line is drawn in the sand. The men possess opposing points of view. Barnabas was interested in building the character of John Mark. He was concerned about the man. Luke writes, "Barnabas was desirous of taking John, called Mark, along with them also" (15:37). That word "desirous" appears in the Greek in the imperfect tense, meaning "to will something forcefully." Barnabas not only willed it, the text suggests he may have even demanded it. "The young man is going. He has every right to take the trip with us. Yes, he failed. Admittedly, he walked away. No one's denying it. But, Paul, nobody's perfect. He was young and inexperienced then. And remember, the mission got accomplished. He walked away, but we still made it. His leaving, I agree, made it harder, but *we made it*. He not only needs our encouragement, he could also benefit from our endorsement. What else are mentors for, if not to give encouragement and affirmation to the weak?"

If you've been blessed by the ministry of a mentor, you appreciate their willingness to stand beside you, back when the chips were down. They were there. Barnabas said, "This is our opportunity." Don't forget, they were cousins (Colossians 4:10). Blood always runs thicker than water. Barnabas was bound and determined to include John Mark on the mission.

Paul's reaction was far different but no less passionate. Luke used the imperfect tense again here to say that Paul "kept on insisting" they should not take him along. Can't you just hear Paul?

"He has proven himself a quitter. Faithfulness is job one in God's eye's and in mine as well." Remember Barnabas was concerned about the man. Paul was protecting the mission. Barnabas looked to the future. Paul wasn't over the past.

For Paul the issue boiled down to a lack of dependability. They'd need strength and stability, someone with a proven track record they could count on when life became unpredictable. Paul knew how hard the journey was the first time around. He could only imagine the increased difficulties they would encounter on the next arduous trek. The opposition will have had time to regroup. The obstacles would be even greater. This next trip offered no time for wimps or quitters!

If they were going to lean on any man and rely on him to be there when they needed him, Paul wanted someone who could go the distance. In his eyes, John Mark definitely was not that man.

But wasn't Paul the preacher of grace? Paul, himself, was once a persecutor. Surely he appreciated the opportunity of a second chance.

It's tough, isn't it? There was no quick-and-easy solution. Be careful.

You may be feeling overly generous at this point. I mean, what was Paul thinking? Give the kid a break!

Before you get too magnanimous, allow me to ask you a few of questions: Would you loan money to a person who didn't pay off the first amount he borrowed from you? Or would you loan your car again to some kid in the youth group who wrecked it the first time around? Or would you let your sister's son use your condo in Vail, if he trashed the place on spring break last year? Funny how perspective changes, isn't it? Now you feel the tension. That's why such a "sharp disagreement" arose between those two men.

Paul could have quoted Proverbs 25:19: "Like a bad tooth and an unsteady foot is confidence in a faithless man in time of trouble." That fits, doesn't it? Literally, "Putting your trust in an unreliable man is like chewing on a broken tooth or trying to run on a sprained foot." Ever done that? You don't get very far. Barnabas, on the other hand, could have quoted from David's psalm: "Bless the Lord, O my soul, and all that is within me, bless His holy name. Who pardons all your iniquities; Who heals all your diseases; Who redeems your life from the pit; Who crowns you with lovingkindness and compassion" (103:1, 3–4). (Don't scripture verses come in handy when you need to buttress your side of the argument? You're smiling.)

When my wife and I have an argument (every decade or so!) I like to point her to verses of scripture that help her see my point of view. Then I have to get used to sleeping on the patio for a while until she finally lets me back in the house.

No doubt about it, God offers second chances. But He also holds us accountable. He's a God of grace, but He also represents justice.

With these two strong-willed bulldogs there was no compromise. Their convictions would not be softened, so their differences could not be eliminated.

This was nothing short of a heated, ugly, all-out clash of viewpoints. A "sharp disagreement." *Paroxusmos* is the Greek word Luke used. *Paroxuno* means "to sharpen," as you would the blade of a knife. I suggest you could cut the tension with a knife. We're talking one intense quarrel. They spoke, they stared, neither blinked. It ultimately led to separation—a permanent breakup of the dream team from Antioch. You never read again of the companionship of Paul with his longtime friend, Barnabas.

John Pollock writes these wise words: "There must have been serious wrong in the situation which made the lovable, even-tempered Barnabas use angry words, and Paul had far to go before he could write, 'Love is patient and kind . . . Love does not insist on its own way.'"[6]

Those words are right on target. I don't like having this scene in the Bible anymore than you do. But it's here, in all its raw, naked emotion. I'd like to take it out, but I can't. I can't do that any more than I can erase the argument you've had and the pain it caused you and your loved ones. You may still hold the anger. Perhaps you continue to harbor bitter grudges.

I know Christians who refuse to talk to each other because of their differences. Christians! I suppose they've decided to wait for heaven to free them from all those sinful hang-ups. Give me a break. Is that any way to live? Can you imagine the resentment and the bitterness that then spreads to children and grandchildren? It's time all of us grow up in grace!

Renowned New Testament scholar A.T. Robertson writes insightfully, "No one can rightly blame Barnabas for giving his cousin John Mark a second chance nor Paul for fearing to risk him again. One's judgment may go with Paul, but one's heart goes with Barnabas."[7]

That's about where we have to leave it.

We need a solution. This story aches for resolve.

MULTIPLICATION BY DIVISION

The story ends in a most remarkable way. Luke tells us that, "Barnabas took Mark with him and sailed away to Cyprus. But Paul chose Silas and departed, being committed by the brethren to the grace of the Lord. And he was traveling through Syria and Cilicia, strengthening the churches" (15:39–41). Don't miss something extremely significant here. *God multiplied by dividing.* Only He can do that. Check Map One. Barnabas and Mark sail southwest, and Paul and Silas travel north on foot. Two teams, armed with the Gospel, pressed on. The latter was commended to God's grace by His people. I find that extremely encouraging. Only God can take something that seemed so final, so much like a dead end, and transform it into a powerful force for good. That's a lesson we all need to learn. But let's not stop with that one . . .

LINGERING LESSONS FROM YEARS OF EXPERIENCE

Let's be painfully candid here. I've had my own share of arguments, and you've had yours. I've had some that were never reconciled. Thankfully, most ended in a renewed friendship. I've learned through the years a few strategies that have proven effective in facing difficult disagreements. I want to give them to you as I bring this chapter to a close. The next time you're engaged in a heated conflict, you'll want to remember these four lessons that have taken me many years to learn.

1. *When in a disagreement, work hard to see the other point of view.* That begins with listening. Include in the formula three qualities that don't come easily: honesty, objectivity, and humility. That's the full package for handling conflict God's way. None of that comes naturally. They come to full bloom as products of the Spirit-filled life.

In Paul's own words, "Do not merely look out for your own personal interests, but also for the interests of others" (Philippians 2:4) That's the ticket. It's hard work to put yourself in the other person's shoes. But that is a major and essential route to reconciliation.

2. *When both sides have validity, seek a wise compromise.* For those who were reared as I was, even the thought of compromise makes you bristle. If you've got backbone, you don't give in. You stand firm, regardless. I appreciate an individual with backbone—true grit. But one who *never* bends, one who refuses to negotiate toward resolution? Hardly. I admire more someone who willingly and graciously seeks a suitable solution to disagreement, without in any way compromising biblical principles.

I wonder why our men from Antioch didn't do just that? Paul or Barnabas could have offered a reasonable compromise. Giving in would not have meant heresy. There was no hard-and-fast doctrinal issue at stake. Paul might have said, "We'll tell him he's on a temporary period of probation; if he doesn't stay strong and stable during the early months, we'll send him back home."

Or Barnabas could have conceded, "We definitely need faithful workers on our team; let's give Mark a minor assignment here in Antioch to see if he fulfills the responsibilities. Meanwhile we'll go ahead on our journey. If he measures up, we'll send for him and he can join us later on."

They could have agreed on a contingent plan. "Let's take Mark and a few others also. If Mark defects again, we'll have the others to fall back on." Those would have been appropriate compromises.

Diplomacy solves disagreements at the table, not on the battlefield. My dad used to say, "Be careful. You have two fists and one mouth." We tend first to swing our fists. Calm, intelligent people don't go there; they use their mouths. As usual, my dad was right. Appropriate compromises alleviate a lot of needless pain.

The words of David Augsburger bear repeating: "Conflict is natural, and everyone should be willing to come part way in an attempt to resolve things. A willingness to give a little will lead to a working solution which is satisfactory to everyone.

"Compromise is a gift to human relationships. We move forward on the basis of thoughtful, careful consensus and compromise in most decisions in conflict. But it calls for at least a partial sacrifice of deeply held views and goals which may cost all of us the loss of the best to reach the good of agreement."[8]

3. *When the conflict persists, care enough to work it through rather than walk out.* Slamming a phone down in the middle of a conversation or breaking through the screen on the front door as you stomp into the street solves nothing. Nor does a lengthy, manipulative silent treatment benefit either party. Or bolting from a marriage. Or quitting your job in a huff. That's not how to handle disagreements. Work it through. Stay at it. It's some of the hardest work you'll do, but it's also the most rewarding.

4. *When it cannot be resolved, graciously agree to disagree without becoming disagreeable.* I think Paul and Barnabas did that. Paul never takes a shot at Barnabas when he later wrote to the churches they had planted. In all of his letters you'll not find one slam against his former companion. And there's no evidence of Barnabas licking his wounds either.

Can I add three more words of advice? *Get over it!* It's funny, but growing up and going through school in Texas, I didn't know the South lost until I was in the eighth grade! I thought the South ran out of time and ammunition and resources. Finally, a reliable American history teacher set me straight. When I heard the truth I got over it.

I'm amazed at how so many people brood over past injustices. They may bleed from a wound that was suffered way back in 1977. Or they'll pull the scabs off a marriage that ended in 1982.

Whatever it is that holds them in its grip, they've never gotten over it. As we've learned, Paul and Barnabas didn't serve together again. But it all worked out in the end. They got over it.

Honestly, not all separations lead to bad endings. Some of the greatest seminaries were birthed from a crucible of conflict. Some significant churches started as a result of an ugly split. It's never too early to start moving on.

Phillip Melanchthon, that persuasive tempering force in Martin Luther's life, put it best in these few words: "In essentials *unity*. In non-essentials *liberty*. In all things *charity*."

A FINAL THOUGHT

"Father, forgive them for they don't know what they're doing." Jesus managed to utter those penetrating words through bleeding, cracked lips, swollen from the noonday sun. Impaled on that cruel, Roman cross, He interceded on behalf of His enemies. What a magnificent model of forgiveness!

He paid the penalty in full for the sins of the world, the just for the unjust. As a result of His sacrificial death, reconciliation was made between man and God. He's our model for correctly resolving disputes. Ultimately, it's a matter of forgiveness.

"Father, forgive them . . ."

What a way to live!

Before going on to the next chapter, you may have some honest reflecting to do. I invite you to revisit your own unhealed wounded past. It may date back many years, it may bring to mind the face of a parent or a child or a friend, a former mate, a fellow employee, a boss, a coach, a pastor, or a sibling. They've wounded you. The pain has lingered all these years. You can't even hear their name or see a photograph without all the anger and mistrust flooding your soul like a river overtaking its banks.

My friend, it's time to move on. Seek a solution. Get help from someone else, if you must. But get on with it. Whatever it takes to be free, do that.

Right now, I invite you to stand all alone at the foot of the Cross, look up to Him, and deliberately release it all. See Him hanging there, bleeding and dying, and embrace His forgiveness, for you and for your enemy. By forgiving, you're not condoning their sin. You're simply leaving that to God. That's *His* turf, not yours. That's grace. And you can offer it to others because you don't deserve it either.

Got a little homework to do? Get started on it before it gets too late and you lose your way home.

CHAPTER THIRTEEN

Traveling as Paul Traveled

The much-loved British pastor and prolific author F. B. Meyer wrote these words: "If in an unknown country, I am informed that I must pass through a valley where the sun is hidden, or over a stony bit of road, to reach my abiding place—when I come to it, each moment of shadow or jolt of the carriage tells me that I am on the right road."[1]

Those words are a fitting summary of the life and journeys of Paul. The hardships he has faced thus far, and those he will soon endure with increasing intensity, all evidence the fact that God's missionary missile is right on course.

I firmly believe God's Word has been preserved, not merely as a collection of historical documents and geographical studies, but as a trustworthy resource—a place we turn to for assistance in living our lives in ways that honor Christ.

In the pages of Scripture, God has given us models—people, believe it or not, who are just like you and me, who, despite the odds, lived lives pleasing to Him. By faith. In obedience. With courage. Above the fray. They are people like Moses and Samuel, Esther and Ruth, Isaiah and John and, as we are discovering, Paul.

Paul, the man who *traveled* well. We will see that unfold in the pages that follow—snapshots of obedience from his second missionary journey.

Grab your camera, make sure you have enough film, put on your imagination cap, don't forget your binoculars to help you get a closer look, and hop on board. This will be yet another thrilling and harrowing adventure, as we join the first-century church planter traversing the land of the Bible, heralding the good news of Christ.

A FRESH VISION AND A NEW TEAM

The journey begins, you'll remember, in Antioch. Paul, perhaps shaken a bit over his separation from his longtime friend and co-laborer, had been spending time recovering there. With Barnabas already en route to Cyprus and John Mark at his side, the church at Jerusalem appointed Silas, a seasoned disciple, and a Roman citizen, to accompany Paul on his second trip. Delighted with their choice, Paul sent word to Silas inviting him to meet up with him as soon as possible. Armed with the Jerusalem Council's mandate regarding Gentile salvation and a few personal belongings, Paul headed off alone up the well-worn road leading from Antioch toward his hometown, Tarsus (See Map Two, *Paul's First and Second Journeys,* p. 354).

Paul journeyed through familiar country, stopping to strengthen churches he'd founded along the way. Like a magnetic force, the towering Taurus range, which he no doubt could see in the distance, drew him gradually to the place of his birth. Perhaps lonely, without the companionship of his close friend, he longed for the familiar sights and sounds of Tarsus. Whether he stopped there or not, we are not told. At some point, he shook off any lingering nostalgia regarding Tarsus and pressed northward. There were souls to reach and lives to touch. As the warm spring sun shone brightly, the brilliant snowcapped peaks of the Taurus Mountains gave way to fresh mountain streams plunging downward into a convergence of rivers leading west to the Mediterranean. He stayed on that familiar Roman road, which cut stubbornly through the rugged terrain, eventually leading him to Derbe—the likely rendezvous spot with Silas, his new partner.

Together they delivered and interpreted the Jerusalem Council decisions to surrounding cities, making sure the new believers were receiving needed instruction and pastoral care. They moved northwest to Lystra, where Paul no doubt introduced his new companion to another thriving community of young Christians.

Among them was Timothy, a zealous disciple, whom one author refers to as "a complicated character. A youthful man, who had a weak stomach, looked very young, and was not a muscular Christian."[2]

That was Timothy. Two of the New Testament letters bare his name. The son of a Jewish woman, a believer, and a Greek father, no doubt a pagan intellectual, Timothy had been nurtured by his mother and maternal grandmother. In the beginning of Acts 16, Luke writes, "And he came to Derbe and Lystra. And behold, a certain disciple was there, named Timothy, the son of a Jewish woman who was a believer, but his father was a Greek, and he was well spoken of by the brethren who were in Lystra and Iconium" (16:1–2). Impressed by his teachable spirit and love for God's truth, Paul invited Timothy to join his team.

Something about Timothy must have intrigued the seasoned church planter. Often, that's how the Lord assembles His teams. You meet some people, and they don't fit. With others, there is instantaneous rapport. Most times, kindred spirits blend rather quickly. Paul saw sterling qualities in Timothy that eclipsed his youthful countenance: That did it – he recruited him on the spot.

Timothy stepped into a whirling missionary internship, filled with adventure and exciting frontline experiences. His learning curve would soon be stretched like never before. What a choice opportunity to travel alongside Paul! Luke writes, "Now while they were passing through the cities, they were delivering the decrees, which had been decided upon by the apostles and elders who were in Jerusalem, for them to observe. So the churches were being strengthened in the faith, and were increasing in number daily" (16:4–5).

Timothy's frail arms must have ached from pinching himself, wondering if it were all a dream! To his amazement, God chose him, in all his childlike zeal, to join two seasoned practitioners, in a rigorous church planting effort that would span two worlds, guided by the Holy Spirit. One of his first major discoveries would come as a surprise: No matter how hard you try, not all doors open widely to the gospel.

WITHOUT EXPLAINING WHY, GOD SOMETIMES SAYS NO

> And they passed through the Phrygian and Galatian region, having been forbidden by the Holy Spirit to speak the word in Asia; and when they had come to Mysia, they were trying to go into Bithynia, and the Spirit of Jesus did not permit them; and passing by Mysia they came to Troas.
>
> Acts 16:6–8

Passing to the north they made their way into Phrygia and Galatia. They prayed for open doors and hoped for ready hearts in that region, but the Scripture says, "They were forbidden by the Holy Spirit to speak the word in Asia."

You've probably had a similar experience. Despite your best attempts to step out in faith and make headway for the Lord, the doors close— sometimes slamming shut. Though no reason was given, they were barred by the Spirit from entering Asia.

Undaunted, they marched on to Bithynia. Again, without explanation, the door closed there as well. Eventually they streamed west and hit Troas, a coastal city on the easternmost shores of the Aegean Sea. Interestingly, Luke offers no insight into how the three men responded to the series of dead ends. It must have seemed strange. What we do know is that they continued despite them, directed by the Spirit of God.

Often God's answer is a plain "No." We don't want to hear it, but it's true. "No. No. No. No." Four doors slam. Phrygia, Galatia, Mysia, Bithynia. Yet, instead of turning and making tracks back to Antioch, they continued, guided by the Spirit, and lured by the sounds and smells of the sea. Once in that westernmost city of Troas, something remarkable happened.

Paul had a vision. The record doesn't say it also appeared to Silas. Apparently, only Paul saw the vision. Before the Scriptures were complete, God communicated His will, sometimes in visions, often in dreams. Dreams came at night, visions could come at any time. And, in this case, the vision appeared to Paul in the night, in the form of "a man of Macedonia" (Acts 16:9).

Now would be a good time to pause and look at Map Two, located on page 354 in the back of this book.

It's a helpful habit to discipline yourself in your personal Bible study to locate on a map those significant places mentioned in Scripture. I beat that drum religiously to our flock at Stonebriar Community Church. Maps help us turn names on a page into actual places on the globe.

Across the blue waters of the Aegean, you'll see Macedonia. While Paul is at Troas (Did you locate Troas?), he sees a vision of a man imploring him, "Come over to Macedonia and help us."

A light went on in Paul's head: *That explains all those closed doors in Asia! Now I know why we weren't able to penetrate Phrygian or Mysia or Bithynia with the good news.* The flashback made crystal clear the reason God brought them to Troas. It was all about a wider outreach.

Paul envisioned a journey to places he had already been. God's plan included an entirely new continent being exposed to the claims of Christ where no one before had ever been—that is, no one armed with the magnificent message of hope in Christ. That's what I call expanding your borders! And may I remind you? Another *change!*

The visionary apostle wasted no time in obeying God's directive. New places did not frighten him. The unknown, in fact, excited him. There was no wrestling with the details. No waiting for peace. No weak excuses like, "Oh, Lord, I get seasick when I have to sail that far! I'm not sure I can handle that much sailing." Or "Oh, Lord, that's too far from home. I'm not sure we have the funds." No sooner had God said "Go," than they left *immediately.*

It is clear to the close observer that it was at this juncture Dr. Luke, the writer of Acts, joined company with Paul, Silas, and Timothy. Luke most likely gave up his practice of medicine to join ranks with these missionaries on the move. Four of them now headed out, as Luke describes it, "to go into Macedonia, concluding that God had called *us* to preach the gospel to them" (Acts 16:10).

CLOSED DOORS AND OPENED HEARTS

Glance again at the map—it will help. Trace the trip with your fingers. From Troas they sailed across the Aegean, past Samothrace, to the port city of Neapolis located on the busy European artery known as the Egnatian Way. In the heart of Macedonia, their destination would be Philippi, one of the region's premier cities. Little did they know that their first Philippian convert would be a prominent businesswoman, worshiping God in an unlikely place.

Lydia: Down by the Riverside

Philippi, named after Philip of Macedon, whose son was Alexander the Great, had become a military outpost after Octavius Augustus soundly defeated the murderous band of infidels, responsible for Caesar's assassination. The bloody battle raged just outside Philippi. Crawling with Roman troops, the city enjoyed the reputation of being considered a miniature Rome. Philippi was self-governing and in many ways autonomous. Understandably, the ancient metropolis was not a hub of Judaism. Therefore, when Paul sought out his usual venue for preaching, he came up short. No synagogue existed, hard evidence that not even ten Jewish males lived within the city limits.[3]

If there were any Jews or proselytes in the city, they would meet regularly by the river, using the abundance of water for ritual cleansing. So Paul and his associates, made their way to the banks of the Gangites River, where they joined a small group of women preparing for worship.

> And on the Sabbath day we went outside the gate to a riverside, where we were supposing that there would be a place of prayer; and we sat down and began speaking to the women who had assembled. And a certain woman named Lydia, from the city of Thyatira, a seller of purple fabrics, a worshiper of God, was listening; and the Lord *opened her heart* to respond to the things spoken by Paul. And when she and her household had been baptized, she urged us, saying, "If you have judged me to be faithful to the Lord, come into my house and stay." And she prevailed upon us.
>
> Acts 16:13–15 (italics, mine)

The household mini-revival must have been a thrilling scene. Perhaps still confounded by the closed doors in Asia, the missionary team watched in amazement as the Lord opened the heart of a prominent woman, paving the way for a church to be born in Philippi. It was all part of God's leading and Paul's obedience. What he lacked earlier in understanding, he compensated for in obedience. The reward awaited him in Philippi.

No one could have predicted that the foundation for one of the first century's most strategic ministries would flow from the riverside conversion of a middleclass woman.

But don't get too comfortable. God had a few more surprises in store for the Macedonian missionaries.

A Demoniac Girl and an Uproarious Miracle

The four men continued their Philippian crusade, enjoying the warm hospitality and encouragement showered upon them by Lydia and her household. Each day they met at the river for fervent prayer and dynamic worship. On one particular walk to the familiar site they encountered a demonized slave girl, who persisted in taunting them during many days that followed. Day after day, Paul somehow managed to ignore her vile ranting, until finally, he could take it no more. Luke paints the scene with his usual economy of words.

> And it happened that as we were going to a place of prayer, a certain slave girl having a spirit of divination met us, who was bringing her masters much profit by fortunetelling. Following after Paul and us, she kept crying out, saying, "These men are bond-servants of the Most High God, who are proclaiming to you the way of salvation." And she continued doing this for many days. But Paul was greatly annoyed, and turned and said to the spirit, "I command you in the name of Jesus Christ to come out of her!" And it came out at that very moment.
>
> Acts 16:16–18

I would have loved to witness that confrontation. Paul, patiently enduring the repeated and annoying comments of this unlikely witness, finally had his fill of it. One day he turned and faced her head-on. In one compelling sentence, he uttered, "In the name of Jesus Christ, come out of her." With that, he delivered the girl of the demon. No ifs, ands, or buts about it. He spoke, it fled. Talk about grit! The crowd stood stunned as the once wild-eyed girl sat serene and silent. Thanks be to God who always gives us victory through our Lord Jesus Christ!

Not everyone was as ready as I to praise Paul's miraculous deed. Angered by their sudden economic downfall, the slave girl's greedy masters roused the crowd to riot. Paul and Silas were immediately seized, viciously beaten with rods by lictors, and thrown deep into a Roman dungeon with their feet fastened in stocks.

Wait a minute. Earlier they are reaping the rewards of obedience, but within minutes they're bleeding and locked up in jail. Did they wonder, *I thought this is where God wanted us to be.* It is! *But we're beaten with rods and thrown in jail.* That's part of the plan.

Turmoil, difficulty, persecution, and hardship are not essential indicators of being out of God's will. On the contrary, there are times those things mean you are, in fact, in the nucleus of His plan. It helps to remember that—another lesson learned in our travels with Paul.

The Philippi plot gets even better.

A Philippian Jailer and an Earth-shaking Conversion

Stop here and picture the scene. On the surface, it's bleak. Paul and Silas are trapped in a damp, dark cell, with open wounds that haven't been washed. Their feet are shackled to a wooden bar, forcing them to sit upright in the most excruciatingly uncomfortable position. The traumatic events have left them sore and in shock. All that has a way of erasing the warm memories of celebration in Lydia's home only a few days before. But these two men refused to let their circumstances determine their attitudes. Watch the remarkable events that followed.

> About midnight Paul and Silas were praying and singing hymns of praise to God, and the prisoners were listening to them; and suddenly, there came a great earthquake, so that the foundations of the

prison house were shaken; and immediately all the doors opened, (don't miss that last phrase!) and everyone's chains were unfastened. And when the jailer had been roused to sleep and had seen the prison doors opened, he drew his sword and was about to kill himself, supposing that the prisoners had escaped.

Acts 16:25–27 (parentheses, mine)

Is that a great scene, or what? As the men started worshiping their Lord, the throbbing pain from the lictor's blows began to wane. Prisoners all around them sat baffled by their cellmates' strange response to such vicious torture. Sitting there in leg stocks, they broke into song. Perhaps they sang the words to the familiar Hebrew song:

> I waited patiently for the Lord;
> And He inclined unto me, and heard my cry.
> He brought me up out of the pit of destruction,
> > out of the miry clay; and He set my feet upon a rock
> > making my footsteps firm.
> And He put a new song in my mouth,
> > a song of praise to our God;
> > Many will see and fear, and will trust in the Lord.

Psalm 40:1–3

Before the Jailer had time to kill himself, knowing that instant death awaited him when the prisoners escaped, Luke tells us that Paul "cried out with a loud voice saying, 'Do yourself no harm, for we are all here." The shocked jailer called for lamps to be lit. He wanted to see this with his own eyes. It must have been a blur as his eyes blinked in amazement, struggling to focus on the missionaries who were smiling by now! Without hesitation he fell to his knees and begged for a way to be saved.

And after he brought them out, he said, "Sirs, what must I do to be saved?" And they said, "Believe in the Lord Jesus, and you shall be saved, you and your household." And they spoke the word of the Lord to him together with all who were in his house. And he took them that *very* hour of the night and washed their wounds, and immediately he was baptized, he and all his *household.* And he brought them into his house and set food before them, and rejoiced greatly, having believed in God with his whole household.

Acts 16:30–34 (Italics, mine)

Can you imagine the confident, contagious faith of those men? Would you have done all that they had done, with your back covered in scabs? Had I been there when those jail doors broke open, I would have run like a spotted ape. "I'm out of here! Let that jailer take care of himself!" Not Paul. He traveled under the control of the Spirit of God, start to finish. He left no opportunity to chance. Best of all, his obedience was not conditioned on his comfort or salary package. He didn't go over the benefits summary before launching his missions career. His goal was simple and clear: to preach Christ where He had not been named. If that meant being shackled to a Roman dungeon, and choking on his blood, so be it. Back in Troas, when he said yes to that vision, it was an unconditional yes.

A man from Macedonia had said, "Come over and help us." God had in mind a seller of purple, an exploited slave girl, and a rugged, brutal Roman jailer. When you travel as God would have you travel, like Paul, you're sensitive to doors that open and at peace with doors that close.

Later, Paul appealed to Rome. Upon discovering he had tortured Roman citizens, the ruling magistrate shook with fear. Realizing he had illegally acted against these two men, the official begged Paul and Silas to leave Philippi to avoid further civil unrest. The missionary team shrugged it off and pressed on, anticipating the next episode of the Lord's power and presence. What amazing men they were!

A BRIEF SYNOPSIS OF PAUL'S REMARKABLE TRAVELS

Teaching in Thessalonica

The consummate church founder forged ahead, flanked by the faithful companionship of his co-workers. Next stop: Thessalonica. Paul, in keeping with his m.o. returned to his preferred place to start, in the synagogue. Many believed, including a large number of Greek men and influential women. That was sufficient to stir jealousy among the Jewish leaders, to the point that Paul and his team were forced to escape under the cloak of darkness (17:10).

Buffeted in Berea

From there, they entered Berea and again preached in the local synagogue. A more sophisticated crowd than the folks in Thessalonica, the Bereans' eagerness led them to examine "the Scriptures daily, to see whether these things were so" (17:11).

I can't pass up this opportunity to say what a fine example they were to emulate. No matter how gifted or charismatic or well-trained and experienced your Bible teacher or pastor may be, form the healthy habit of checking what is being said against the Scriptures.

Architects and construction people use precise measurement to ensure a precise result. They don't go by how they feel. Both carefully mark their work by inches and by feet. Not even seasoned builders rely on guesses and hunches. They stay with the standard. The Scriptures are your measuring tool for making sure the teaching you receive is straight and true. Keep comparing.

As you grow in your spiritual life, the triangles need to be congruent between what's being said and what has been written in the Bible. If you can't support it with the Scriptures, there's something missing in the teaching. Don't believe the teacher. If he or she contradicts the divine standard, you're building on sand. Stay with the Scriptures. They remain your ultimate authority for faith and life.

Now, back to Berea. The result of their tireless ministry was the founding of another church in that city. But it was not all peaches and cream. Luke, who keeps us riveted to reality, quickly adds, "When the Jews of Thessalonica found out the Word of God had been proclaimed by Paul in Berea, they came there as well, agitating and stirring up the crowds" (17:13).

Don't assume critics in one place won't follow you to another. If they are determined, they will dog your steps. If they didn't like you in Dallas, they probably won't like you in New Orleans. And when you move on to

Miami, they'll show up there too. Critics proliferate! That's especially true if you're being used effectively and people are embracing the truth. Critics hate truth because it sets people free. Their hope, therefore, is to silence the message every way possible. Berea is a classic case in point.

Finally, the believers in Berea figured they'd had enough of that and encouraged Paul to head for the Aegean coast. Silas and Timothy would remain in Berea with Luke to settle the restless community.

Alone in Athens

The next scene opens with Paul in Athens, alone. Athens was the intellectual center of the world. The city of the Academy. The birthplace of democracy. To make matters worse, the busy metropolis was covered with idols. One Athenian poet wrote there were more idols in the city than there were people. We can hardly imagine such a place. (Bangkok, Thailand, today may come close in resembling Athens back then.) The demonic presence was oppressive as the godly apostle strolled the streets. His attempts to penetrate the darkness proved unsuccessful. (More on Paul's visit to Athens in the next chapter.)

Challenged in Corinth

He left Athens and traveled a short distance to Corinth, where Luke writes, "He settled there a year and six months" (18:11). Rejoined by Silas and Timothy (and Luke, of course), Paul enjoyed a fruitful stay in Corinth, meeting Priscilla and Aquila, who would become close allies in the work, along with Crispus, a brilliant young synagogue leader, who surrendered his heart to the Messiah (18:8). The work was challenging—never a dull moment in Corinth—but rewarding as Paul introduced the one and only God who is Holy to the fast-lane crowd of that carnal city.

Encouraged in Ephesus

The second missionary journey came to a glorious end, following a brief stay in Ephesus. What a fruitful place to minister! After preaching there and leaving Aquila and Priscilla to carry on, Paul sailed south to Caesarea to meet with the church in Jerusalem, and then he traveled on to Antioch.

He came full circle. Thousands of miles and many months later, Paul returned to his sending base to report the remarkable wonders, thanks to the grace of God.

A REALITY CHECK AS WE REFLECT

For a few final moments in this chapter, let's do some realistic reflecting. Think how rugged conditions must have been for these missionaries. Traveling was downright tough. Today we slide into an air-conditioned car with smooth leather seats, CD player, windows closed tightly, full speed ahead. When we grow weary of the road, we pull over and check into a comfortable place for overnight lodging. We have a choice, with all the nice amenities.

Those rugged warriors of the cross walked. If they rode, it was on crude, wooden-wheeled carts or straddling the back of sweating beasts for miles, enduring the extreme weather conditions.

Food rations were slim. They knew no modern health care. If it hadn't been for Luke, Paul would have fainted along the way. That must have been a major reason Luke decided to join the team at Troas; to be his personal physician. And we dare not forget the hostility. They lived and ministered in harm's way almost every day. Still, Paul and his companions pressed on.

Western Christians have become a soft-bodied lot of folks. We look out for ourselves, our rights, and our conveniences. We have little tolerance for anything that interrupts a life of ease. Sacrifice rarely crosses our minds. When we're called upon to consider paying a heavy price, we wince and stammer and politely excuse ourselves. Or we say we'll help support those who are called to go.

Try to imagine life in the sandals of Paul . . . without air conditioning! Would you have been his companion? Would you have struck out with him when he left Antioch for places unknown? Would you have left a successful practice at Troas? I've asked myself the same questions. They force us to probe below the surface of our comfortable world.

Though not that old, Paul already has scars from Philippi. Bruises from Lystra. Memories of the mob in Thessalonica. Wounds from Berea. And still he continued. I find that kind of spiritual grit not only inspiring, but deeply convicting.

Remarkably, by the time he reaches age sixty, he makes plans for a *third* missionary journey. I mean, this man is absolutely *addicted!* And before you can catch your breath, he's underway, compelled by the grace of God.

Traveling back through Syria and Galatia, he settled in Ephesus, where he discipled many new believers and enjoyed a lengthy, fruitful ministry. For more than two years he labored among the people of Ephesus, teaching truth, performing miracles, combating the adversary, and leading many Gentiles to Christ.

While at Ephesus, Paul wrote First Corinthians. After leaving there he journeyed back through Macedonia where he wrote Second Corinthians. While back in Corinth he picked up his pen again and wrote what we have today as the New Testament letter to the Romans. And then it gets even more exciting, which we'll examine later.

The ground Paul covered in this third journey alone is mind boggling. Look again at the map marked *Paul's Third Journey* on page 355 in the back of the book. Spend a few moments tracing Paul's footsteps on his final missionary campaign. He comes all the way around. Trace it with your finger. Imagine the miles! From Ephesus all the way down to Miletus to Cos and Rhodes and Patara and Tyre and Ptolemais and Caesarea then back to Jerusalem.

By the time he arrives in Jerusalem, he has finished the third journey. Souls were saved. Churches were founded. Lives were transformed. Though arrested, beaten, persecuted, jailed, and slandered, Paul finished that course. He gives a glowing report of all that God had done to those assembled to greet him (20:17–25).

Not suprisingly, the Sanhedrin threw their heads back and howled. They caused such a commotion in opposition to his reports that the Roman authorities were called in to quell the uprising. Paul stands before Felix, Festus, and King Agrippa—all officials of the Roman government. In a triumphant display of faith and courage, he exclaims to Agrippa, "I would to God, that whether in a short or long time, not only you, but also all who hear me this day, might become such as I am, except for these chains."

Agrippa was nearly converted.

Still, Paul remained in his chains. He's sent as a prisoner aboard a merchant ship bound for Rome. Of all things, he gets shipwrecked (that's Acts 20!) Graciously, the Lord spares his life and brings him safely to Rome. There, while under house arrest, and chained to a Roman guard, he writes Philemon, Colossians, Ephesians, and Philippians. They're called the "prison epistles." They're in your Bible, because Paul refused to quit. Obediently, he pressed on.

PRINCIPLES FOR TRAVELING WELL AS PAUL DID

Whether you are traveling as a missionary or in the midst of your personal profession, God would have you travel as Paul traveled. I observe four enduring principles that will help you maximize your effectiveness for Christ, wherever you may go. To make them easy to remember, let's start each with the words, "When you travel . . ."

1. *When you travel, don't go alone.* Stay close to at least one other person, ideally your mate. If not your mate, a family member. If not a family member, a close companion. But stay close. Think back. Call to mind those with whom Paul traveled. He took Barnabas, John Mark, Silas, Timothy, Luke, Aquila and Priscilla. And don't forget Sopater, Aristarchus, Secundus, Gaius, Timothy, Tychicus and Trophimus. Oops, we almost overlooked Erastus. Those are names you don't spend much time thinking about, but they were indispensable to the man of grace and grit. If at all possible, avoid traveling alone. If you're lonely, a companion is there to lift your spirits. If you get into trouble, a companion is there to help get you through. Two are better than one. Three are better than two.

2. *When you travel, don't lose touch with home.* Stay accountable. Paul's heart stayed close to home. While away, he stayed in touch. When he returned he gave his reports. When he was with his men, he willingly gave an account of his ministry. When he wrote the letters, he was often vulnerable. It's quite possible he kept a journal. You may consider keeping a journal. It's one of the great legacies you can leave your children. When our family lays us to rest it would be wonderful if all of us had in our library several handwritten journals of the things the Lord taught us in our lives. A journal,

not a diary. It's not about what we've done, minute by minute, day by day. That's a diary. Journals are written thoughts given to us by our Lord. How meaningful to those who follow in our footsteps! They are the lessons we've learned in our journey with the Father. Paul's letters were, in some ways, like inspired journal entries. Though gone for long periods, he stayed accountable.

3. *When you travel, don't believe everything you hear.* Someone has said, "An authority is anyone who's one hundred miles away from home." Because I'm fairly well known, when I travel, people show up thinking they're going to be impressed. If they were around me more, they'd know better. When you travel, occasionally you'll meet folks who will almost worship you. (It happened to Paul.) Don't let them. On the opposite extreme, others will reject and mistreat you. Don't be derailed by naysayers. A few may even conspire against you. Keep your eyes on the goal. Focus on the Lord and none of that will get you down.

Some of the best people who ever lived have been mistreated, misunderstood, and maligned. It's part of what God uses to prepare His servants. I don't wish it on anybody, but I'm not the director. That's the Lord's work.

The life of Abraham Lincoln comes to mind once again. Talk about tough times!

Lincoln was slandered, libeled, and hated more intensely than any man ever to run for the nation's highest office. In his book *Lincoln on Leadership,* author Donald Phillips writes,

> He was publicly called just about every name imaginable by the press of the day, including a grotesque baboon, a third-rate country lawyer who once split rails and now splits the Union, a coarse vulgar joker, a dictator, an ape, a buffoon, and others. The *Illinois State Register* labeled him "the craftiest and most dishonest politician that ever disgraced an office in America." Imagine the slander. Ironically, we built an enormous memorial to that remarkable man. Those who lived in his day despised him openly.[4]

Paul stands out today as a man of God and a model for all of us to follow. His message gave hope to all who would listen. Why? Grace. Amazing grace. He too was despised in his day. None of that swayed him. Why? Grit. Absolute grit.

4. *When you travel, don't become aloof.* It's easy in the busyness of travel to become a wax figure. Untouchable. Picking up the "circuit lingo," the clichés of the road and losing touch with reality. Resist that sort of superficiality. Stay available. Stay real. People need a real, authentic *you.* Not perfect, *authentic.*

Paul says he "wanted Timothy." That's real. When they were in prison he sang with Silas. He didn't ask Silas to sing *to* him. He sang *with* Silas. When one of his friends was being mistreated, Paul wanted to step out in front of a mob in the public theater at Ephesus. His friends had to hold him back. That's real. When he poured his heart out to the elders at Ephesus, they wept and kissed him repeatedly. That's an accessible man.

THE END OF ALL JOURNEYS

Down through time people who have traveled often wrote of those travels. One of my favorites is John Steinbeck's *Travels with Charlie*—a simple account of his travels with his dog, driving his pick-up truck. Great story. Another favorite is *Blue Highways* by William Least Heat Moon. It's a wonderful story of a man who, after losing his job, gassed up his van and took off across the back roads of America. He chronicles the lessons he learned from ordinary folks in nameless places, all on journeys of their own.

No matter the story, and no matter the journey, the traveler is forever changed. Life is full of journeys. Some are dull excursions we grudgingly take out of sheer duty. Others are thrilling adventures we embark on with eyes of faith. But changes await you . . . changes in you.

Throughout this chapter we have been on the road again, and again, and again. We've journeyed with Paul over vast land masses. But, like Paul, we have also journeyed inwardly. We've done some self-examination along the way. That always happens during any meaningful journey.

Phil Cousineau, in his splendid volume *The Art of Pilgrimage*, writes, "Whether you are embarking on a grueling walking pilgrimage a thousand miles across Europe . . . setting off on a long-delayed journey to your ancestral roots, or taking that first step on the long-spiritual journey . . . your journey is about to change you."[5]

He is correct. No journey is more life changing than your inner spiritual journey back to the Cross. In all your travels, have you gone there? If not, are you willing to take that first step? It's a journey you will never regret, I can assure you, and one you will never forget.

Come on. It all begins with that first step.

CHAPTER FOURTEEN

Preaching as Paul Preached

Question authority. That battle cry prevailed in the sixties and lingered well into the seventies. Most adults today remember those torrential decades. It made no difference your role or title, if you pulled authority over anyone, they bristled and questioned it. It was true of the teacher in the classroom. It was true of the cop on the corner. It was true of the parent in the home. It was true of the boss at the office. The ultimate occurred when it became true of the preacher in the pulpit. The collective refrain rang out, "Hey, I've got my rights. Who do you think you are to stand up there and talk to me like that, without giving me equal time?" By the early 1970s, it got downright ugly.

As a ministry professional, I have observed with sadness this erosion of authority occurring in our ranks. Though Christianity has certainly survived the sixties and the seventies, some churches today still evidence that "question authority" mentality. Critical statements leveled against both preachers and preaching are commonplace. Those are often the same churches that turn to the interesting and entertaining style rather than standing and delivering the timeless truths of God's Word.

I read a statement recently that made me frown: "Preaching is a dying art." Since that happens to be one of my gifts, does that mean I'm dying? "Preaching is a dying art, an outmoded form of communication—an echo from an abandoned past," said this alleged authority. In many contemporary circles preachers are viewed as dinosaurs on the loose. To them, sermons are considered rather pathetic attempts at pulling rank on people who do not believe in the message they herald, and question the importance of the role they fill. In short, preaching is old fashioned.

Sometimes, the lack of esteem is of the clergyman's own making. That problem is not new. Just ask sixteenth-century, Italian painter Raphael. While he was working diligently on his Vatican frescoes, two rather arrogant cardinals walked up and, as usual, sneered and began to criticize his work. While studying the artist's painting one of them whined, "The face of the apostle Paul is much too red." With hardly a glance at his malevolent patrons, Raphael replied, "He blushes to see into whose hands the church has fallen." I think he would still blush. Some of God's spokesmen, to this day, are arrogant. If not arrogant, some have left the role of preacher and allowed themselves to become talkshow hosts or stand-up comics. Believing that people won't come unless they're given what they want, they now do that.

In too many places, the church has become a local entertainment center attempting to rapture the attention of busy parishioners away from the glamour and clamor of society. The strategy often disintegrates into not getting too specific or pointed in our messages, lest our customers get offended and take their business elsewhere. The result in most cases is that people are left chewing on spiritual junk food. That's not original with me. I found it in Eugene Peterson's paraphrase of 2 Timothy 4. Read his words in *The Message* carefully and thoughtfully. As you do that, see if this sounds like what's happening today.

> I cannot impress this on you too strongly. God is looking over your shoulder. Christ himself is the Judge, with the final say on everyone, living and dead. He is about to break into the open with his rule, so proclaim the Message with intensity; keep on your watch. Challenge, warn, and urge your people. Don't ever quit. Just keep it simple.

You're going to find that there will be times when people will have no stomach for solid teaching, but will fill up on spiritual junk food—catchy opinions that tickle their fancy. They'll turn their backs on truth and chase mirages. But *you*—keep your eye on what you're doing; accept the hard times along with the good; keep the Message alive; do a thorough job as God's servant.[1]

I love that expression "spiritual junk food." It's what we say to our kids: "Don't fill up on junk, we're having supper in the next hour." Too many twenty-first-century churches deliver little more than sermonettes. Sermonettes create *Christianettes*. That type of watered-down diet leads only to spiritual malnutrition, or worse, starvation. I should add, the cults have a field day when they come across starved sheep.

Martin Luther's conversion to Christ alone through faith, gave impetus to the Reformation. Luther's dramatic conversion began a personal crusade of restoring the Scriptures as the ultimate authority in the life of every believer. Naturally, that emphasis found its way into Christian worship. Not surprisingly, the proclamation of the Word would become the central focus of the corporate worship experience. The Reformation elevated the pulpit above the altar. Luther taught that through the Word of God the elements are given sacramental significance. Furthermore, the preaching of the Word is essential to establishing the life of spiritual freedom and grace. Strong preaching became the catalyst of true worship.

Luther's passionate convictions on the primacy of Scripture in the life of the church alchemized into nine virtues which he charachterized as "good preaching."

I'm not big on promoting simplistic formulas or step-by-step methods for anything that ultimately depends on the work of God's Spirit. But Luther's nine virtues are worth mentioning.

1. He should, of course, teach systematically.
2. He should have a ready wit.
3. He should be eloquent (forceful, clear, and expressive).
4. He should have a good voice.

5. He should have a good memory.
6. He should know how to make a beginning, and when to make an end.
7. He should be sure of his doctrine.
8. He should venture and engage body and blood, wealth and honor in the Word. (passionate)
9. He should suffer himself to be mocked and jeered.[2]

Luther's ninth virtue represents, at least in his mind, the ultimate test. The preacher must be willing to risk ridicule, the loss of wealth, even his life if necessary, if he's to become a worthy spokesman for Christ. That doesn't sound like someone serving up spiritual junk food to me. That kind of virtuous preaching not only gives life, it sustains it.

Make no mistake about it, it was that kind of preaching that characterized the apostle Paul. Though simple in form, his preaching cut through the complexities of his own pluralistic society as he magnified the supremacy of Christ. Those of us in vocational Christian work would be wise to take our cues from him. If you are not called to do God's work, professionally, it would be discerning of you to use Paul's example as the kind of model you should seek from the one who shepherds your flock.

A SIMPLE MODEL FOR OUR COMPLEX AGE

A quick survey through the early chapters of Acts, which record the beginning of Paul's ministry, demonstrates his passion for communicating the message of Christ without hesitation or apology. Paul *spoke* boldly. Paul *preached* the Word. Paul *taught* with conviction. Paul *connected* with the needs of his hearers.

Not until Acts 17, however, do we have a complete *sermon*—a sermon worth a closer look, from preparation to delivery.

The Preparation

As we learned toward the end of the last chapter, by the time Paul reached Athens, he was alone. While awaiting the arrival of his missionary partners, perhaps to pass the time, Paul ventured into the crowded streets of that storied metropolis. Hoping to soak up the sights and sounds of sophisticated Greek culture, he shook his head in dismay. What he encountered was Greek culture at its worst. It vexed him deeply. In Luke's words, "His spirit was being provoked within him as he was beholding the city full of idols."

Paroxuneto is the Greek word Luke uses to describe Paul's inner turmoil: It means "to sharpen, to irritate, to stimulate." He churned within himself. The prevalence of idols and the resulting commercial windfall they spawned gnawed at the straight-thinking preacher's soul.

Most likely your travels abroad have brought you into the presence of an idol. I've been in places where there were not only idols, there were idol worshipers—sincere people bringing their treasures and offering them to gods of stone and wood. I've seen them weeping and begging, at times cutting and mutilating themselves, all as offerings to their lifeless gods. Invariably they are hoping for approbation. The tragedy is this: Earthly gods are never satisfied. Filled with superstition and blinded by fear and ignorance, idol worshipers live their lives wondering if they've satisfied all the demands, if they've won the favor of the right gods. It's so heartbreaking that you churn within. That was Paul at Athens.

The city was a junkyard of idols. What surrounded the stranger on those busy streets was a veritable forest of stone, wood, and precious metals all carved into altars, an endless array of shrines of strange gods shaped into faceless images. One monotonous monument after another.

At the same time, ancient Athens was a city unsurpassed in sculpture and architecture. It boasted a sixty-thousand-seat stadium. Art galleries existed in rare abundance. Lavishly decorated music halls and respected Academies lined the stone-laid streets. In many ways, it stood as the cultural centerpiece of the entire Greek world.

Pliny wrote, "In the time of Nero, Athens had well over twenty-five thousand public statues, and another thirty thousand in the Parthenon alone." "It was easier to find a god than a man in Athens," added Petronious.

The city was a philosopher's dream. Wealthy families sent their children to Athens to learn philosophy and to be enriched by ear-tickling myths of fanciful gods and goddesses. The native home of Socrates and Plato,

Athens was also the adopted home of Aristotle and Epicurus. Paul took it all in. There must have been moments of open-mouthed amazement. His spirit grew more restless by the minute. Paul was about as at home in Athens as a bust of Luther would be in the Vatican. Between the furrowed lines on the faces of the brilliant and thoughtful intellectuals of that city, Paul could read messages of confusion and despair. As the churning subsided, a sermon began to brew within him.

The final voice of authority on all this high-brow philosophizing came from the direction of the Areopagus, the hill of Mars, which still stands in solid marble today. In that lofty place sat philosophers and scholars, teachers and historians, each of them so unsettled and unsure in their thinking that no room was allowed for anything absolute. Truth to them was relative. Dogmatism amounted to intellectual suicide. Though Paul's soul perceived the evil around him, his spirit ached for the spiritual blindness and emptiness of the Athenians.

John Stott provides a fitting analysis of the apostle's assessment of the spiritual darkness of Athens:

> Paul's reaction to the city's idolatry was not negative only but also positive and constructive. He did not merely throw up his hands in despair, or weep helplessly, or curse and swear at the Athenians. No, he shared with them the good news of Jesus. He sought by proclamation of the gospel to prevail on them to turn from their idols to the living God and so to give to him and to his Son the glory due their name. The stirrings of his spirit with righteous indignation opened his mouth in testimony.[3]

Not only did careful observation play a vital role in Paul's preparation for preaching, he also engaged in an exercise of thoughtful interrogation, interacting one on one with the people of Athens.

The People

Paul was no mere tourist in Athens, he was an intelligent and engaged student of culture. Being a people person, Paul chose to carry on a series of town-hall meetings, utilizing two familiar public platforms: the synagogue and the marketplace. Luke writes, "He was reasoning in the synagogue with the Jews and the God-fearing Gentiles, and in the marketplace every day with those who happened to be present" (17:17).

He continued vigorously dialoging with the citizens of Athens, while gathering information soon to become the stuff of his preaching. Nothing passed unnoticed to this keen-thinking scholar.

He likely adopted the Socratic method of questions and answers, listening intently to those with whom he spoke. He would ask questions to passers-by and listen intently to the answers, only to follow up with yet another question. From pedestrians to trained philosophers, Paul engaged them all.

First, he went to the synagogue to speak to the Jews and then into the market to interact with Gentiles. The Agora was the central place of public life in Athens and, thereby, the meeting place of philosophical talk, idleness, leisure, general conversation, and business negotiations. Paul wasn't picky about his audience. Effective preachers don't care who is listening. Their aim is to win a hearing with people, then help them interact with truth. Paul continued for days, undeterred by intellectual snobbery or downright rejection.

You can't silence a called and gifted preacher. In fact, I challenge you to try. Paul understood the crucial nature of that appointment in Athens. Squandering such a God-ordained opportunity never crossed his mind. He needed to be ready at a moment's notice to defend and proclaim the gospel. It wasn't long before his audience included some rather sophisticated thinkers: "And also some of the Epicurean and Stoic philosophers were conversing with him."

Who were they? You're probably familiar with our English word "stoicism," which derived from the teaching of ancient Stoic philosophers. Stoics taught that a man should strive, fearless and proud, to accept the laws of the universe, however harsh. They were to work toward a world state founded on reason. They believed the soul survived the body, but only in a kind of ethereal state, bodiless and free. Emotionally, they remained passive, disengaged.

The Epicureans, on the other hand, taught that happiness and pleasure were the highest good. Both were to be pursued with unbridled passion.

"Eat, drink, and be merry, for tomorrow we die," is classic Epicurean sentiment. We simply die like animals, without the fear of judgment or consequence. "So, live it up!"

Stoics and Epicureans smugly stroked their beards as they listened to the strange speaker from Tarsus tell of a foreign deity. Their questions were invited, answered, and countered by further questions.

Paul was in his element.

There are few things more dangerous than a preacher in his element—dangerous in the sense of the world's culture. No amount of sneering or pompous name calling would deter God's man of grace and grit from fulfilling his call to proclaim the gospel. While reasoning with the townspeople, he was joined by a growing group of philosophers who sneered, "What would this idle babbler wish to say?"(17:18).

Notice the slang nickname. We'd say today "gutter snipe"—a seed picker, like a nervous little bird that picks up french fries on the parking lot at McDonald's. To them, Paul was little more than a scavenger of profound thoughts. Shy of his own material, he fed off others' verbal scraps.

All this talk of Jesus and resurrection seemed strange to the idolatrous philosophers. After all, none of their gods boasted such powers. Interested in pursuing these strange new ideas, they granted him a formal hearing. They invited him to speak on a higher plane—literally. They escorted him up the hill called Mars.

His moment had arrived.

The Platform

Paul didn't need a pulpit to preach. The platform mattered little to him. All he desired was an audience. But surely at this moment he realized his place of preaching in Athens was no insignificant location.

On the prominent Areopagus, this august body of intellectuals amounted to a preacher's dream. It was akin to being invited to preach in the hall of Congress or to stand and speak for Christ before the United States Supreme Court. There the sharpest minds and most respected judges of the land would listen to every word you'd say. Such was the Areopagus. It represented one of the choicest opportunities Paul would ever have.

A few years ago I had a similar opportunity. Four-Star General Charles Krulak, then the commandant of the United States Marine Corps, invited me to speak at the National Cathedral. In the audience would be not only a group of recently graduated officers from Quantico, Virginia, but also numerous high-ranking officers in the Marine Corps. It was a significant gathering of military officials. Sitting in front of me were rows of two-star and three-star generals, including the commandant, himself, all in uniform with chests full of medals. As a former Marine myself, I was both excited and honored to be in the presence of those real officers.

General Krulak loves Christ. Before I rose to speak to that impressive group of people, he met me in the back room, embraced me and prayed, "I commit this man to you, Lord Jesus Christ. I pray that Your Spirit will work through your Word as You speak to him and he speaks to us. Give us not only hearts to listen but wills to obey."

I found it's hard to hug a commandant while standing at attention! After a stirring rendition of *Amazing Grace*, played on bagpipes by the drum and bugle corps, I rose to preach. My message was on "Integrity." God had provided a remarkable and unique platform from which I had the privilege to preach His Word. It was that sort of thing for Paul on Mars Hill. What a magnificent moment it must have been.

You can visit the site today. The marble is slick from the overuse of tourists' shoes. The steps that lead up to it are quite dangerous because they are not only slippery, they are now worn into a steep slope. You're forced to crawl up on all fours. Paul didn't crawl apologetically onto that platform. He mounted it, with a combination of humble trust and courageous determination to deliver the sermon of his life.

The Proclamation

Looking directly into their eyes, he began, "Men of Athens, . . ." And he was off and running. What a message he proclaimed!. It wouldn't take you three minutes to read the entire sermon as Luke records it. He begins where they were and, like all good preachers, he led them to where they needed to go. They stood riveted to his words. Their minds never wandered.

The reason Paul could speak as he did was because he felt what he felt.

And he felt what he felt because he saw what he saw. Great sermons begin with the insights drawn from seeing what others no longer see and feeling what the majority no longer feel. He spoke to these intelligent men who, if degrees were given then as they are now, would have had numerous letters strung past their names. No notes, no *Ryrie Study Bible* to coach him along, no cue cards or teleprompter. He simply stepped up and delivered: "Men of Athens, I observe you are very religious in all aspects . . ."

What a courteous beginning. No insult, no doubled-up fist, no frowning put down. He simply tells them what he had observed over the last several days while visiting their beloved city. He had talked to a cross-section of Athenian citizens and observed them as a "very religious" people. He didn't say "Christian," he said "religious." There's a major difference. They no doubt, received Paul's opening line as a compliment.

Here's a free piece of advice for budding preachers: Pay close attention to the first sentence you deliver in your sermon. Paul's message wasn't going to center on the meaning of the universe or the political histories of the ancient world—his topic was religion. Pure and simple. They got it in the first words out of his mouth. It will help you to remember that a well-thought-through opening line helps break the ho-hum mentality of your audience.

Paul continued, "For while I was passing through and examining the objects of your worship, I also found an altar with this inscription, 'TO AN UNKNOWN GOD.' What therefore you worship in ignorance, this I proclaim to you" (Acts 17:23).

Quite likely, every man listening to Paul had seen that very altar. They knew about the Unknown God. It may have been a source of anxiety for some, who wondered if they had missed one of the gods. They wouldn't want to overlook a god, after all. So they dedicated an altar to a nameless god, just in case. (And they called *Paul* a babbler!) They knew precisely which altar Paul had in mind. They could picture the image now glowing hotly in their minds.

Paul began with the familiar so that he might explain the unfamiliar. Superb technique. He knew his plan but his audience didn't. In a brilliant display of creative transition he exclaimed, "What you worship in ignorance, I proclaim to you." If I may: "Guess, what, men of Athens? You know that unknown god down there on the corner of Zeus and Perecles? I know that God's name. All these years the weather has turned the old altar black with age, but I'm here to introduce you to Him today."

Evangelist Billy Graham prepares for his crusades just as Paul did in Athens. He studies the city. He, no doubt, meets the mayor and, when possible, the governor of the state. He gets to know the media outlets, the sports personalities, and acquaints himself with the teams that are popular in that city. He begins by laying a foundation of familiarity, preparing to lead his audience into unfamiliar territory most have never visited before. So he leads them in his sermon. It's a genius plan that has worked for over fifty years. Good preaching starts with the familiar, then builds bridges to where folks need to be.

Paul spoke of that unknown God and immediately built a bridge to make Him known. "The God who made the world and all things in it, since He is Lord of heaven and earth, does not dwell in temples made with hands; neither is he served by human hands, as though He needed anything, since He Himself gives to all life and breath and all things" (17:24–25).

Who is this unknown god? Well, He's *Theos*, the Creator of heaven and earth. The true God. The one and *only* God. Don't miss the definite article: He is *the* One who made the world and all things in it. He is *Kurios*: "Lord!" That's what his audience called Caesar. Paul exclaimed, "I not only want to introduce to you *the* God, I want to tell you that He is Lord and Master of the earth. Do not be mistaken: He doesn't dwell in man-made temples. *How could there be a god who doesn't dwell in temples made with hands?* they must have wondered. He's holding their attention.

Paul's describing the God of heaven, the God you and I are familiar with. But, understand, those eggheads had never heard of Him. Paul's audience was intelligent and religious . . . but as lost as wounded geese in high grass. So he continued to build his bridge by saying, "He Himself gives to all life and breath and all things; and He made from one, every nation of mankind to live on the face of the earth, having determined *their* appointed times, and, the boundaries of their habitation . . ." (17:25b–26).

Not only is God omnipotent, He is sovereign. He sets the boundaries. He sets the limits. He is the immeasurable One who measures all. He is Lord—the true *Kurios!*

Paul's warming to his climax: "That they should seek God, if perhaps they might grope for Him and find Him, though He is not far from each one of us; for in Him we live and move and exist, as even some of your own poets have said, 'For we also are His offspring'" (17:27–28).

A deafening silence overcame the crowd. This is preaching at its best. Paul knows precisely where he wants them to go. They only know where they've been and where he is now. The man is describing a deity they've never met.

Remember, Paul had little time to prepare or to write out his sermon. He began to prepare it during his days on the street. He finalized it in his head during the brisk climb up the marble steps to Mars Hill. Did you notice? He quotes one of their own poets, who said, "For we are His children." "But let me tell you," says the apostle by implication, "It is not Zeus." Just in case anyone started to doze off, he did a little seed picking of his own by quoting a familiar poem written about Zeus. Stoic philosopher, Aratus of Soli (third century, B.C.) had originally written,

> Zeus fills the streets, the marts,
> Zeus fills the seas, the shrines or the shores, and the rivers!
> Everywhere our need is Zeus!
> We also are his offspring.

It was that last line Paul borrowed. The God whom Paul proclaimed was not Zeus. All their learning had led them down a dead-end street. This was no cheap marketplace god, whose image appeared for sale on vendors' carts and in storefront windows. Paul was introducing to them the God who created the universe and demanded a response from His wandering. Having bated and hooked his audience, he now cautiously reeled in his catch with masterful skill.

The Proposition

> Therefore having overlooked the times of ignorance, God is now declaring to men that all everywhere should repent, because He has fixed

a day in which He will judge the world in righteousness through a Man whom He has appointed, having furnished proof to all men by raising Him from the dead.

Acts 17:30–31

The "R" word! There wasn't a Stoic or an Epicurean in the bunch who wasn't by now squirming in his toga. "Repent? You've got to be kidding. Me change *my* mind, relinquish all my training and my position as judge in Athens?" If they at one time wondered if the man was deluded, what they just heard had removed all doubt. Paul boldly proposed that the God of heaven expected a heartfelt response from the ones He had lovingly created. Then came the final blow. He used that other "R" word—*raised* from the dead? Yes! The one-and-only God had proven Himself by raising Jesus from the dead.

With that, the whole lot of them threw their heads back and howled. They couldn't believe their ears. "*Resurrection*? Preposterous!" They showed this guttersnipe the door. *Enough!*

Paul slipped the resurrection in before they could turn him off. (Skilled preachers know that technique). He had been telling people on the streets about the Savior, Jesus, since he had arrived through the gates. Perhaps the news of Paul's teachings had crossed the Aegean Sea and made its way into the Athenian marketplace. They figured the corpse of this Jesus was now rotting in the grave. Paul told them otherwise. He was, in fact, alive. They'd consider no such nonsense.

Look how quickly they tuned him out.

Now when they heard of "the resurrection of the dead," some *began* to sneer, but others said, "We shall hear you again concerning this." (17:32)

And a very small group believed.

The same response happens today. Every effective sermon results in some sneering and rejecting—an immediate negative response. Some are intrigued enough to return for a second hearing. A small group of others believe. Among those whom Paul persuaded are Dionysius and Damaris (17:34).

THE QUESTION

You, too, are in one of those three categories. Which one? You have a choice: Reject truth, you're intrigued by truth, or you believe truth. In other words, you respond in faith to God's Word.

Paul didn't wait around for "a show of hands." Having delivered his message, he stepped off the marble platform and "went out of their midst."

No singing of seven verses of some song. No emotional appeal for a conjured-up response. No begging or threatening or manipulating. No apology for being unprepared. None of that. He ended his sermon and left. What a magnificent model. Signed by God, sealed by the Spirit, delivered by a servant. It's that simple. Now let's make it even more practical.

A FOUR-PART PLAN FOR POWERFUL PREACHING

You may be reading this chapter as a fellow preacher. Perhaps you are a teacher or leader of a Sunday school class or small-group Bible study. Maybe you are a youth pastor or lay leader. You might be involved in counseling at a camp, evangelism, or on-site, true-blue missionary work. If you are responsible for communicating biblical truth, consider yourself a preacher (at least for the next couple of pages)—you are a communicator of God's Word. If that describes you, these next four principles are especially for you. Pay close attention, read thoughtfully and carefully, as I apply this to whatever may be your ministry.

First, always stay on the subject—Christ. For Paul it was always about Christ. Though explaining the altar of the unknown God of Athens, everything for Paul pointed to Christ. Preaching that doesn't exalt Christ is empty preaching. Paul wrote to the Corinthian believers, "For I determined to know nothing among you except Jesus Christ, and him crucified" (1 Corinthians 2:2). For Paul, to live was Christ and to die was gain. Christ is the answer to our deepest needs. Great preaching carries a theme, and that theme is Christ. When Christ is preached, lives are transformed. Mark that down. Don't ever forget it!

Second, always speak the truth without fear. Do not be overly impressed with those who have come to the class or who sit in the church where you serve. Makes no difference how much they're worth or how little they contribute. Makes no difference their gender. Makes no difference their level of interest. Makes no difference their response. Forget what they're wearing. Ignore their academic pedigree. Get beyond their notoriety. Your task is to speak the truth without fear. Learn that from one who didn't hear it early enough in his ministry. One of your primary responsibilities is to be unintimidated when you speak the truth. Often, the most brilliant among us have never put it all together in their minds. What they need (and what they will appreciate) is a fearless witness, well prepared, who knows where he's going.

Third, always start where your audience is. Paul hooked those men in his first sentence. You can too, if you spend some time thinking about it. Know your audience well enough to build a bridge quickly. Find a way to get into their world and then build a bridge to Christ. Remember: You're beginning with the familiar in order to acquaint them with the unfamiliar.

Fourth, always surrender the results to God. Once they have heard the message, your part ends. Your task is to communicate truth. It's God's job to draw people to Himself. You prepare the patient; He does the surgery. They don't need manipulation. There's enough of that going on. You don't need to follow them out to their car or push them into a corner. God will reach them, just as He did in Athens. When you finish your message, graciously greet those who linger, and walk out of their midst. You pray. You care. You show genuine interest. You entrust the results to God. Don't keep score; that's His job. God can handle the rest. Trust Him. Trust the power of His Word. Trust it to haunt them and humble them. Your job is to love them and speak truth to them, graciously and wisely. Leave the results to God.

Paul spoke what he spoke because he felt as he felt. And he felt as he felt because he saw what he saw. That makes for good preaching. Good preachers see what the majority don't see. Usually it's the invisible. It's that which is hard to get your arms around. It's the gnawing emptiness of the human soul that the preacher somehow sees, understands, and then effectively articulates. Paul was provoked in his spirit. Being provoked, he was led to say what he said. When he said it, he connected. It's just that simple.

When your heart is right, it's amazing what you're able to see. And when you see it clearly, it's remarkable how God can give you the words to say. You may be amazed how God uses you, just as He did Paul in that ancient metropolis so many years ago. When his moment arrived, he was ready.

When your moment comes, stand and deliver. God will give you courage as you tell others of his Son. There is no greater honor on earth.

CHAPTER FIFTEEN

Leading as Paul Led

We call it "Black Tuesday" around our house. September 11, 2001, the ultimate 9-1-1 wake-up call. The world watched in horror the chilling video tape of two American Airlines jetliners slamming at full speed into the Word Trade Center in lower Manhattan. Within less than two hours, both towers imploded, crumbling into heaps of torn metal and melted steel. Thousands were killed. Hundreds more perished as another jetliner slammed into the Pentagon, and still another fell to the earth in southwest Pennsylvania, not far from Pittsburg.

There'll never be another morning like that, by God's grace. It rocked us back on our heels. Since we never expected it, we weren't ready for it. The nation sat stunned, emotionally paralyzed, in shock. America needed leadership. If there was ever a time our national leaders needed to step up and provide a command performance, it was then. The need of the hour was a series of clear and reassuring words about responsibility, vision, and courage. It was no time to sit and stare, immobilized by confusion and fear. Those savage acts of aggression called for words and actions that would bring confidence and reassurance to a country caught off guard. We also needed hope. Remaining silent and neutral at a time of crisis were not options. Political rhetoric, screams of rage, and panicked responses would have left the nation seriously crippled. Heavy weights of hope and resolve hung on the thin wires of courageous leadership.

Thankfully, George W. Bush, our president, rose to the occasion. The speech he delivered on the Thursday night following the attack was one of the finest I have ever heard. Cynthia and I cheered and applauded as he delivered a courageous, compassionate, and calm response to the chaotic situation we faced. He spoke of resolve, determination, faith, hope, compassion, and justice. When he finished, I looked at Cynthia, and said, "Whoever helped him write that speech deserves a significant raise!" Whether or not he composed that speech or others assisted him, one thing was certain: The courage, comfort and hope, which he offered to all of us, came from deep within the man's soul. From the rubble and ruin of a fractured people, a strong leader had emerged. A grateful nation rallied to his side. That's *leadership*.

I appreciated the words that appeared in a special edition of *Newsweek* that reveal a great deal more about the man we call Mr. President. Word on the street at that time was that those assigned to the meeting called by the president were prepared for disappointments. What they received came as a complete surprise. The President had found his voice. Clearly, it was a voice of leadership. An excerpt from the article states, "They all got more than they bargained for. The meeting didn't last minutes but half an hour. The President was relaxed and in control. As for their aid request, 'I'm with ya,' the President said eagerly, and it was approved by Congress the next day. The Virginians got promises of aid, too, and the warlike words that all yearned for. "When I take action," he said, "I'm not going to fire a two-million-dollar missile at a ten-dollar empty tent and hit a camel in the butt. It's going to be decisive!" That's true grit. My kind of leader.

The *Newsweek* reporter added this comment: "Winston Churchill might not have used those words, but he'd have loved the sentiment and admired the maturation of the man who uttered them."[1]

Most people of my generation would name Winston Churchill as one of the world's greatest leaders. We remember the qualities that great British war hero not only wrote about but emulated in his life. Optimism. Kindness. Magnanimity. Gratitude. Independence. Justice. Self-criticism. Loyalty. Calmness under stress. And the rare ability to face and communicate bad news squarely. Every age enjoys a few remarkable individuals who, in times of crisis, rise to the occasion and lead with courage and integrity. Our man Paul was no exception. He is, in my opinion, in a league of his own.

Frankly, I am more impressed with Paul than I am with any other leader I've ever studied. He never led a nation in time of war, or stood toe to toe against a madman who desired to control the world. However, he was constantly buffeted by the powerful forces of Satan and his domain as he set in motion a Christian enterprise that would impact the entire world for centuries.

Like fine gold thread, excellent leadership qualities weave their way through Paul's ministry life. Admittedly, an entire study of those outstanding qualities requires more space than I'm allotted in this book. That's why I'm limiting my discussion to those qualities implicitly stated in a letter he wrote to the Thessalonians while on his second missionary journey. During his extended stay in Corinth, some trouble in Thessalonica compelled him to write a pastoral letter to encourage that flock and defend his apostolic authority. The letter is filled with grace and grit. We'll focus on eight essential leadership qualities I observe in the first twelve verses of 1 Thessalonians chapter 2. The first four are negative; the last four are positive.

THE LEADERSHIP STYLE OF THE APOSTLE PAUL

For you yourselves know, brethren, that our coming to you was not in vain, but after we had already suffered and been mistreated in Philippi, as you know, we had the boldness in our God to speak to you the gospel of God amid much opposition. For our exhortation does not *come* from error or impurity or by way of deceit; but just as we have been approved by God to be entrusted with the gospel, so we speak, not as pleasing men but God, who examines our hearts. For we never came with flattering speech, as you know, nor with pretext for greed—

God is witness—nor did we seek glory from men, either from you or from others, even though as apostles of Christ we might have asserted our authority.

1 Thessalonians 2:1–6

Before addressing those eight qualities, let me make a general observation, followed by a couple of impressions. I observe that the Thessalonian Christians knew Paul and his ministry well. He was no distant celebrity; no aloof executive in a pinstriped suit who communicated solely through interoffice memos. On the contrary, he walked among them and worked alongside them. Quite likely, he had enjoyed Sunday afternoon meals in their homes and getting to know their families. He knew them intimately and allowed them to come "up-close and personal" with him.

Several times in the opening verses he makes statements suggesting their personal knowledge of him and his work.

For *you yourselves know*, brethren . . . (v.1)

After we had already suffered and been mistreated in Philippi, *as you know* . . . (v.2)

We never came with flattering speech, *as you know* . . . (v.5)

For *you recall*. . . (v.9)

You are witnesses . . . (v.10)

And on it goes. They knew all about his suffering, understood his words, and trusted his motives. He was no stranger to those folks.

Over and over he implied, "When you look back on my ministry with you, you remember, you know, you were witnesses, you were there, you saw it in action." They knew the founder of their flock intimately. He was truly a shepherd among them. Now my impressions.

First, Paul was not offering them leadership ideals. He didn't write a theoretical textbook on Christian leadership. He wrote a personal letter, appealing to his readers' intimate knowledge of him and his ministry among them. When he wrote them he reminded his readers of significant leadership essentials they would remember seeing at work in him. They are attainable qualities for all of us and worth the time to cultivate.

Second, Paul's style of leadership was neither aloof nor secretive. He lived *among* them. They knew his address. He talked to them. He didn't preach a sermon and then conveniently slip out the back door during the benediction. He remained approachable, accessible, and real. His life was an open book. Most would agree, that kind of leader is refreshing. They've got nothing to prove, no secrets to hide, no pretense or air of self-importance, never feeling compelled to remind you of their qualifications for the job. That was Paul. He was believable.

John Stott writes, "Paul's ministry in Thessalonica had been public. It was exercised in the open before God and human beings for he had nothing whatever to hide. Happy are those Christian leaders today, who hate hypocrisy and love integrity, who have nothing to conceal or be ashamed of, who are well known for who and what they are, and who are able to appeal without fear to God and the public as their witnesses! We need more transparency and openness of this kind today."[2]

A leader who lives his life in the open has nothing to guard or fear. But if he is always on the move, forever hiding behind locked doors and drawn blinds, the public has reason to suspect he's not genuine. Be careful about following a leader who is inaccessible and invulnerable.

In Paul's letter to the Thessalonian church, he looks back on his ministry there and writes, "You yourselves know, brethren, that our coming to you was not in vain." How encouraging that must have been for them to hear! Many a pastor looks back on former ministries and sighs, "That was a frustrating ministry, a sad disappointment." Paul thought the opposite about the Thessalonians. He enjoyed pleasant memories of effective service and loving fellowship.

Please remember, however, his ministry was no bed of roses. He literally limped into Thessalonica, his body bruised and tender from being beaten and imprisoned in Philippi. Thankfully, I've never had to endure such brutal persecution. Paul did. But here's the good news: It didn't impede his resolve. He writes, "After we had already suffered and been mistreated in Philippi, as you know, we had the boldness in our God to speak to you the gospel of God amid much opposition" (2:2)

One of the secrets of the man's success can be stated in three words: *He plodded on.* He led the same way whether the winds were at his back or blowing hard against him. Opposition and hardship didn't matter. The only priority that mattered was that Christ was proclaimed. Every trail he blazed led others to the Cross.

Since Paul stands as the Bible's sterling example of spiritual leadership, we would be wise to take a closer look at several of the qualities that made him the leader he was.

LEADING AS PAUL LED

I see eight principles for leading as Paul led. Four are negative, four positive. Let's look first at the negatives. I call them negative because of Paul's use of the word "not" or "nor" or "never." In other words, the following principles demonstrate what spiritual leaders are *not* to be.

The Negatives

First, spiritual leaders are not deceptive. Paul writes, "For our exhortation does not come from error or impurity or by way of deceit" (2:3). Look closely at the word *error.* The original Greek word means "wandering" and was used often to describe what appeared to be an aimless moving of planets through space. The word was eventually used when referring to people suffering under delusion. Paul reminded the Thessalonian flock that there was nothing manipulative about the way he led. He used the word "impurity" to buttress that point. Nothing off-color or under the table characterized his ministry. No religious traces. No double-talk in fine print designed to trap the unsuspecting. He played it straight. The words "not . . . by way of deceit" simply mean "nothing devious in method or motive." Paul didn't conceal the cost of discipleship. He told them it was a rugged journey. Neither did he hold out a promise of fraudulent blessings and benefits. No name-it-and-claim-it theology—as if God promises to double your money each time you give to some fund-raising appeal. That's nonsense. Paul knew it and said so. Some people give their lives in places of obscurity and never realize on this earth any significant return on their investment. More often than not, tangible rewards are deferred.

Paul avoided sleazy tactics. He deliberately stayed off the slimy paths of manipulation. He operated on higher ground. No verbal voodoo. No lies. No schemes. Honesty was his middle name. Integrity marked his steps.

General Dwight Eisenhower wrote, "To have followers, one must have their confidence. Hence, the supreme quality for a leader is unquestionable integrity. If one's associates find him or her guilty of phoniness, if they find that he lacks forthright integrity, he will fail. His teachings and actions must square with each other."[3]

Second, good leaders are not people pleasers. A sure sign of personal insecurity is wanting to be liked by everyone. Peace at any price. Remaining neutral lest someone be offended. Paul had learned to resist that trap by speaking not "as pleasing men but God, who examines our hearts." Would that all ministers and ministries could resolve to maintain such a standard! Paul understood the perils involved in telling people what they *wanted* to hear, rather than declaring what they *needed* to hear. To him, the stakes were eternal. His motive for ministry wasn't complicated: Please God, not people.

Years ago, while serving a previous church, I got caught between a rock and a hard place. A sticky issue had presented itself, and the board had reached an impasse. A vote was called to resolve the issue democratically. Of the seven of us voting on the elder board, three voted in one direction, and another three voted in the opposite direction. The tying vote would be cast by the pastor—yours truly. It was your classic no-win situation. We adjourned for twenty-four hours to pray, but mainly to give me time to sort out the matter.

I went home and said to Cynthia, "I'm going to get away for some time alone. I'll spend the night thinking and praying about the dilemma somewhere other than at home. I need a change of scenery."

A good friend of mine, a pharmaceutical salesman I had come to respect, was spending the night in a hotel an hour away. I planned to spend some time in prayer with him and hopefully benefit from his wise counsel. En route to his hotel, a passage of Scripture hit me square between the eyes. I nearly drove off the road as I read from the Bible perched on the steering wheel. Pulling off to the side of the road I read aloud Paul's words to the Galatians: "For am I now seeking the favor of men, or of God? Or am I striving to please men? If I were still trying to please men, I would not be a bondservant of Christ" (Galatians 1:10).

Boom! Like a heat-seeking missile, the truth of that passage detonated deep within in my heart and destroyed every objection to doing what I knew to be right. For me it was a turning point. It was time for me to be true to my convictions. Either I served Christ or men. You cannot be a faithful bondservant of Christ and spend your life making people happy. I made a U-turn and headed back home.

When I returned after less than an hour on the road, a surprised Cynthia met me at the door. "I know exactly what I need to do." With some embarrassment, I admitted, "I knew what my heart was telling me; I just didn't want three of those men not to like me."

Some feared a church split over the sensitive matter. I didn't let that intimidate me. Twenty-four hours later I voted my conscience, and the Lord honored that decision. Not only did we not split the church, attendance soared during the next eighteen months.

A warning is in order. Don't take this as an opportunity to justify your abrasive style. I can almost hear some deacon slapping his knee, thinking, *Hot dog! Now I've got a biblical reason for offending as many people as I possibly can. The Bible teaches I'm not supposed to please people.* Stop! Don't go there. That's an extreme reaction which will help no one.

Notice also the word "flattering" in verse 5. You might ask, "How do I please God and honor people without resorting to empty flattery?" Glad you asked. Paul says focus on the Lord "who examines our hearts" (2:4). You listen closely to Him. If you don't know, admit that. If you're certain, say it like you believe it. Some may get up and walk out of the meeting. (Rarely have I preached a sermon where someone didn't walk out of the place.) I see anger reflected on some people's faces at times. Disapproval and disagreement aren't uncommon either. The fact is, I've gotten to the place where when I don't see opposition to truth, I'm a bit surprised. Invariably when you come down strong on an issue, you'll have some who won't like it. And they leave in a huff. My response? *Adios!* At my age you get a little ornery.

Leaders who focus on pleasing God gain people's respect.

Third, spiritual leaders are not greedy. I like Eugene Peterson's paraphrase in *The Message* of verse 5: "We never used words as a smoke screen to take advantage of you."[4]

Godly leaders avoid putting up verbal smoke screens. Sadly, some leaders, who call themselves "Christian," use their giftedness to manipulate and mislead God's people. Greed is a vicious master. And it's not always related to money. You can be greedy for desire or power. You can be greedy for your own agenda. Greed can be a hidden motive that causes you to orchestrate events to move in your direction. Greed flows out of discontentment. Actions spawned by greed usually backfire, causing more heartache and pain for everyone involved.

A couple I read about recently was having a double celebration. Both of them were celebrating their sixtieth birthdays, and their fortieth wedding anniversary. During their quiet evening together, a fairy appeared and said, "Because you have been such a loving couple all these forty years, I want to grant each one of you a wish. The fairy pointed her wand to the woman first. Being a faithful, loving spouse, the wife wished for an all-expense-paid cruise to a romantic Caribbean island for her and her beloved. Whoosh! Instantly the tickets appeared in her hand. She squealed and beamed with delight. Next the fairy turned her wand to the husband to grant whatever he asked. The man pulled the fairy aside and whispered, "In all honesty, I'd love to have a wife thirty years younger than I am." The fairy wiggled her nose, waved her wand and poof! He was suddenly ninety years old.

Greed backfires. When people follow greedy leaders, they get hurt. Ministries suffer. Worst of all, Christ is dishonored.

Finally, spiritual leaders are not self-serving. Apostles were a rare breed. To qualify, they had to have seen the resurrected Christ. They performed miracles and founded churches. They possessed supernatural discernment and wisdom. They served as the Lord's chosen men at crucial junctures during first-century church history. Paul stood in their ranks.

By the time he wrote to the Thessalonians, he had proven himself a worthy apostle and exclaimed with a clear conscience that he did not "seek glory from men, either from you or from others, even though as apostles of Christ we might have asserted our authority" (2:6). I admire that sense of authoritative restraint. One of the marks of genuine humility is the restraint of power; it's what's held in check that reveals true leadership. No throwing their weight around. No taking unfair advantage. Paul said they could have done that, but they didn't.

In his excellent book *Empowered Leaders*, Hans Finzel writes, "There is nothing about leadership that says we have to make people think we are powerful and important. On the contrary, servant leadership finds great strength in serving the needs of followers . . . Top-down leadership is out of place in the church."[5]

Hans' words cut across the grain of current church leadership trends. The apostle says, "We never once sought the glory of men." That's a remarkable statement. Good leaders are not self-serving. They are passionate about meeting the needs of others.

Enough of the negative. The final four principles for leading as Paul led are positive in tone. The contrast occurs in verse 7 with the tiny-though-powerful word "but." (Anytime you see that word in Scripture, prepare yourself for a sharp contrast.) Where deception, flattery, greed, and pride did not mark Paul's ministry, gentleness, affection, authenticity, and encouragement did. The final four principles represent what good leadership is supposed to be.

The Positives

First, good leaders are sensitive to the needs of others. Paul compared his ministry to a mother, who tenderly cares for the needs of her children. I love that word picture. I watched my wife nursing our children when they were tiny, without giving one thought to her own needs. It has been my joy as well to witness my grown daughters caring for our grandchildren too. It's a precious sight to behold.

Watching my wife and daughters gently cradle their little ones close to their breasts, and lovingly providing for their needs, helps me understand what Paul meant by "gentleness." His ministry was marked by a gentle nurturing of the flock. Paul says, "I was like a mother nursing a child, in my manner among you."

If God has placed you in a leadership responsibility, I urge you to cultivate a spirit of gentleness. It is after all a fruit of the Spirit (Galatians 5:23). Your tenderness will work wonders in the lives under your care.

In the aftermath of the September 11 tragedy, the world watched in wonder as powerful leaders spent time tenderly listening to the gut-wrenching stories of rescue workers and grieving New Yorkers. Mayor Rudolph Giuliani impressed the world day after day standing before the people of that great city chronicling the grim progress reports from ground zero. He spoke softly and compassionately, sometimes with tears, as the gruesome figures stuck in his throat. Somehow he made it through each meeting. Holding back his tears seemed as futile as trying to recover victims from the ten-story mound of twisted Trade Center rubble. Americans needed to see gentle leaders weep.

So do Christians. Spiritual leaders need to be just as real, as gentle, as understanding, and as empathetic. You and I appreciate spiritual leaders who consistently reveal their human sides. Contrary to popular opinion, Paul, the strong-hearted, passionate, gritty leader was also known for his gentleness and grace.

Second, good leaders have affection for people. Paul writes, "Having thus a fond affection for you, we were well-pleased to impart to you not only the gospel of God . . ." (2:8). Is that great, or what? Paul didn't shrink from sharing his emotions with his flock. That strong man, an apostle of Christ, looking back on the Thessalonians said, "Oh, what an affection I had for you. How dear you were to me." Those are affectionate words of intimacy.

To keep this simple and easy to remember, I want to suggest that affection for people can be demonstrated in two ways: *Small yet frequent acts of kindness* and *stated and written words of appreciation.* Those you lead should have a few notes of appreciation and encouragement from you by now. They should be growing accustomed to your expressions of affection that include small yet frequent acts of kindness. No one is so important that he or she is above kindness. That aspect of leadership takes courage and a spirit confident in God's grace.

I came across a couplet that summarizes this point nicely:

> Life is mostly froth and bubble.
> Two things stand in stone.
> Kindness in another's trouble.
> Courage in your own.

I'm grieved by strong leaders who consistently walk over people. We wonder how people like that make it into significant places of influence. Here's some free advice. If you don't enjoy people, please, do us all a favor, don't go into leadership. Choose another career stream. Everyone will be better off. Say no when you're offered an opportunity to lead.

Neither the world nor the ministry needs more bosses. Both need more leaders—servant-hearted souls to lead as Paul led, with sensitivity and affection toward others. Love and affection, when appropriately given, fills the gap when words alone fail to comfort. If people know you love and value them, they'll go to the wire for you. Paul told the Christians at Thessalonica that he loved them. They never got over it.

Third, good leaders demonstrate authenticity. Paul continued, "We were pleased to impart to you not only the gospel of God but also our own lives." He reminded the believers at Thessalonica that he gave them *himself.* I can already hear your question: "Chuck, are you saying that the gospel isn't important?" I'm not saying that. I am saying the gospel *alone* isn't enough. Simply delivering truth doesn't make you a leader. A computer or commentary can do that. So can tracts and tapes. Paul went a step further and said, "I had such affection for you, when it came time to serving I gave you my whole life." How refreshing!

It gets better.

Paul continued, "For you recall, brethren, our labor and hardship, how working night and day so as not to be a burden to any of you, we proclaimed to you the gospel of God." Hey, this is Macedonia. Not Newport Beach. Times were hard. Thessalonica didn't enjoy the strong, vibrant economy of Corinth. Folks lived lean, dirt-poor lives. Paul wrote, "Knowing that it was hard for you I paid my own way. I earned my own living."

He's not bragging; he's reminding them of his diligence and sacrificial commitment to them and to the ministry. He had a job to do and he did it. Plain and simple, he had no expectations.

A leader who isn't authentic will never break through the tough layers of self-preservation so prevalent in our culture. Being real melts away those barriers and lets in light.

Fourth, good leaders are enthusiastically affirming. Again, Paul writes, "You are witnesses, and *so is* God, how devoutly and uprightly and blamelessly we behaved toward you believers; just as you know how we *were* exhorting and encouraging and imploring each one of you as a father *would* his own children" (2:10–11). He started with a *mother* tenderly caring for her children. Now we see a *father* encouraging and exhorting his kids.

Ever sat on hard bleachers, in front of the father of the high school quarterback? He's his own cheer section. Why? He's a dad! The kid on the field's going, "Dad, come on, knock it off." But his old man's standing up there, yelling at top volume, loving very minute of it.

Perhaps you've longed for more affirmation from your father. Let's face it, encouragement goes a long way in preparing a child for life. No one should be getting more encouragement from us than our own children.

Pretty convicting stuff, isn't it?

What's true of children is true of all God's people. Good leadership balances the tender nurturing of a mother with the loving affirmation of a father. Encouragement is like an oasis in the desert. It brings needed refreshment to weary individuals whose souls are parched from time spent in the desert of self-doubt. There's also the desert of failure when we've tried so hard to succeed and the desert of no progress when we so wanted something to happen. And there's the desert of family rejection, abuse, and a thousand other arid, barren landscapes of life.

In those desert experiences you long for an oasis where you're able to get a cool drink of water. Though it didn't come from your father, at last it comes from the affirming words of a leader, who, in speaking, dips his ladle deep in ice water, and as he pours it out, it cools your spirit and refreshes your soul.

Paul understood the importance of enthusiastic affirmation. It motivated people to better living. In fact, that's the goal of all these leadership distinctives. Paul writes, "so that you may walk in a manner worthy of the God who calls you into His own kingdom and glory" (2:12). That's it. *We lead like this so others will live like that!*

Question: Where did Paul learn how to lead like that? He started out as Saul of Tarsus, that once arrogant, pretentious Pharisee. Remember? He was a vicious savage around Christians back then. What happened to transform that vengeful, Christian-hating crusader into a dynamic model of Christian leadership? He met his Master. He went from being in charge, to submitting to another. Again, I invite you to consider the words of Hans Finzel: "Servant leaders must be willing to live filled with submission on many levels: submission to authority, submission to God the Father, submission to one's spouse, submission to the principles of wise living, and submission to one's obligations. Though conventional wisdom says everyone should submit to their leaders, the real truth is that leaders, to be effective, must learn to submit."[6]

What happened to the proud, self-sufficient Paul? It was the same thing that happened to Joseph and Moses and Joshua and Samuel and the magi and Peter and John and Mary and Martha and Cornelius and Lydia. He met the Master. He came under new management. He met the Master! And after meeting Him, he surrendered control to Him. That's the first step to leading as Paul led.

> I had walked life's way with an easy tread,
> I had traveled where pleasures and comfort led.
> Until one day in a quiet place,
> I met the Master face to face.
> With station and rank and wealth for my goal,
> Much thought for my body but none for my soul,
> I had entered to win this life's mad race,
> When I met the Master face to face.

I built my castles and reared them high,
Till their towers had pierced the blue of the sky;
I had sworn to rule with an iron mace,
When I met the Master face to face.
I met Him, and knew Him and blushed to see,
That His eyes full of sorrow were fixed upon Me;
I faltered and fell at His feet that day,
While my castles melted and vanished away.
Melted and vanished and in their place,
Nothing else could I see but the Master's face.
My thoughts are now for the souls of men,
I've lost my life to find it again;
Ever since that day in a quiet place,
Where I met the Master face to face.[7]

Somewhere between the Damascus road and the visit from Ananias, Paul's life was transformed forever. He started taking orders from Christ his King. He advanced on his knees.

BRINGING IT HOME TO YOUR PLACE

Searching stuff, isn't it? What is it going to take to convince us that the last will be first and the first will be last? For some it will take a lifetime, for others only a few semesters in seminary.

Each May, at the end of the spring term at Dallas Seminary, we have the joy of listening to the school's top preachers. They're nominated and selected by pastoral-ministry professors. One year a talented young man preached on that pivotal passage in John 13 where Jesus washes His disciples' feet. After a compelling exposition of that simple text, the young senior class preacher leaned low into the microphone, looked across the faces in Chafer Chapel, and asked his fellow students, *"Do you want to have a great ministry . . . or do you just want to be great?"*

The packed-out chapel went silent. Nobody blinked. I'll never forget his question. None of us will. I hope he never does either.

In a single question he captured the crucial issue: Greatness. Not as the world defines it. But greatness according to the standard of Almighty God. Great leaders are servants first. Like Paul . . . like his Master Jesus Christ.

This is for you and this is for me. If you've never submitted fully to the Master, this is your moment. If you're still arrogant, you probably won't be struck down with blindness or find yourself shackled in a Roman prison. That was Paul's experience. But now that I have your attention, I suggest you take a good look within.

You do know how strong-willed and proud you are. So do the people you lead. You know how slow you are to encourage and how reluctant you are to affirm. They do too. You know if you're greedy. You know if you're self-serving. Frankly, it's time to give all that up. We're back to the crucial question: *Do you want to have a great ministry, or do you just want to be great?*

How you answer will determine how you lead.

CHAPTER SIXTEEN

Responding as Paul Responded

I f you ever meet Charlie and Lucy Wedemeyer, you'll never forget them. Charlie was an all-star football player from the state of Hawaii. He was such a good athlete, he probably could very well have played professional football. Unfortunately, all that changed when he was stricken by Lou Gehrig's disease. The disease has ravaged his central nervous system to the point that today he is able only to move his eyelids.

At his side day in and day out stands his beloved wife, Lucy, loving him and melting you with her contagious smile as she interprets the flutter of her husband's eyelids. Remarkable people. We don't admire the Wedemeyers simply because of Charlie's debilitating illness. That saddens us. Our hearts go out to him for that. We admire them because of how they have responded to the disease that has robbed them of so much of life. At some point in their past, they made that crucial call—"This will not destroy us. Instead, it will make us into the people God would have us be."

Most Christian people know the name Joni Eareckson Tada. As a young girl she loved to ride horses, dance, and enjoy life with her other high school friends. All that changed in a diving accident in 1967 in which she snapped her spinal cord. From that moment until now Joni has been paralyzed. She now spends her days in a wheelchair living as a quadriplegic, but what a remarkable attitude! Joni and her husband Ken live their lives intertwined with one another, traveling the world on behalf of her ministry to the disabled known as *Joni and Friends.*

Each time she tells her story the audience sits silently in awe. But it isn't simply the paralysis that makes us admire Joni. That part of her story saddens us. We admire her for her *response* to the paralysis. She made that crucial call. That's what gives her greatness.

Most people *don't* know Lisa Beamer. Lisa lives in Cranbury, New Jersey. On the morning of September 11, 2001, she received a chilling call from her husband Todd secretly revealing that his plane had been high-jacked.

Todd was among three others who joined together in a strong-willed, heroic fight against the terrorists on Flight 93 at 32,000 feet, which ended when the plane and all its passengers plunged into the Pennsylvania countryside. No survivors. From what we're able to decipher from the cell phone calls, those men kept the plane from crashing into yet another government building, saving hundreds of lives by their heroism. Lisa stood stunned by the news. She was several months pregnant at the time. Now her husband is gone, his life snuffed out by an atrocious, vicious attack on innocent people.

When Lisa Beamer was asked how she felt about her husband's courageous act, she responded, "It made my life worth living again." She made that call. We admire Lisa Beamer, not simply because she lost her husband. That saddens us. We grieve with her and her fatherless children. We admire her because of her remarkable response to that enormous loss.

It is response to adversity that becomes the stuff of greatness. It boils down to that call.

I've said for years that life is ten percent what happens to us and ninety percent how we respond to it. Ten percent of Charlie Wedemeyer's life is Lou Gehrig's disease. Ninety percent is how he and his wife are responding to it. Ten percent of Joni Eareckson Tada's life is paralysis. Ninety percent of her life is her attitude in responding to it day after day. Ten percent of Lisa Beamer's life is the loss of Todd, her beloved partner and father of their children. The other ninety percent flows from a beautiful response to that horrible day. That's true greatness.

It's that same greatness we observe in the character and ministry of Paul—that remarkable man of grace and grit.

A PORTRAIT OF GREATNESS

If we were to study a portrait of Paul painted by a realistic artist, we would first notice his scars and bruises. Depending on when the portrait was finished, some wounds would be red and swollen, a few still bleeding. Paul writes of those wounds at the end of his letter to the Galatians. In an unguarded moment he picks up the stylus and writes, "See with what large letters I am writing to you with my own hand" (Galatians 6:11.) Whoever read from the autographa, the original letter from Paul's own hand, would have noticed a change in handwriting toward the end of the letter. They could see the difference with their own eyes. It must have brought an emotional stirring to read that part of his original letter to the Galatians.

The oversized writing may have been due to Paul's extremely poor eyesight, or a raging migraine may have blurred his vision. Perhaps he had permanent nerve damage to his arm. Whatever the reason, he wrote larger letters. He was determined to allow his emotions to bleed onto the page. My preference is to write out, by hand, my books or articles that I'm preparing for publication. Sometimes in the passion of writing I push the pen so hard it digs through the page. Paul may have done just that when he wrote by hand, "From now on let no one cause trouble for me, for I bear on my body the brand-marks of Jesus" (Galatians 6:17).

I appreciate Paul's candid appeal. I'm convinced he had grown a bit impertinent by this point in his ministry. He's had it with troublesome folks. He says in effect, "Don't mess with me. Back off. I'm writing this letter bearing in my body the marks of one who has suffered greatly for you. I've paid for the right to instruct you. I carry around on my body the scars, the wounds, the marks, physical evidence of torture—these brands of Christ."

In the first century, slaves had the names of their owners burned onto their bodies. They were branded like cattle. Roman soldiers would often tattoo on their arms the names or numbers of the military units in which they served. In the same way, devotees of false gods tattooed the names or symbols of their gods across their flesh. But Paul's scars were different. His brands signified his sufferings for Christ. That's why he was stoned. That's why he was punched in the face. That's why he was beaten with rods. And every one of those scars was a permanent reminder that he belonged to his Master, Jesus. He, alone, was his *kurios*.

Author Jay Sidlow Baxter writes, "What were the *actual* marks on Paul's body, which he here speaks of as 'brands'? There can be no doubt about the answer. They were those scars and sears and, maybe, long-continuing sores, which had come upon him during his costly and heroic service for the sake of Christ and the gospel.

"Every time I'm around veteran prisoners of war I stand a little straighter. I want to shake their hands a little firmer. They bear in their bodies the marks of liberty. They deserve my utmost respect."[1]

That was Paul. Crippled from the unjust blows of his enemies, he stood broken in body but never in spirit. In fact, rarely does he even call attention to his scars. On the few occasions he does, it's never about him, it's always about the Savior. That's greatness. It isn't about the actions that were done against him or even the accomplishments he achieved. His greatness is revealed in his responses to those hardships.

THE PRESSURE OF MINISTRY

Few individuals have experienced the degree of suffering that comes near to the magnitude Paul endured. The pressure he lived with was borderline unbearable. He writes about that in his second letter to the Christians at Corinth. He weaves through that letter what amounts to a litany of hardships he endured during his ministry experience and missionary journeys: "For we do not want you to be unaware, brethren, of our affliction which came to *us* in Asia, that we were burdened excessively, beyond our strength, so that we despaired even of life; indeed, we had the sentence of death within ourselves . . ." (2 Corinthians 1:8–9).

The word translated here "affliction" is the Greek term for "pressure." Pressure from opposition. Pressure from rejection. Pressure from physical and emotional strain. Paul writes that he was "burdened excessively," to the point he despaired of life. The full load of intense pressure weighed so heavily upon him, he felt he had reached the end. Maybe you've been there. On a very few occasions, I've been there. For Paul the pressure felt like a death sentence. Given enough time it would eventually finish him off.

If we're going to study the life of Paul and learn lessons from his life and ministry, a major lesson to be learned is how to respond to pressure. I use *pressure* and *hardship* interchangeably. The way he responded to hardship is the way I want to respond. Rarely do any of us face adversity with such determined resolve. We view hardship as an unpleasant interruption. It's an unfair circumstance brought upon us by difficult people or oppressive situations.

Paul responded differently. His secret of endurance lay in his "divine perspective." Let's explore that idea.

He Trusted God Alone

Paul allowed the affliction to strengthen his trust in God alone. He writes, "Indeed, we had the sentence of death within ourselves in order that we should not trust in ourselves, but in God who raises the dead; who delivered us from so great a peril of death, and will deliver *us*, He on whom we have set our hope. And He will yet deliver us" (1:9–10).

He *has* delivered us, He *is* delivering us, He *will* deliver us. Get the picture? He focused on God's ability to handle the circumstances from start to finish. That freed him to lean on and tap into God's power alone.

I think the apostle reached the place where he realized he wasn't capable of altering anything. He wasn't competent enough to fix the problem or smart enough to solve the mystery. His confidence drained away to the point he despaired of life itself. At that critical juncture he found supernatural strength by looking up. He said, "Lord, right now I am unable to go on. I'm not capable. I'm not competent. I'm not confident in anything in myself to relieve this pressure. I trust You and You alone." That's what I call "divine perspective." Grit under pressure.

An Old Testament story flashes across my mind. There is a similar episode in David's life recorded in 1 Samuel 30, when the pressure could have wiped him out. David is not yet king. Yet he's in the midst of the wilderness battling the enemies of Israel. The Scriptures transport us to the scene: "Then it happened when David and his men came to Ziklag on the third day, that the Amalekites had made a raid on the Negev and on Ziklag, and had overthrown Ziklag and burned it with fire; and they took captive the women and all who were in it, both small and great, without killing anyone, and carried them off and went their way" (1 Samuel 30:1–2).

David and his men lived at Ziklag. They had left home to go fight a battle. On their return, after scaling the final ridge, they stared in disbelief: The smoldering remains of what was once their home lay before them. It would be like driving home after a long day at the office, and as you turn the final corner you notice fire trucks parked all over your neighborhood, and fire personnel scrambling all around the houses, including yours. You then notice black smoke billowing from the roof of your residence. Your home and several of your neighbors' homes are engulfed in flames. To your horror when the smoke clears there's nothing left but a pile of charred rubble.

That's the scene David and his men happened upon, only it was worse. The entire village was gone and all of the homes burned. In addition, to their horror, the entire area was desolate. The women and children had been taken. For all they knew, they had been slaughtered, and they would never see them again.

The Scripture continues, "And when David and his men came to the city, behold, it was burned with fire, and their wives and their sons and their daughters had been taken captive. Then David and the people who were with him lifted their voices and wept until there was no strength in them to weep. Now David's two wives had been taken captive, Ahinoam the Jezreelite and Abigail the widow of Nabal the Carmelite. Moreover David was greatly distressed because the people spoke of stoning him, for all the people were embittered, each one because of his sons, and his daughters" (1 Samuel 30:3–6a).

Welcome to leadership. I'm sure some on their mounts looked over in David's direction and sneered, "You're the one who took us on this fight. If we had not gone we could have stayed here and defended our families. We left because you urged us to leave. *You're* responsible for what happened here." On top of the loss of his own family and children, David faced mutiny. I call that pressure at maximum level.

Notice the next eight words. They represent the man's response: "David strengthened himself in the Lord his God."

Been there? Nothing around you provides strength. Not even your closest friends seem reliable. Your situation is bleak. Your future is threatened. You're all alone. You're at a loss for wisdom. At that time of crisis all you can do is look up. That's how David responded.

And that's exactly what Paul did. When the whole world seemed set against him, he looked up and God came through. He learned that God was trustworthy. Later he exclaims, "We have this treasure in earthen vessels, that the surpassing greatness of the power may be of God and not from ourselves" (2 Corinthians 4:7).

We don't have the power we need to face life's worst blasts. Left to ourselves we cave in. The kind of power we need comes from God only, regardless of our circumstances. To describe his life of ministry, he used words like *afflicted, perplexed, persecuted,* and *struck down.* That was Paul's life as an ambassador for Christ. More often than not, he was like a sheep ready for slaughter. Any takers?

Again, it's not his affliction we admire, but how he handled it. That's the greatness we appreciate. "We are afflicted in every way, but not crushed; perplexed, but not despairing; persecuted, *but* not forsaken; struck down, but not destroyed; always carrying about in our body the dying of Jesus, that the life of Jesus also may be manifested in our body. For we who live are constantly being delivered over to death for Jesus' sake, that the life of Jesus also may be manifested in our mortal flesh" (2 Corinthians 4:8–11).

In my more-than-thirty-year study of Paul, I've discovered he never once blamed God for his affliction. He never shook his fist at the heavens in frustration. I find that absolutely incredible. He received it all as part of his commitment to Christ and trusted God to handle those moments when he came to the breaking point. He confidently relied on his Lord. What a wonderful response. But there was another dimension to Paul's perspective.

His Focus Remained on Things Unseen

Paul viewed whatever happened to him through the eyes of faith. That remarkable trait allows him to be numbered among giants of the faith like Moses, who according to Hebrews 11, "left Egypt, not fearing the wrath of the king; for he endured, as seeing Him who is unseen" (11:27). Like Moses, Paul endured the hard times by focusing on the eternal. He used his trials as reminders to focus on things not seen. When your heart is right you can do that.

Not long ago Cynthia and I traveled to Houston for an Insight for Living event. While there we enjoyed a brief visit to the home of some good friends. Being down in the city in which I was reared reminded me of a home she and I had been in many years before. The place had a huge stone fireplace, big enough to crawl into. I relish those rare occasions when I can sit by a roaring fire and read or listen to classical music. I'm a fireplace guy!

Anyway, etched into the massive piece of timber that formed the mantle of that magnificent fireplace were these words:

"IF YOUR HEART IS COLD, MY FIRE CANNOT WARM IT."

Cynthia and I will never forget those words above that great stone hearth. There's no fire in the world that can warm a cold heart. A cold heart stays riveted on the hardship and refuses to see beyond the present. Paul's heart blazed with the fire of faith, allowing him to see the unseen. That's what kept him together under pressure. His heart stayed warm.

Nothing of what touched Paul externally would cool him deep within. Rather, it fueled his inner flame. The longer the persecution continued, the hotter his fire for God. He focused on the One who works His eternal purposes in the unseen realm when all around him gave way. Adversity strengthens our faith, consuming the dross of fear and unbelief as it melts away doubts.

By the way, focusing on the unseen is a learned trait. Some years ago I heard my friend, Jim Dobson, tell a very moving story about a lovely, large African-American lady, picturesque and strong-hearted. Every day without fail she came to the hospital to be with her five-year-old son, who was dying of lung cancer.

Before she arrived one morning, the nurse heard the little boy's voice coming from his room, "I hear the bells. I can hear the bells. They're ringing." Again and again the same words could be heard by the nurses and the staff on the floor where the little boy's room was located.

When his mother arrived later that same morning, she asked one of the nurses how her son had been doing. The nurse sighed and replied with a shrug, "Oh, he's been hallucinating all morning; it's probably the medication. He's not making any sense. He says he's hearing bells."

That beautiful mother's face beamed with understanding. She waved her finger in the face of that nurse and said, "You listen to me. My boy is not hallucinating, and he's not out of his head because of the medication. I told him weeks ago that when the pain in his chest got so bad that it was hard to breath, it meant he was going to leave us. It meant he was going to go up to heaven, and when his pain got really bad, I told him to look up into the corner of his room toward his new home in heaven, and listen for the bells because they'd be ringing for him."

With that she turned and marched down the hall and swept her little boy into her big, soft arms and rocked him until the sounds of the ringing bells were only quiet echoes and he was gone.

Focusing on the unseen helps us endure what would otherwise be unbearable. That's what Paul did, and it kept him strong in troubled times. And in all of that he learned the greatest lesson of all. He discovered for himself . . .

THE POWER OF WEAKNESS

Paul pressed ahead through a mind-boggling series of intense hardships, which he lists later in the same letter (2 Corinthians 11:22–28).

> Are they Hebrews? So am I.
> Are they Israelites? So am I.
> Are they descendants of Abraham? So am I.

Are they ministers of Christ? I have more claim to this title than they. This is a silly game but look at this list:

I have worked harder than any of them.

I have served more prison sentences!

I have been beaten times without number.

I have faced death again and again.

I have been beaten the regulation thirty-nine stripes by the Jews five times.

I have been beaten with rods three times.

I have been stoned once.

I have been shipwrecked three times.

I have been twenty-four hours in the open sea.

In my travels I have been in constant danger from rivers and floods, from bandits, from my own countrymen, and from pagans. I have faced danger in city streets, danger in the desert, danger on the high seas, danger among false Christians. I have known exhaustion, pain, long vigils, hunger and thirst, doing without meals, cold and lack of clothing.

Apart from all external trials I have the daily burden of responsibility for all the churches.[2]

On top of all that, the Lord gave him a thorn in the flesh. The Lord answered his desperate prayers to remove the thorn—whatever it may have been—in a most unexpected manner. The Lord simply answered, "My grace is sufficient for you, because power is perfected in weakness."

Surprised? "You mean, I don't have to be super-strong and endure each trial relying my own resources?" It's not like that at all. In fact, the only way you qualify to receive His strength is when you admit your weakness, when you admit you're not capable and strong, when, like Paul, you're willing to boast in nothing but *your* weakness and *God's* power.

We'd rather admire Paul for his strength in trials. We want to applaud his fierce determination against vicious persecution. If the man were alive today, he would not tolerate our congratulations. "No, no, no. You don't understand. *I'm not strong.* The One who pours his power into me is strong.

My strength comes from my weakness." That's no false modesty. Paul would tell us, "Strength comes from embracing weakness and boasting in that." It is that kind of response that brings divine strength and allows it to spring into action.

J. Oswald Sanders, in his book *Paul, the Leader,* writes, "We form part of a generation that worships power—military, intellectual, economical, scientific. The concept of power is worked into the warp and woof of our daily living. Our entire world is divided into power blocs. Men everywhere are striving for power in various realms, often with questionable motivation."[3]

The celebrated Scottish preacher, James Stewart, made a statement that is also challenging: "It is always upon human weakness and humiliation, not human strength and confidence, that God chooses to build His Kingdom; and that He can use us not merely in spite of our ordinariness and helplessness and disqualifying infirmities, but precisely because of them."[4]

That's a thrilling discovery to make. It transforms our mental attitude toward our circumstances.

Let's pause long enough here to consider this principle in all seriousness. Your humiliations, your struggles, your battles, your weaknesses, your feelings of inadequacy, your helplessness, even your so-called "disqualifying" infirmities are precisely what *make* you effective. I would go further and say they represent the stuff of greatness. Once you are convinced of your own weakness and no longer trying to hide it, you embrace the power of Christ. Paul modeled that trait wonderfully, once he grasped the principle. His pride departed and in its place emerged a genuine humility that no amount of hardship could erase.

REFLECTING ON YOUR RESPONSES

So much for Paul. How about you? Fast forward to the twenty-first century. Are you afflicted and burdened *excessively?* Do you feel as if you're under such intense pressure these days that you, too, are close to despair? I have some surprising news: You're exactly where God wants you to be. It took all these years to get you this low, this needy. Now, *look up!*

Are you feeling crushed and confused, misunderstood and beaten down?

Resist the temptation to roll up your sleeves and muster a self-imposed recovery plan. This is your opportunity! Rather than fighting back, surrender. Embrace your weakness. Tell your heavenly Father that you are trusting in the strength of His power. If Paul could do it, so can you. So can I.

At this moment I am facing a few impossible situations. No doubt, so are you. To be honest, I'm too weak to handle any of them. So are you. I'm often near tears. I'm frequently discouraged. There's hardly a week that passes that I don't slump into a mild feeling of discouragement. Sound familiar? Admit it! Some nights I don't sleep well. There are times that I absolutely weep out of disappointment in some individual's failure . . . or my own. You, too? You and I need to face the fact that we will never be able to handle any of these pressures alone. When we acknowledge this, and not until, His strength will be released in us.

Florence White Willett penned these beautiful words that help me keep life in proper perspective:

> I thank God for bitter things;
> They've been a 'friend to grace';
> They've driven me from paths of ease
> To storm the secret place.
>
> I thank Him for the friends who failed
> To fill my heart's deep need;
> They've driven me to the Savior's feet,
> Upon His love to feed.
>
> I'm grateful too, through all life's way
> No one could satisfy,
> And so I've found in God alone
> My rich, my full supply![5]

Now that you and I are beginning to grasp what Paul modeled so well, strength in weakness, I suggest we truly embrace it. You and I have slugged our way through life long enough. What do you say we stop that habit?

Let's both come before the Lord and say, "Lord, if You don't come through, I'm sunk. If you don't open that door, it isn't going to open. My situation is in Your hands. I'm tired of pushing and shoving and relying on myself. I surrender." When we do that, we hear Him say, "My grace is sufficient. My strength is perfected in your weakness."

Are you ready to face the next battle with a new strategy? Okay, *start by surrendering*. Instead of returning to your same-old method—doing a month of mental push-ups, talking yourself into looking strong and acting brave, putting on the gloves and stepping into the ring with swagger, relying on your own strength to win and succeed and impress. *Stop* and *surrender*. Drop to your knees and cry out to God. Admit your inadequacies and declare your inability to keep going on your own.

If you're finally ready to step aside and let Him have His way, say so; then do it. He will honor your admission of weakness by showing Himself strong through you. But if you don't, He won't.

It's your call.

CHAPTER SEVENTEEN

Thinking as Paul Thought

Something happened to a good friend of mine recently that illustrates the value of thinking straight. Dr. Ron Allen, a colleague of mine at Dallas Seminary and close friend for many years, is a brilliant scholar. He has not only mastered the biblical languages of Hebrew and Greek, he is a wonderful Bible expositor, historian, collector of antiquities, and a respected contributor in the area of worship and sacred music. He's a real Renaissance man, some would say. Besides all that, he grows beautiful roses on his little farm in Oregon and is an avid cyclist.

Not long ago, he hit a patch of loose gravel, lost control of the bike he was riding, and slammed onto the pavement beneath him. Thankfully, he always wears a helmet, and that, no doubt, saved his life. He hit hard on his head and broke several ribs. His recovery was slow and painful. Several weeks passed before he began noticing some difficulty in his hand-and-eye coordination. He also experienced brief seizure-like episodes that seemed to be intensifying. He finally decided to get it checked out. An outstanding neurologist discovered an enormous hematoma on the surface of his brain. You can imagine his shock when he heard the two words "brain surgery."

The operation went very well. Shortly after his surgery I visited Ron in the ICU. Through layers of white gauze wrapped tightly around his head, he managed to open one eye and peer across the room at me standing near the doorway. As he did, he immediately smiled and said, *Yic-toll, tick-toll, tick toll, tick tollee, eck-tol. Yic-tallu tick toll nah, tick-tallu-ticktoll na, nick-toll.* I couldn't believe what I was hearing. He wasn't speaking in tongues—the guy had conjugated the imperfect tense of a Hebrew verb! After he finished I laughed out loud (you know me!) as he said, "I just wanted to make sure I'm still thinking straight."

Funny, isn't it? To prove that he was thinking straight, he didn't laugh or weep, or demonstrate some other emotion. He didn't tell me of an experience he had had several weeks ago. He went to something evidential, something factual, strictly intellectual. That helped him (and me) to know he was thinking straight. He then named all of his grandchildren, along with all of their birthdays, one right after another. Bev, his wife, stood near me, smiling and shaking her head. That wise scholar knows that neither emotions nor experience, valuable though they may be to all of us, are reliable proofs of straight thinking.

Author Don Miller, in his excellent book *The Authority of the Bible*, writes, "Experience in itself is too subjective, too changeable, too inner, too fleeting, too tied to physiological factors to be a trustworthy guide for faith. To trust our experience is to put our faith at the mercy of our liver, or our endocrine glands, or the quality of our sleep on any given night, or the state of our digestion, or the problems of our work. Experience must always be subjected to the authority of the saving work of God in Jesus Christ as set forth in the Bible."[1]

What significant words in our world of sloppy thinking! If you rely on emotions and experience alone, you're treading on thin theological ice. It's about as reliable as judging a situation by how well you slept the night before. It makes no sense.

The Bible exhorts all believers to be ready to "give a defense" for our faith (1 Peter 3:15). The Greek word for "defense" is *apologia*. Our word "apology" derives from that Greek term. In our English language, an apology is an excuse. But in the Greek, it carries the idea of setting forth evidence.

The point is clear: We need to be ready to provide compelling evidence for what we believe. That requires straight thinking.

By the way, could you do that? If a friend happened to be struggling to find the truth, or a coworker challenged your belief system, could you deliver enough evidence to provide a compelling defense? That's worth serious consideration. It's part of being a calming witness in a world spinning wildly off center.

STRAIGHT THINKING FOR CROOKED TIMES

We need more straight thinking Christians like Dr. Ron Allen or, far more significantly, like Paul. Straight words come from straight minds, especially in a day when society insists on twisting, altering, distorting, and compromising the truth. Paul didn't tolerate relative reasoning—not in himself, not in others.

It wasn't long after his final missionary journey that Paul faced his own, unique set of challenging situations that called for some straight-thinking grit.

RETRACING OUR STEPS

By the time we reach the middle of Acts 21, all three of Paul's missionary journeys have ended. He is back in Jerusalem. By now, that bustling city was as familiar to him as Tarsus, his hometown. The visit began in a spirit of delightful joy. Paul greeted the brethren as they welcomed him back, and they glorified God together for "the things which God had done among the Gentiles through his ministry" (21:19).

Unfortunately, the celebrating ended quickly. Luke writes, "And when the seven days were almost over, the Jews from Asia, upon seeing him in the temple, began to stir up all the multitude and laid hands on him" (21:27).

The party was over. Paul's enemies from Asia had followed him all the way back to Jerusalem. After seeing him in the temple, they decided they had endured enough of his menacing presence. They devised a murderous plot to rid themselves of Paul once and for all.

Keep in mind, these aren't disgruntled souls, who simply disagree with him intellectually or who wish to confront him on a few of the finer points of his theology. They have murder on their minds. So they incited the crowd, shouting, "'Men of Israel, come to our aid! This is the man who preaches to all men everywhere against the people, and the Law, and this place; and besides he has even brought Greeks into the temple and has defiled this holy place.' For they had previously seen Trophimus the Ephesian in the city with him, and they supposed that Paul had brought him into the temple" (21:28–29).

Once again, they leveled criticism not based on facts. Not thinking straight, they were building a head of steam among the crowd, hoping to arouse their support for a stoning. The commander of the Roman cohort quickly received word that "all Jerusalem was in confusion" (21:31). Talk about exaggeration. That's all the Roman official needed to hear. Rome despises uprisings.

By now the mob was out of control. The beating of Paul was so severe he almost reached the point of unconsciousness. It must have been a terrifying experience.

Thankfully, word of the riot reached the ears of the Roman cohort responsible for maintaining order in Jerusalem. He didn't need another bad report going back to Rome; so he acted promptly. And it was a good thing for Paul. He ordered his soldiers and centurions to mount up and head for the center of town.

Centurions were seasoned officers in the Roman guard responsible for one hundred armed men. Within a few minutes several hundred of those armed men on horseback came upon the scene and could see Paul being beaten by the crowd.

There's something about a large police force in uniform on horseback that breaks up a crowd. The beating stopped immediately. Paul stood there dazed, bruised, and bleeding. The Roman official, simply by doing his job, had saved the apostle's life. Luke writes that this commander "ordered him to be brought to the barracks" (21:34). Antonia's barracks would be the safest place for Paul.

Just then something startling happened.

> When he got to the stairs, it so happened that he was carried by the soldiers because of the violence of the mob; for the multitude of the people kept following behind, crying, "Away with him!" And as Paul was about to be brought into the barracks, he said to the commander, "Do you know Greek?" "Then you are not the Egyptian who some time ago stirred up a revolt and led the four thousand men of the Assassins out into the wilderness?" But Paul said, "I am Jew of Tarsus in Cilicia, a citizen of no insignificant city; and I beg you, allow me to speak to the people."
>
> Acts 21:35–39

How's that for straight thinking? Paul figured this was his opportunity not only to speak to the crowd but also to build a relationship with the Roman commander. You can't think any straighter than that. The cohort is surprised that Paul is not the infamous troublemaker from Egypt.

Josephus, the ancient Jewish historian, tells us that three years earlier an Egyptian appeared in Jerusalem claiming to be a prophet. He managed to recruit several thousand men to help him overthrow Roman rule. The Romans narrowly escaped a coup by stamping out the uprising.

Paul denied any connection to that scene. He also spoke to the officer in Greek, informing him that he hailed from Tarsus and was, in fact, a citizen in good standing. What he wanted more than anything was an opportunity to proclaim Christ to the hissing mob.

I find that sort of straight thinking absolutely amazing. Talk about grit under pressure. Most of us would have sought a secure place to hide and called for our attorney. Not Paul. He says, "I'd really like to have an opportunity to talk to these people."

"Permission granted," nodded the stunned Roman officer.

As Paul turns to speak, a hush falls on the crowd. They're surprised. He speaks to them in Aramaic, the *lingua franca* among Palestinian Jews. He'd just finished speaking Greek, and now he speaks fluent Aramaic to begin his defense. What an amazing scene! The man didn't miss a beat. The mob, now a bit more subdued, listens on tip-toe.

A GOLDEN OPPORTUNITY

"Brethren and fathers, hear my defense which I now offer to you." And when they heard that he was addressing them in the Hebrew dialect, they became even more quiet; and he said, "I am a Jew, born in Tarsus of Cilicia, but brought up in this city, educated under Gamaliel, strictly according to the law of our fathers, being zealous for God, just as you all are today. And I persecuted this Way to the death, binding and putting both men and women into prisons."

Acts 22:1–4

These people are thinking, *So far so good. Our kind of guy.* They're all on the same theological page. They, too, were Jews. They, too, despise the Christians. Nothing he has said so far gives them cause for alarm.

"And I said, 'Lord, they themselves understand that in one synagogue after another I used to imprison and beat those who believed in Thee. And when the blood of Thy witness Stephen was being shed, I also was standing by approving, and watching out for the cloaks of those who were slaying him.' And he said to me, 'Go, For I will send you far away to the Gentiles.' "

Acts 22:19–21

Did he say *Gentiles?* Yes! The man used the G-word. *Boom!* That's all the volatile crowd needed to hear. What an explosion! They had heard enough. "This man is now concerned about Gentiles. We don't talk to Gentiles. We don't relate to Gentiles. Our children don't go to school with Gentiles. We refuse to live among Gentiles." Gentiles were like a pack of wild dogs. That's all it took—the place erupted in dust.

The Roman commander stepped in and rescued Paul, ordering him to be brought inside the barracks and prepared for a flogging. He was determined to teach the preacher a lesson.

Paul was stretched over a stump, wrists and ankles bound with leather thongs. In only a few moments Paul would feel the stinging smack of the bone-edged straps tearing into his already scarred back. Though about to be scourged, his keen mind never once flinched. Managing to turn his head and speak in the direction of his tormentor, Paul calmly asked, "Is it lawful for you to scourge a man who is a Roman and uncondemned?"

Is that thinking straight under pressure, or what?

Imagine the shock on the lictor's face. He had no clue the man was a Roman citizen. They immediately reported it to the cohort, who promptly halted the torture. Under Roman law citizens were not to be tortured without a trial. They were on the verge of committing an infraction punishable by death. Lysias, the cohort demanded, "Get him off the rack, don't whip him. Take off those chains." It must have been an exasperating experience for the high-ranking officer. Recalling the stiff bribes he paid for his own claim to Rome, he snorted, "I acquired this citizenship with a large sum of money." Without blinking, Paul replied with an eye-opening statement: "I was born a Roman." Case closed.

The issue would go to the Jews' supreme court. Straight thinking again paid off in spades.

A CLEVER ESCAPE

Another kangaroo court scene opens in Acts 23 with an emergency meeting of the Sanhedrin. Lysias, after piously escorting Paul to the august chamber, waited outside the door. With creative skill, John Pollock summarizes the scene:

> Paul stood in the precise spot where Stephen had stood and the seventy-one judges included a few surviving from the time of Stephen's trial. The president was Ananias ben Nedebaeus, high priest since A.D. 47, one of the most rapacious men ever to disgrace the office. Paul did not know him by sight, and the damage done by the mob's violence made sharp vision difficult. It had not, however, reduced the strength of personality he could exert through his eyes. He gripped the council with the intense gaze which had quelled Elymas the Cypriot long ago, and thereby he seized the initiative and opened the proceedings himself.

"My brothers," he began, "I have lived all my life, and still live today, with a perfectly clear conscience before God. I—" The president barked an order.

One of the court ushers struck Paul a stinging blow on the mouth.

The old Paul flared at such totally illegal behavior. Forgetting his own teaching, "When we are cursed, we bless, when insulted we answer with kind words," he shouted at the indistinct figure of the president: "God will strike you, you whitewashed wall! You sit there and judge me according to the Law; yet you break the Law by ordering them to strike me!"

The ushers were horrified. "You are insulting God's high priest!"

Paul was abashed. "My brothers," he said mildly, "I did not realize he was the high priest. Scripture says, 'You must not speak evil of the ruler of your people.' "[2]

Realizing his mistake, Paul sought to make amends. He had not forgotten, though, the present danger. Again his straight thinking prevailed over fear. He quickly devised a clever escape plan.

Knowing the room swelled with Pharisees and Sadducees, he sought to divide and conquer. Luke writes, "But perceiving that one part were Sadducees and the other Pharisees, Paul began crying out in the Council, 'Brethren, I am a Pharisee, a son of Pharisees; I am on trial for the hope and resurrection of the dead'" (23:6).

The place erupted in confusion as the Pharisees and Sadducees were pitted against each other. Sadducees were rationalists and did not believe in angels or supernatural things, let alone resurrection. Pharisees believed in all the above. Paul's strategy worked beautifully.

Meanwhile, Lasius, the Roman cohort was having a major Maalox moment outside the door. He hears yet another uproar inside the judging chamber. Nothing was working for this guy. His only solution was to keep Paul behind bars until he could come up with a workable, safe plan. Once again Paul lands hard onto the floor of a damp Roman dungeon.

He wouldn't be alone for long.

A DIVINE PROMISE OF PROTECTION

Sitting alone in the barracks, having had his lights punched out by a mob, Paul may have wondered if any of it mattered. He hung his battered head in prayer, when suddenly, "The Lord stood at his side and He said, 'Take courage; for I have solemnly witnessed . . . just as you have solemnly witnessed to My cause in Jerusalem, so you must witness at Rome also' " (23:11b).

You know what that is? Look again at the statement within the single quotation marks. That's a promise. The Lord assured Paul of his continued safety. In addition, Rome would be his destination. What comfort that must have been to the man who, again, bore the marks of torturous treatment.

Survival seems next to impossible, until the Lord intervenes. At that point, we realize He has a bigger plan than we could possibly have imagined. Often, in the midst of great pain, on the heels of mistreatment, the Lord appears in His Word, providing peace through His Spirit. He whispers, "I've got everything under control. You're right where you're supposed to be. Just as you've served me faithfully *here*, you're going to be My witness *there*." Amazing, isn't it? About the time Paul might think it's curtains in Jerusalem, He's promised a guaranteed ticket to Rome.

I think Paul slept like a baby. Divine reassurance is a great cure for insomnia.

AN UNLIKELY ALLY

But while Paul dreamed of Rome, a murderous conspiracy was being plotted against him. His Jewish enemies planned an ambush, vowing not to eat or drink until the apostle was dead. But once again, the Lord had a plan of His own.

> And when it was day, the Jews formed a conspiracy and bound themselves under an oath, saying that they would neither eat nor drink until they had killed Paul. And there were more than forty who formed the plot. And they came to the chief priests and the elders, and said, "We have bound ourselves under a solemn oath to taste nothing until

we have killed Paul. "Now, therefore, you and the Council notify the commander to bring him down to you, as though you were going to determine his case by a more thorough investigation; and we for our part are ready to slay him before he comes near the place." But the son of Paul's sister heard of their ambush, and he came and entered the barracks and told Paul. And Paul called one of the centurions to him and said, "Lead this young man to the commander, for he has something to report to him."

Acts 23:12–17

Not one assassin but forty of them! Forty determined terrorists, operating under cover of secrecy. All of them vowing, "We will not eat or drink until we've killed him." The plan was treacherous and set in motion by those who wanted him dead. What they hadn't counted on was an unlikely ally for Paul. His nephew had overheard everything and made tracks to warn his uncle.

Remarkably, Paul's nephew plays a major role in his survival. He is not mentioned by name, and we never hear of him again. Then how did he know about the ambush? Only God knows.

The Lord, who neither slumbers nor sleeps and always is at work on behalf of His own, pulls a nephew from the middle of the ambush plot. It's possible the youth overheard the plot while standing among them. Perhaps he got word of the plan from an informant. It doesn't matter. The good news is that he believed it was true and did something about it.

Meanwhile the Roman commander was feeling relieved, proud of his wise handling of the situation. His musings were interrupted by a reluctant knock at the door. The news couldn't be good. One of his centurions reports that the young man with him has some important information about a conspiracy to kill Paul. The Roman commander wasn't about to let some scrappy band of fanatics spoil his plan to bring Paul safely to Rome. So he pulled out all the stops.

Therefore the commander let the young man go, instructing him, "Tell no one that you have notified me of these things." And he called to him two of the centurions, and said, "Get two-hundred soldiers ready by

the third hour of the night to proceed to Caesarea, with seventy horse-
men and two hundred spearmen." They were also to provide mounts to
put Paul on and bring him safely to Felix the governor.

Acts 23:22–24

Do the math:

$$
\begin{array}{r}
200 \text{ soldiers} \\
200 \text{ spearmen} \\
70 \text{ horsemen} \\
\underline{2 \text{ centurions}} \\
472 \text{ bodyguards}
\end{array}
$$

Uniformed, armed, and trained soldiers. Four-hundred seventy-two to
forty rag-tag conspirators. Nice odds. *Talk about overkill.* The guy would not
be outdone. He made sure no one could get to Paul. Remember God's promise? "You must witness at Rome." This is just part of that divine plan. It was
as if God said, "I know what I am doing. I will escort you down to Caesarea
by the Sea with full protection. You are in My hand." A massive official
escort—that would work just fine.

What a comforting story. Despite the odds stacked against him, Paul
was never removed from God's protective hand. And neither are you.

Are you feeling alone, mistreated, misunderstood, forsaken? Remember
this true account. God's at work. He's there, working behind the scenes.
He'll work it out. He has a plan. Just when you're convinced the bottom is
about to drop out from under you, He steps in and lifts you to safety. For
Paul he used an unlikely and virtually anonymous ally, a nameless nephew
who comes out of the shadows at precisely the right time. God's timing is
always perfectly synchronized with His will. Remember that.

By dawn, Paul was en route to see the governor, safely surrounded by
four hundred seventy-two bodyguards. Next stop, Caesarea by the Sea.

The Lord is in charge of this man's life. But you wouldn't know it if you
looked around for visible evidence. From the time the Lord visits him in a
vision until the last trial, you do not see Paul anxious or uneasy. He gives
every evidence of being perfectly relaxed. God's promises are true. Paul

fixed his mind on what God had said, firmly believing it was true. That's straight thinking at its best.

Have you ever felt the ground move under your feet? Do you know what it's like to pitch from side to side in a small boat on strong seas? Have you ever had to run for cover, dodge bullets, or duck out of the way of advancing troops? Remarkably, some people around the world could answer, "Yes!" to all three questions. Most of us only imagine such scenes.

Still, everyone sooner or later faces the reality of feeling as if life is spinning out of control. That may describe you today. Left unchecked, fear will run its course and paralyze you to the point of helplessness. If you're not careful, you'll spend your days wringing your hands and obsessing over your encroaching circumstances. That will cause you to focus on what might happen instead of what God has promised.

Not Paul. He understood something about the sovereignty of God. That clear understanding allowed him to think straight and remain calm in crisis. That kind of straight-thinking calmness is rooted in the promises of God's Word. Take, for example, the promise in Psalm 46: "God is our refuge and strength, a very present help in trouble. Therefore we will not fear, though the earth should change, and though the mountains slip into the heart of the sea; though its waters roar and foam, though the mountains quake at its swelling pride" (Psalm 46:1–3).

Do things seem a little bit out of control these days? We all felt that way toward the end of 2001. It started on September 11. Several days later I went out to get the mail and Cynthia said, "Don't open anything yet. Anything look suspicious?" The whole anthrax scare associated with the terrorist attack on America made all of us a little paranoid for awhile.

Guess what? Cynthia and I turned to Psalm 46. We decided to take God at His word. Now, we are sleeping like babies. Nothing anyone or anything can throw at us will erase that promise (or any promise) of God.

Nothing. Our final home is not planet earth. Our future is sure. In the meantime, God is in control. Make that in *full* control.

Like Paul, we need to learn to think straight, even if the foundations of the earth shift beneath our feet. That takes a heart willing to trust His Word, submit to His plan, then deliberately and consciously relax.

The literal rendering of Psalm 46:1 goes something like this: "God is our refuge and strength; abundantly available for help in tight places."

In a tight place? Don't fear. You are right where He wants you. Furthermore, He will see that you arrive precisely where He wants you to be.

If He is able to stir up four hundred seventy-two earthly bodyguards to get Paul from Jerusalem to Caesarea, safely and securely, He will have no trouble getting you from here to wherever, safely and securely. After all, how many angels are there?

And by the way, when you think straight about all this, you realize you need only one.

CHAPTER EIGHTEEN

Dealing with Critics as Paul Did

A tender heart and a tough hide—that's the ticket. It's not an easy balance to maintain, especially if you're engaged in ministry and your face is on others' mental dartboard. Frankly, the tough hide is harder to cultivate than the tender heart. For those of us who concentrate most of our attention on spiritual matters, a tender heart is almost a given. Developing a tough hide can take years.

Cynthia and I don't have plaques or mottoes adorning our home, but I do have a statement taped to the wall of my study that I read almost every day. William Henry Ward wrote the four-liner:

> For every achievement there is a price.
> For every goal there is an opponent.
> For every victory there is a problem.
> For every triumph there is sacrifice.

Reading those words regularly helps me stay realistic and toughen up. Among my reading habits, I'm on a hunt for insights, techniques, and stories that describe how other people maintain that delicate balance. Abraham Lincoln was one who seems to have mastered dealing with criticism. How did he handle all the flack? He admits, "If I were to read, much less answer, all the attacks made on me, this shop might as well be closed for any other business. I do the very best I know how—the very best I can; and I mean to keep doing so until the end. If the end brings me out all right, what is said against me won't amount to anything. If the end brings me out wrong, 10,000 angels swearing I was right would make no difference."[1]

Like Lincoln, I've tried my best not to let it get to me. Usually I succeed . . . sometimes, not.

I've also benefited from Charles Haddon Spurgeon's insights. He writes, "Get a friend to tell you your faults, or better still, welcome an enemy who will watch you keenly and sting you savagely. What a blessing such an irritating critic will be to a wise man. What an intolerable nuisance to a fool."[2] Well, that hasn't always worked for me, either.

To be candid, sometimes criticism comes from people who are just plain ornery, whose words are not worth considering. Frequently, folks criticize without knowing all the facts. Once they get more information, they usually lighten up. Not always. That's when having a tough hide pays off.

People in ministry are like lightening rods. Every pastor, every Christian leader, every Christian musician, every Christian author I know can tell his or her own stories of times they've been verbally assaulted. I have found the more effective the ministry, the larger the number of critics. Without a tough hide, you're an emotional wreck.

Paul, the man we are studying, understood that reality. On one occasion he comes right out and declares, "a wide door for effective service has opened to me, and there are many adversaries" (1 Corinthians 16:9). That's encouraging to me. He experienced both sides and came up with an axiom: *Effective ministry and opposition go hand in hand.* Mushrooming opposition from others accompanies meaningful work for God.

We're back to that line, "For every goal there is an opponent."

A friend of mine recently reminded me, "Our Lord was nailed to a cross; so you can count on being nailed to the wall." That's good counsel for us in the ministry.

FOUR SPIRITUAL FLAWS OF NEGATIVE CRITICISM

For years I've appreciated the insight and writing skills of my longtime friend, David Roper. Dave and I were seminary students together back about the time the earth's crust was cooling. He and I went to Peninsula Bible Church in Palo Alto, California, to serve alongside Ray Stedman. I was there just for the summer of 1961; David stayed on as part of the staff and remained there many years before leaving to serve the Cole Community Church in Idaho. One of the fine books he has written is titled *A Burden Shared.* In it Dave lays out four truths about criticism that are right on target. I would call them the Four Spiritual Flaws of negative criticism.

First, criticism always comes when we least need it. I've certainly found that to be true, haven't you? It never seems to come when you're on top, but rather at the bottom. After you've blown it and you're on your face, some grinning church brother or sister comes along and kicks you again, in "Christian love," of course.

Second, criticism seems to come when we least deserve it. Often after an honest mistake or an off-the-cuff comment, said without malice, some dear soul (with the gift of criticism) blasts us with a shot of stinging words. Never fails.

Third, criticism comes from people who are least qualified to give it. Then who's qualified to give constructive criticism? The people who know you the best—those who love you the most. Not strangers. Not folks who have no relationship with you.

Let me offer you some free advice here: If you don't really know the person you're getting ready to criticize, or if you're not fully apprised of the facts, just pass up the opportunity. Let it be. Loving someone begins with knowing him. That's why Solomon wrote, "Faithful are the wounds of a friend" (Proverbs 27:6.) In Hebrew the verse is even more specific: "Faithful are the bruises caused by the wounding of one who loves you."

For those relatively few people who truly love me and understand me and who have labored alongside me for enough time to know me well, their words are invariably worth hearing. They may hurt, but they're reliable. People like that don't criticize inappropriately. Those I often get criticized by don't even know my middle name.

Fourth, criticism frequently comes in a form that is least helpful to us. Sometimes the critical words sting with anger, jealousy, and envious rage. Seldom is criticism offered lovingly and graciously. More often than not, the words are delivered anonymously, like unsigned letter bombs that appear harmless, but when detonated do unbelievable damage.

We're back full circle: If you plan on surviving and remaining effective in ministry for the long haul, cultivate a tough hide. As I mentioned above, we have a wonderful model in the person of Paul. He faced any number of growling critics with unusual grace and characteristic grit.

A LONG LINE OF RELENTLESS CRITICS

Paul's critics dogged his every step from Antioch to the Macedonian coastline and all the way back to Jerusalem. He rarely knew a moment of reactionary peace. Even as we move toward his later years, a time when, for most others in ministry, things began to settle down, Paul's troubles with critics intensified. They were downright relentless.

You would think by now that there would be at least a few applauding crowds heralding the mammoth achievements of this missionary statesmen. Not so. Instead, we find Paul having to thicken his hide. Remarkably, his heart has grown softer with age. No bitterness. No jaded edgines in his attitude toward the ministry found within the ranks of Christian leaders today. None of that. Here is a man who maintained a tender heart while, at the same time, a tough hide. He's more compassionate and understanding. Yet, he's full of grit, determined to hang in there to the end.

He has finished his third missionary journey. He went where no tourist group would ever want to go. And he did what no novice would ever undertake. Beaten. Mistreated. Maligned. Misrepresented. The apostle Paul, while in the process of writing letters to churches, had established and mentored the younger men who would follow in his steps. He returns to Jerusalem, ragged and weary from the battlefield. But there was no ticker-tape parade. No applause. No church opened the doors to say, "Welcome back, you hero. You have been our model while you've been gone." Instead, he's forced to contend again with a group of harsh critics, who had followed him like a bad dog all the way from Asia. Those Jewish critics didn't even live in Jerusalem. They went out of their way to make life miserable for him.

After a narrow escape from ambush, Paul found himself en route to Rome, compliments of Caesar. The trip to Caesarea-by-the-Sea would be the first leg of a journey fulfilling the Lord's urgent plan for him to "witness at Rome also" (Acts 23:11). Who was in Rome? Why, the ruler of the world, that's who. The Roman Emperor, Nero, sat proudly on his throne in Rome. But before he'd meet Nero Paul would encounter a trio of the state's more beguiling political characters—Felix, Festus, and Agrippa—a motley crew of governors, pompous in their outward displays but weak in character and prejudiced in their dealing with anyone who was Jewish.

Felix is an otherwise obscure figure in history. Had it not been for his encounter with God's ambassador of grace to the world, he would have slipped into eternity as a quasi-unknown.

What you may not realize is that he's Pontius Pilate's successor. Pilate served as the Roman procurator (like our state governors) of Judea during the trials of Jesus. Felix succeeded Pilate. There was no improvement of government as a result. Paul's defense before him would commence a spiraling series of kangaroo trials, rife with empty accusations and unfair criticism. Remarkably, Paul handled every act of brutality and false accusation with remarkable ease. Not once did he flinch at all the wild swinging of fists and slinging of words.

A HELPFUL STRATEGY FOR HANDLING RELENTLESS CRITICISM

As I observe Paul in these settings, I find no less than seven ways he handled criticism. They're not that complicated; in fact, they will be useful for you when you find your face pasted to someone's dartboard in the future. These things we observe are proof positive that Paul, while sensitive within, had developed that tough hide I referred to earlier.

Let's begin in Acts 24 where Paul is awaiting his trip to Rome in Caesarea. Through an interesting chain of events, he found himself standing before Felix, the governor of Judea.

And after five days the high priest Ananias came down with some elders, with a certain attorney named Tertullus; and they brought charges to the governor against Paul. And after Paul had been summoned, Tertullus began to accuse him, saying to the governor, "Since we have through you attained much peace, and since by your providence reforms are being carried out for this nation, we acknowledge this in every way and everywhere, most excellent Felix, with all thankfulness. But, that I may not weary you any further, I beg you to grant us, by your kindness, a brief hearing.

Acts 24:1–4

In Texas that kind of overdrawn flattery is called "blowing smoke!" Tertullus, the pompous windbag hired by the conspirators, waddles up to the platform in his oversized toga and blows smoke all over the courtroom. He reminds me of a guy we might call "Fast Eddie," sort of a shady lawyer, working behind the scenes doing the dirty work for the crooks. What a scene for Paul to witness.

Felix warmed to the glowing flattery of Tertullus's opening remarks as the dull ring of his pontificating wafted over his head and faded in the roar of the Mediterranean. Pollock suggests that Felix and Tertullus were a match made in heaven. He writes, "Tertullus knew perfectly well that since the appointment of Felix in A.D. 52 Judea had suffered widespread bloodshed from the insurrections he provoked, and from the increase in political murders after he had arranged for the ex-high priest Jonathan to be assassinated in the Temple itself. Felix's greed was notorious. He had been born a slave, had risen to power on the shoulders of his brother, the freedman Pallas, a favorite of Claudius, and his character is well summed up by Tacitus: 'He exercised the power of a king with the mind of a slave.'"[3]

The guy's a crook! Corrupt to the core. Pollock continues, "Tertullus puffed out his cheeks and hitched his robes in the immemorial manner of advocates with weak cases."[4]

He saunters up to the bench, puffs his cheeks, and dumps out a verbal smoke screen. The whole thing's a sham. Paul saw through it all. Secure and calm, he patiently waited his turn. He allowed Tertullus sufficient time to crawl out on that limb of false and exaggerated accusations from which he would soon saw him off with a hard set of facts. You can hear the exaggeration in the trumped-up charges.

> We have found this man a real pest and a fellow who stirs up dissension among all the Jews throughout the world, and a ringleader of the sect of the Nazarenes. And he even tried to desecrate the temple; and then we arrested him. [And we wanted to judge him according to our own Law. But Lysias the commander came along, and with much violence took him out of our hands, ordering his accusers to come before you.] And by examining him yourself concerning all these matters, you will be able to ascertain the things of which we accuse him.
>
> Acts 24:5–8

You recall Lysias, the Roman commander, never used violence. He properly protected Paul against the murderous plot devised by the Jewish leaders. After the smoke settles from Tertullus's overblown address, Paul calmly steps up to give his defense. His words are brief, accurate, and well paced. It is in these courtroom settings I find those seven principles for responding to criticism I mentioned earlier. You may find, as I have, that they come in handy when the darts fly in your direction.

1. He refused to be caught up in the emotion of the charges. The opposite is a typical first mistake that most of us make. Not Paul. As you will note, his opening line is disarmingly pleasant: "I cheerfully make my defense."

Cheerfully? By now the man ought to be blazing with indignation. Even though he'd been labeled "a real pest" and called "a ring leader of a cult," Paul graciously acknowledges the opportunity to give a factual reply. It is immediately obvious how he could respond with such reasoned ease: He refused to let his emotions take the lead. That's lethal in any argument, especially in a courtroom.

When we lower ourselves to the over-charged emotions of accusers, our anger is unleashed and straight thinking caves in to irrational responses and impulsive words. Paul doesn't go there.

2. He stayed with the facts. In essence, he said, "You can check my record. Twelve days ago I went up to worship. You can ask those who were there." In a deliberate, logical manner, Paul reviews the events to which his accusers referred. He reports, "Neither in the temple, nor in the synagogues, nor in the city itself did they find me carrying on a discussion with anyone or causing a riot. Nor can they prove to you the charges of which they now accuse me."

The apostle never blinked. He merely unwrapped the facts—one, two, three. That strategy not only kept him on target, it enhanced his credibility in the eyes of Governor Felix.

3. He told the truth with a clear conscience. This bears a close watch. With laser-like confidence, Paul states, "But this I admit to you, that according to the Way which they call a sect I do serve the God of our fathers, believing everything that is in accordance with the Law, and that is written in the Prophets; having a hope in God, which these men cherish themselves, that there shall certainly be a resurrection of both the righteous and the wicked. In view of this, I also do my best to maintain always a blameless conscience both before God and before men" (24:14–16). Brilliant! Paul fueled his defense with carefully chosen words that caused his hearers to identify with his position and not feel alienated from it. Trust began to grow. Credibility finds its origin in integrity.

Allow some space here on behalf of you who find yourself accused and needing a solid defense to convince a critic. Two words come to mind: *Avoid falsehoods.* If you've already breached the truth, go back now and correct it. Admit your wrong. Stepping over a lie or ignoring a misdeed weakens your case. It will give you needed courage to do that if you will remember *the truth sets us free.* Go with the truth every time.

Cynthia and I have used that principle in rearing our four children. We've employed the same approach in churches we have served, as well as throughout our marriage relationship. I've sought the truth and then told only the truth each time I've had to provide counsel or mediate interpersonal conflicts. Telling the truth means saying it straight. You take no backdoor exits. You allow yourself no end-runs around your opponent, no embellishment of the facts. If you know the truth, say it. Yes, *every time.*

That's exactly what Paul did when answering his accusers. He told the truth with a clear conscience. That freed his mind to set forth his defense in a most-convincing manner. By now, his accusers are starting to squirm.

4. He identified the original source of the criticism. "Now after several years I came to bring alms to my nation and to present offerings; in which they found me occupied in the temple, having been purified, without any crowd or uproar. But there were certain Jews from Asia—who ought to have been present before you, and to make accusation, if they should have anything against me" (Acts 24:17–19).

Now that's what I call putting one's finger on the crucial nerve.

And he was as right as rain. In effect, "Where are my accusers?" The only ones present were people with second-hand information: Tertullus, the high priest, and a group of onlookers who were playing the false role of eyewitnesses. Paul exposed the absence of his original critics, leaving the case against him based on hearsay.

Few situations create more problems than shadow boxing with absent critics. Spreading the venom of anger against someone to people completely unrelated to the matter is an insidious, cowardly strategy. Paul deals with that vile tactic head on as he contends, "I know my accusers are the Jews from Asia." Bringing other people into the situation to offer casual, unreliable opinions only complicates things. Credibility gets undermined and truth vanishes like the morning fog. Paul gave it to them straight by fingering the original source.

I don't know where you find yourself in this story. Obviously this is a first-century setting far removed from your present situation. But if you are in the process of casting stones of criticism, throw them only at the ones with whom you have a dispute. Then when held accountable, have the integrity to say, "I threw that stone." If you can't do that, take your stones and stick them in your pocket and go home. Everyone will be better off.

I have rarely been hurt by the original source. My deepest wounds have been inflicted by second- or even third-hand sources. Paul knew the futility of lobbing countermeasures at ambiguous targets. He locked onto the original source while unloading his arsenal of facts.

5. He would not surrender and quit. I love that about Paul. That, alone, convinces me he is a man of grit. He's like a pit-bull on a thief's leg. The man will not let go! I find such tenacity invigorating, especially in the face of my own relentless critics. He squinted his eyes and roared, "Let these men themselves tell what misdeed they found when I stood before the Council" (24:20).

He wanted them to name his wrong. State it plainly for all to hear. Their silence at that point was eloquent. He knew their hollow accusations fell flat like dead wood hitting pavement. He was never tempted to walk off the scene in exasperation. Never once threatened to quit amid the injustice of it all. He stayed calm and courageous. Even after numerous beatings, another string of false accusations didn't faze him. He stood firm in the truth.

Paul managed to get up and get going by counting on God to carry him to where he couldn't go on his own. You say, "I'm walking as best I can, and the road is getting steep." From Paul's example, my advice is hang on, don't quit. The Lord will honor your resolve.

As Paul stood firm, little beads of sweat popped out of Felix's forehead. His knees weakened as he stood to his feet. He caved and ordered that the court session be adjourned. He realized that to proceed meant a long fall off that weak limb, thanks to Paul's sharp set of facts. Governors don't like losing face. And since he knew more than he was letting on, he dodged the truth and declared a recess.

Some time later his Jewish wife and he, together, listened to more of Paul's convictions regarding Christ Jesus. Again, the truth penetrated. And Felix again went pale. Frightened by Paul's convicting words about "righteousness, self-control, and the judgment to come," he shut down the proceedings. Luke records the response in vivid terms: "Felix became frightened and said, 'Go away for the present, and when I find time, I will summon you'" (24:25b). He often spoke with Paul following that session, but we know nothing of those conversations. After two years, Felix's ears went deaf to the truth. He moved on to obscurity, leaving Paul alone and cold in a prison cell.

Felix's successor was the infamous Festus. Felix modeled beautifully what a human weasel might resemble. His successor, Festus, shared a similar distinction. We've already covered the peril of following people-pleasing leaders.

Though Luke tells nothing of Paul's response, his silence on the matter leads me to believe he handled that with the same remarkable attitude.

That brings me to my next observation on the way Paul handled criticism. It may be the most amazing of all. Go back long enough to remember the words "two years."

6. He did not become impatient or bitter. For two years he pounded the drums of truth before Felix, and nothing happened in his favor. Nothing. He waits for a break. A year passes. Nothing changes. No response. Another cold winter. Another spring. Still no movement. Finally, he hits the two-year mark, and Felix leaves office, ignoring Paul, who is still sitting in prison. Luke records nothing that leads us to believe Paul suffered from any level of depression, bitterness, or regret. Luke records nothing of this because there wasn't any.

Then Festus takes office and his first order of business was a trip up to Jerusalem to meet the same sorry band of Jewish leaders breathing charges and threats against Paul. The plan of those dim bulbs was to lure Paul back to Jerusalem for a hearing, ambushing him en route. Though determined, they were slow learners. Festus agreed to a hearing in Caesarea as he promised to reopen the case against Paul. He ordered a tribunal session in less than two weeks, at which Paul would be present (25:6).

The scene was all too familiar for the seasoned apostle. Surrounded by a group of prejudiced, albeit pious-looking Jewish leaders leveling empty accusations against him, Paul again rises to offer a calm reply. This time he condenses the entire speech to what amounts to nineteen English words: "I have committed no offense either against the Law of the Jews or against the temple or against Caesar" (25:8).

Not a trace of anxiety can be found in his words. No impatience. No bitterness. Actually, it's what he *doesn't* say that's so remarkable. He could have reminded them of his God-appointed apostleship. He could have made a strong case for his academic scholarship. He could have complained about being held in prison unfairly or driven hard the point of his blameless reputation among the Sanhedrin. "Ya-da, ya-da, ya-da." But he didn't. He stood before the new governor and said, "What is said against me is wrong. I have made no offense against the Jews, or against the temple, or against Caesar."

Like his predecessor, Festus capitulated to Jewish pressure and offered Paul an opportunity for defense *in Jerusalem*. It was an easy way out for Festus, maybe, but a bad deal for Paul, for certain.

Paul knew a journey to Jerusalem spelled trouble. His accusers licked their chops with thoughts of ambush. Paul's retort set Festus back on his heels: "I am standing before Caesar's tribunal, where I ought to be tried. I have done no wrong to the Jews, as you also very well know. If then I am a wrongdoer and have committed anything worthy of death, I do not refuse to die; but if none of those things is true which these men accuse me, no one can hand me over to them. I appeal to Caesar" (25:10-11).

Paul remembered the Lord's promise made to him years earlier (23:11). He knew God's plan included a visit to Rome. Knowing that his Heavenly Father keeps His word, Paul rested in God's faithfulness. That leads me to the last of seven principles.

7. He stood on the promise of God. Underneath all the visible stuff, that's how he made it. He clung to the hope of what the Lord had said. That got him through many a dark night. It didn't take Festus long to confer with his advisers and come back with a ruling: "To Caesar you shall go." Paul knew it all along.

No pip-squeak Roman governor could outwit the Almighty. Though at times God's wheels grind slowly, His plan prevailed. Paul would soon find himself on his way to the capitol of the world. But before that would become a reality, there was one more defense Paul must make, before Herod Agrippa. We'll examine that in depth in Chapter 19.

TAKING TRUTH HOME TO YOUR PLACE

Given enough time you may face a situation somewhat like the one Paul endured. It won't have the official intensity of a Roman tribunal or include a plot to end your life, but you'll face your critics. Someday you will encounter those who don't seek your good, only your downfall. You may already be feeling the heat. Whatever the case, those seven principles for handling negative criticism will serve you well in facing similarly harsh days. Who knows? They may prove helpful enough to ensure your safe passage to the other side.

Let's review them briefly, only this time I'll make them much more personal.

When facing negative criticism . . .

- refuse to get caught up in the emotion of the charges.
- stay with the facts.
- tell the truth with a clear conscience.
- identify the original source of the accusations.
- don't surrender or quit.
- don't become impatient and bitter.
- stand firm on the promises of God.

That's a list worth duplicating, don't you agree? You can apply every one of those principles when facing harsh critics of your own. In fact, I urge you to do that. So will I.

A PERSONAL ILLUSTRATION

Long before my mother died she and a neighbor friend compiled a book of God's promises taken from the Scriptures. Each made her own. My mother used that little book as a primer for her prayers. After she died, my brother and sister and I viewed that tender compilation as part of her legacy to us. The book swelled with handwritten promises from the Bible.

She must have written out hundreds of promises drawn directly from the Bible. Promise after promise after promise. My name was connected to some of them. "For Charles, I claim this promise," she wrote on one of the pages. For Orville and Luci she claimed scores of others and recorded them in her book. She included my dad, as well as herself. My mother clung to the promises of God's Word no matter what she faced. They kept her above the fray.

My friend, go back to the Book. Search for the promises God offers you in His Word. I suggest you start with the Psalms. Look for the promises there. They are myriad. Become familiar with them. Live in them. Walk with them. In some special cases, memorize them. Let them be your guide and comfort. Like Paul, you'll be able to withstand the fiercest storms of criticism when you stand firmly on the promises of God. That's the message of this chapter. I hope it becomes the message of your life.

I don't know where you are or what you face today. It's quite possible you're living under the pressure of negative criticism. I know that's true if you're in the ministry. Somebody may be determined to "prove" things about you that you know are absolutely false. My advice is to learn from Paul: Remain calm. Rest your case with your Lord. Take your battles to Him in prayer. With a clear conscience and committed to the truth, lay your case out before Him. Start there. And the Judge of all truth will guide you to your next step. Don't quit. Don't stop. Don't tell yourself that you really are the kind of person others say you are. If what is being said against you is not true, don't believe it. Count on the Lord to give you the strength and the courage to stand on the truth. His grace has brought you safe this far, and it will be His grace that leads you home.

Trust me on that; even better, *trust Him.*

※

Lord God, How thankful I am for Your Book, Your Word that lives and abides forever. Thank You for the way truth comes to life when we see it as print on the pages of the Bible. Thank You for the power of your Word that transforms lives and mends broken hearts and strengthens frightened hearts. May we, in the process of time, begin to feel more and more at home in Your Word, so that the life of another becomes ours and the truth another provides becomes a principle for us to live by. Thank You for coming to our rescue again and again by Your grace. And for those who are most afraid, I pray they will know Your peace and relief from anxiety as they turn to the promises in the Bible and there find hope to go on.

In the all-powerful Name of Jesus Christ, Amen.

CHAPTER NINETEEN

Standing Tall as Paul Stood

It helps to have someone with skin on when we're looking for heroes. Distant myths don't work, no matter how dynamic they were in some legend. We need flesh-and-blood models to pattern our lives after. Paul is one of my heroes in skin, though, certainly there are others who fit the mold.

Webster defines a "hero" as "a person admired for achievements and noble qualities; one who shows great courage." My definition isn't nearly as sophisticated. For me, a hero is someone who stands tall when others shrink back. A hero is someone who swims upstream while the majority of people go with the current. It's someone who speaks up for what's right as others look away, sitting silently on the sidelines.

History chronicles the lives of those rare individuals. Some of the best examples are found in the Bible.

STANDING TALL AGAINST GIANTS

Travel back, for example, to the valley of Elah where young David, still a teenager, took on the giant named Goliath who, marching back and forth, taunted the armies of Israel. King Saul and his entire army stood frozen because of Goliath's stature. His booming voice only added to their fear.

David would not be intimidated. Once on the scene he couldn't believe everyone's fear. He asked, "Who is this uncircumcised Philistine that he should defy the armies of the living God?" His brothers teased him for acting like a tough guy while still smelling of his father's sheep. Their mockery and sarcasm never fazed the teenaged lad. He understood Goliath represented more than a physical threat to a few skittish soldiers. The giant from Gath had the audacity to stand against the God of Israel and defy His power. How dare that happen! David saw the challenge as a cause worth dying for.

Remarkably, one smooth stone slung from the skilled shepherd's sling found its mark, sending the human mammoth crashing to the ground and silencing the Philistine threat. David forgot the odds as he went for the jugular.

That's my kind of hero.

Esther also comes to mind. She faced the threat of her entire nation being exterminated. Mordecai said to her, "You have obtained royalty for such a time as this." She believed him. His stirring words spurred her into action as she exclaimed, "Something must be done, and *I* must do it!" Courageously, she pled her case before the king. As a result, evil Haman was exposed, his plot foiled, and the Jewish people were saved from an ancient holocaust. Esther stood tall against the odds.

Daniel defied the king's edict to bow down and worship him as a god. His refusal resulted in his spending the night in a lions' den. In honor of his courage, divine protection kicked in. Because of his unswerving faith in the Lord God, it became more like the lions spending the night in Daniel's den. The prophet stood tall when others shrank back.

In my study of the Scriptures, I've noticed a pattern with heroes—the men and women who stand tall and refuse to shrink.

First, there's something wrong on the cultural scene. There exists some sort of outside threat that must be challenged.

Second, there's a principle at stake. The closer you examine the situation, the clearer the principle. A fundamental value or belief is at stake.

Third, there's an element of risk involved for taking heroic measures. Besides the physical peril, the risk of being misunderstood, misrepresented, maligned, or mistreated is real. To do nothing, however, makes matters worse. Doing something heroic and risky usually means acting alone.

William Wilberforce stood alone against the evils of slavery. He defied every member of the British Parliament to stay with his convictions. To him, freedom for the enslaved was a principle worth risking everything to uphold.

Patrick Henry spoke those immortal words, "Give me liberty or give me death." That single-minded resolve helped to turn the tide of America's battle for independence.

Martin Luther King, Jr., stormed the American civil rights scene at a time when many folded their arms in indifference and looked the other way. It was easier for most to shrug off the issue of racial equality as someone else's cause. Martin Luther King, Jr., became an American hero for standing tall against deep-rooted prejudice.

Near the end of the year 2001, hundreds of New York and Washington D.C. area firefighters, emergency medical personnel, and police officers stepped into the ranks of genuine heroes. As others understandably ran from the disaster, they ran toward it. Deliberately and selflessly they stormed into harm's way to save the lives of people trapped in the ruins of the World Trade Center. Others performed acts of heroism at the Pentagon. With no concern for their own safety, many lost their lives in those rescue efforts. All who did stood against the odds and paid the ultimate price. A grateful nation mourned their deaths.

A couple of more observations about heroes come to mind:

First, heroes don't seem like heroes at the time they act. Accolades for heroic deeds are typically deferred. At the time, all of those people I've written about had folks around them who questioned the wisdom of their actions. Why make waves? Why risk so much for so few? Some who stood tall were unappreciated at the time for where they stood and for what they accomplished. Time alone revealed the true significance of their deeds.

Second, heroism is not genetic. We'd love to think our children receive heroic genes from us. It doesn't work that way. No one gives birth to a hero. Heroes are forged through time. Often those who overcome the most become heroes in their time.

By the way, I need heroes in my life, don't you? Rarely does a day pass when I don't think about one of my heroes. I'm grateful for all of them. Some are alive; most are dead. Doesn't matter. The memory of another's determination to stand alone motivates me to reach for higher levels of courageous living.

The apostle Paul stood taller than most. His final defense recorded in Acts 26 illustrates his heroic ability to stand alone and determined even under the most extreme pressures. The aging preacher had come a long way from his younger days of persecuting Christians in and around Jerusalem. The Lord laid hold of him and made him into a blazing herald of grace. He never got over his profound appreciation. He had a debt of gratitude to discharge.

Because of that, Paul rose above the pomp and pretense of Rome. With fierce resolve the man stood tall for the eternal cause of Christ. Once underway, nothing would deter him.

STANDING TALL BEFORE KINGS AND QUEENS

At the conclusion to the previous chapter, we left Paul waiting under Roman lock and key inside a cell in the port city of Caesarea. Timothy and Silas had gone off to continue the work of fortifying churches and reaching more Gentile souls for the Savior. Luke stayed with Paul to attend to his physical condition and record the remarkable proceedings.

Festus, the Roman governor of the region, reluctantly agreed to allow Paul a defense before Nero in Rome. While Paul waited, Festus fretted over his situation. Having made his ruling, he now wrestled with how to justify troubling the Emperor of Rome. After all, none of the accusations held water. He needed evidence that would merit Nero's time. He hoped his neighbor, King Agrippa, would have some creative ideas. Therefore, he invited him to examine Paul for himself.

EMPTY POMP AND UNUSUAL CIRCUMSTANCES

The scene opens in Acts 25:13 with the entrance of Agrippa. Festus had enlisted his assistance in preparing Paul's case for presentation before Nero.

Luke wrote his eyewitness account with compelling attention to detail. Picture the scene as you read of it.

> Now when several days had elapsed, King Agrippa and Bernice arrived at Caesarea, and paid their respects to Festus. And while they were spending many days there, Festus laid Paul's case before the king, saying, "There is a certain man left a prisoner by Felix; and when I was at Jerusalem, the chief priests and the elders of the Jews brought charges against him, asking for a sentence of condemnation upon him." (25:13–15)

He continued later . . .

> But when Paul appealed to be held in custody for the Emperor's decision, I ordered him to be kept in custody until I send him to Caesar. And Agrippa said to Festus, "I also would like to hear the man myself." "Tomorrow," he said, "you shall hear him."
>
> And so, on the next day when Agrippa had come together with Bernice, amid great pomp, and had entered the auditorium accompanied by the commanders and the prominent men of the city, at the command of Festus, Paul was brought in. (25:21–23)

You may need a little background on the shallow character of these regal figures. Let's go back a few years. King Herod I, ruling in brutality and wickedness, gained biblical notoriety partly for being the king who attempted to kill Peter. Not long after Peter's escape, Herod died a miserable death. He left several surviving children, all cut from the same soiled piece of cloth. Only three have any significance to this story.

One of his sons was Herod Agrippa II. He's the Agrippa of our story. Though only thirty-two, he enjoyed a certain respect among the Jewish people. Herod I also had two daughters, Drusilla and Bernice. Felix married Drusilla, whom he had lured away from her husband in the heat of an illicit affair. Drusilla's sister, Bernice, was also Herod's sister. Bernice and Agrippa were embroiled in an incestuous relationship. The whole family was a mess of ethical corruption and gross immorality.

Strangely, these are the judges who've come to sit in judgment on Paul. The court was a circus. Character was conspicuous by its absence. Luke must have shaken his head in disbelief as he recorded every sordid detail, including the pompous procession of Agrippa's staged entrance into the open auditorium. The foaming Mediterranean, with its magnificent pounding surf and sweeping coastline gleaming in the sunlight, provided a fitting backdrop for Agrippa's monstrous ego. He loved playing the role of a celebrity.

The stage was set for Paul's final defense. Following a brief but courteous introduction to the noble crowd, Paul stood to his feet. Manacled, he hobbled into place, his chains dragging. Standing before the ruling monarchs, he raised his hand and said, "In regard to all the things of which I am accused by the Jews, I consider myself fortunate, King Agrippa, that I am about to make my defense before you today; especially because you are an expert in all customs and questions among the Jews; therefore I beg you to listen to me patiently" (Acts 26:2–3).

What a gracious, disarming opening statement! No narrow-minded fire-and-brimstone words of condemnation flew from Paul's lips. That wasn't his style. Courteously, he said he considered the entire ordeal a wonderful privilege.

Right out of the chute, we can learn a lesson from our hero Paul. When God grants us the rare opportunity to stand before prestigious people and high-ranking government officials, it is best to demonstrate courtesy and grace. Regardless of their lifestyle, speak with respect. Regardless of their politics or their private world, model grace. Show some class.

To come on like gangbusters will surely be an offense, and the door of opportunity will slam shut. Paul didn't roar at his audience, even though they lived lives altogether different than he would approve. Despite his chains and their differences, he addressed them with kindness and respect.

Not surprisingly, his audience hung on his every word. He looked around and perhaps saw some familiar faces. Maybe he spied a former classmate or two from the school of Gamaliel. The Jews in the crowd were well acquainted with his background. He appealed to the honesty of his audience, reminding them that they were witnesses to his career as a zealous Pharisee and staunch keeper of the Law. He minced no words. He had done nothing in secret. There was nothing to hide.

He then plunged to the point. That he would contend for the doctrine of resurrection should come as no surprise to his Jewish accusers. If his judges were to be honest before the jury, they too would hold to "the promise to which our twelve tribes hope to attain, as they earnestly serve God night and day" (26:7). As the political celebrities stroked their beards in rapt attention, Paul paused, then forthrightly informed them that it was for that hope he stood falsely accused. Nice verbal sword thrust. They sat riveted.

Resurrection remained the primary issue, the main agenda on the table for discussion. To embrace the Messiah would force one to believe that the One crucified was raised from the dead. "How could that be so hard to believe?" Paul wondered aloud.

After all, Gamaliel, a scholar they respected, included that subject on his syllabus for Judaistic Theology 101. Undaunted, Paul pressed the issue. Agrippa hardly moved a muscle. "So then, I thought to myself that I had to do many things hostile to the name of Jesus of Nazareth. And this is just what I did in Jerusalem: not only did I lock up many of the saints in prisons, having received authority from the chief priests, but also when they were being put to death I cast my vote against them. And as I punished them often in all the synagogues, I tried to force them to blaspheme; and being furiously enraged at them, I kept pursuing them even to foreign cities" (Acts 26:9–11).

He hid nothing from Agrippa or the skeptics sitting near. He modeled quiet courage and vulnerable authenticity. Paul resisted the temptation to sugarcoat his past. He painted the canvas realistically for all to ponder— grit on display.

His tone no doubt changed slightly as he testified of his roadside conversion. The audience was now so silent you could have heard a mouse sneeze. Paul's seamless recounting of being conquered by the living Christ caused mouths to open. No one blinked.

> While thus engaged as I was journeying to Damascus with the authority and commission of the chief priests, at midday, O King, I saw

on the way a light from heaven, brighter than the sun, shining all around me and those who were journeying with me. And when we had fallen on the ground, I heard a voice saying to me in the Hebrew dialect, "Saul, Saul, why are you persecuting Me? It is hard for you to kick against the goads."

Acts 26:12–14

A palpable nervousness fell over the crowd, as Paul drilled toward home.

And I said, "Who art Thou, Lord?" And the Lord said, "I am Jesus whom you are persecuting. But arise, and stand on your feet; for this purpose I have appeared to you, to appoint you a minister and a witness not only to the things which you have seen, but also to the things to which I will appear to you."

Acts 26:15–16

Some by now had begun to fidget in the awkwardness of Paul's strange remarks. He spoke of visions and voices connecting with him from the glow of a shining light. In their self-inflated opinions, his comments moved from intriguing to weird.

Even though he noticed the ripple of uneasiness, Paul never wavered. He went on with another verbal sword thrust:

Having obtained help from God, I stand to this day testifying both to the small and great, stating nothing but what the Prophets and Moses said was going to take place; that the Christ was to suffer, and that by reason of His resurrection from the dead, He should be the first to proclaim light both to the Jewish people and to the Gentiles.

Acts 26:22–23

"Stop!" Festus screamed in order to bring a halt to this. Interrupting Paul, he accused him of madness. "Your obsession with learning has rendered you a maniac" (v. 24), he barked in an awkward attempt to break Paul's rhythm. With controlled determination Paul ignored his fidgety host and turned his attention only to Agrippa, who was still staring and thinking. He sensed a choice opportunity to lead the regal ruler closer to the Savior. He would not be dissuaded.

Paul's testimony reflected a life transformed, seasoned over years of faithful, sacrificial service. We can be sure he delivered his defense in the most gentle, sensible manner imaginable. But he was firm.

Ignoring the abrupt interruption, Paul held the floor without skipping a thought. Answering Festus but looking at Agrippa, Paul responded, "I am not out of my mind, most excellent Festus, but I utter words of sober truth. For the king knows about these matters, and I speak to him also with confidence, since I am persuaded that none of these things escape his notice; for this has not been done in a corner. King Agrippa, do you believe the Prophets? I know that you do" (vv. 25–27). Classic verbal sword *twist.*

Momentarily forgetting the difference in rank and status, Paul now spoke face to face with Agrippa. He engaged him on his knowledge of the Scriptures. He then listened for Herod's reply. It was a reply heard around the world: "In a short while you will persuade me to become a Christian" (26:28). What a statement! The apostle's enthusiasm could no longer be contained. In unguarded abandon, he exclaimed, "I would to God, that whether in a short or long time, not only you, but also all who hear me this day, might become such as I, except for these chains."

That may have been the crowning moment of Paul's entire life. Chains on his wrist rattled as the prisoner raised his arms to deliver that closing line. What an epochal moment! His words brought proud Agrippa so close to the throne of grace he nearly bowed before the King of kings!

Rushing back to his senses, Agrippa blushed then awkwardly rose to his feet cueing his rattled guests to do the same. The whole lot of them stepped into the marble hallway, outside the hearing of Paul, to discuss the matter. They were impressed with what they had heard. Surely, the prisoner stood innocent before them. Still, he had appealed to Rome. But for that, Paul could have walked out of Caesarea a free man with a clear record.

Make no mistake, though he remained in chains, Paul viewed the entire meeting as an enormous victory. Those rulers had heard the gospel. The irony is unmistakable. The only one truly free was Paul, who walked back to his cell in chains. The rest left walking unhindered, still chained within their ignorance and unbelief. It was a joyful, pitiful scene.

Having shaken some sense back into his head, Agrippa straightened his robe and attempted to look dignified as he strolled into the open air. The crowd dispersed with a few words of farewell. From all appearances, nothing had changed. For sure, Paul would sail for Rome.

As unpretentiously as he arrived, the stooped prisoner stumbles through the door and disappears. Deep within, he is full of joy, knowing that not even the seaside breeze could blow his words from Agrippa's head. They would haunt the king that night, probably for the rest of his days.

Whether in a short or long time, I would that all who hear me this day, might become such as I am, except for these chains . . . except for these chains . . . except for these chains.

SOME FINAL THOUGHTS FOR MODERN-DAY HEROES

At least two truths emerge from this story.

First, when you stand tall you're so focused that you feel invincible. Now don't allow that thought to slip past too quickly. You may have never experienced that sort of bold abandon because you've not allowed yourself to be in a challenging situation. Most play it safe. It's more convenient to let someone else do the talking. It's easier to let another climb to the heights and risk falling.

However, when the day arrives and you decide to stand tall for what's right, your focus on that all-important issue will give you a feeling of invincibility. The odds will mean nothing. You will be unimpressed with other folks sitting or standing in front of you. Neither credentials nor titles will intimidate you. Your convictions will carry you forward in a strength not your own. Like Paul, you will have become God's voice for that hour.

Second, when you stand tall you are so passionate that you don't realize your ultimate impact. Standing for the principle at stake is all that matters. Paul's audience simply got up and left. On the exterior it looked like the hearing had been a waste of time. Yet who can say? Who knows what Agrippa dreamed of that very night and in the nights that followed Paul's speech? I wouldn't be surprised if compromising Festus continued to squirm at Paul's compelling witness.

Only God knows the true impact of Paul's heroic stand that day by the sea. Ultimately, only God knows the impact of yours as well.

STANDING TALL IN HIGH PLACES

Recently, I read a stirring speech delivered by the late Mother Theresa at the 44th National Prayer Breakfast—a prestigious event that occurred while Bill Clinton served as President. In the course of her speech, delivered without pretense, the gracious nun from Calcutta spoke plainly and courageously about the evils of abortion and the devastation that dreadful lapse in morality continues to have on our already splintered culture. While she read from a carefully prepared manuscript, no one in the room moved a muscle. In fact, many of the well-dressed dignitaries smiled nervously, appearing cool and collected on their refined exteriors, but churning wildly within.

The scene bears an uncanny resemblance to Paul's courageous appearance before Agrippa. Mother Theresa's poignant words were nothing short of heroic. I regret only being able to quote a few of them here. Please read them carefully and slowly, doing your best to transport yourself into that august gathering of Washington's political elite.

> I feel that the greatest destroyer of peace today is abortion, because Jesus said, "If you receive a little child, you receive me." So every abortion is the denial of receiving Jesus, the neglect of receiving Jesus."
>
> Abortion is really a war against the child, and I hate the killing of the innocent child, murder by the mother herself. And if we accept that the mother can kill even her own child, how can we tell other people not to kill one another? How do we persuade a woman not to have an abortion? As always, we must persuade her with love.
>
> . . . Any country that accepts abortion is not teaching its people to love one another but to use violence to get what they want. This is why the greatest destroyer of love and peace is abortion.[1]

Like Paul, the frail figure of a woman spoke her words and exited the room as silently as she entered. As the ancient political officials had sat glaring at Paul, so the nobility of Washington sat silent, their consciences throbbing in their chests.

They had encountered a courageous messenger with a bold message ordained for that moment in time.

I'm convinced that many people given the situations faced by some of the heroes we've mentioned in the last several pages would rise to such heroic deeds. I believe you have the potential in you to stand against enemies of righteousness who defy the power of Almighty God, or to speak out boldly against blatant injustice and outright discrimination. I believe many who pick up this book, would be willing to have been numbered among the brave rescue workers at the Word Trade Center and the Pentagon or even among those who died thwarting another air disaster on the flight that crashed in Pennsylvania.

The challenge comes in those private, unguarded moments when you face opposition to truth . . . in the halls of the university, in a company board room, at the school PTA meeting, in the athletic director's office, or while seated on a plane. In those times, will you stand tall and speak the truth when a principle is at stake? Will you defend what you believe, graciously yet firmly?

It is doubtful that you will ever be summoned to stand before kings and queens or be invited to address the political elite or high-ranking military officers; but you will have your own opportunities to stand and deliver. As you determine in your heart to stand tall, God will lay those opportunities before you when you least expect it. You can count on it.

When He does, will you be ready?

CHAPTER TWENTY

How to Handle a Shipwreck

I've never seen a bumper sticker that read, "I'd rather be shipwrecked." I have seen a number of bumper stickers along the California coast that read, "I'd rather be sailing," but never, "I'd rather be sinking."

The adventure of sailing across the open seas carries a certain exhilarating thrill that can become almost addicting. But there's nothing fun about plunging into the cold waters of the deep, certainly not while caught in a violent storm.

Experiencing shipwreck is not on my resumé, I am happy to report, though I have logged many hours at sea. I enjoy the ocean both as an avid fisherman and a fair-weather sailor (especially when someone else owns the boat). Thankfully, I've enjoyed all that while *on* the deep, not *in* the deep.

The closest I've come to shipwreck was while aboard a troop ship, along with 3,500 other Marines, traveling from San Diego to Japan. Though the ship seemed the size of a large office complex while in dock, after being at sea for four or five days, the immensity of the ocean put the ship's size in proper perspective. Suddenly, it seemed tiny.

About five days into our seventeen-day voyage, we found ourselves in the center of a raging Pacific storm with waves reaching nearly fifty feet at their crest. Pause long enough to realize that's five stories high. In fact, no one was allowed on deck during the worst of the storm, which lasted nearly three days. Days later, after the waters calmed, the skipper of the ship admitted that, at one point, he began to question our chances of survival.

Years later I had a similar experience while fishing several miles off the coast of Miami. After a few hours of pleasant deep-sea fishing, a nasty squall blew in, skies turned an ugly dark gray, and the sea twisted violently in the wind. The storm intensified with each passing minute to the point where water started crashing over the rails. The situation got dicey much too quickly. I prepared myself for the worst. You may wonder how.

Well, to begin with, I confessed every sin that I have ever committed. In fact, I believe I added a few that I hadn't committed just to be sure I hadn't missed one. I then reviewed every Bible verse I had learned since childhood as my fretting mind brought them to my attention. I also remember counting the life preservers and checking the size of the largest one I could find. I stayed close to it!

Eventually, I stumbled to the cabin where the skipper was very busy, Nervously, I asked him, "Do boats like this ever sink?"

"Sure, the whole bottom of this ocean area is strewn with boats like ours that never made it," he answered without smiling.

Then I asked, "How long would it take for us to swim to Miami?"

That brought a sneering smile as he replied, "Are you kidding? We would be dismembered by sharks in less than an hour if we ended up in these waters."

I tried to smile and act as if that was funny.

Frankly, the storm was no joke. No storm on the open sea is. Though we made it to shore safely, it was a treacherous experience for all on board. It was as if our lives hung on very thin wires that could have snapped at any moment. I'll level with you, it was the truth of God's Word that kept me sane and relatively calm during that terrifying ordeal. I deliberately prayed. I consciously remembered several pertinent promises. I leaned hard on them.

Paul knew that same feeling. Luke vividly records their shipwreck experience in Acts 27, especially Paul's reaction to it. By now, you'd think the man had paid all his dues; surely his final ministry years would be smooth sailing the rest of the way. Right? Wrong.

STAYING AFLOAT WITH A REMARKABLE FAITH

Most likely, you're reading this chapter free from the harsh elements of a raging sea. So, the challenge is to place ourselves in the scene as Luke hoped we would when he wrote it. Apart from the narrator's spectacular memory of the details during that perilous voyage, we are left to rely on our imaginations to understand what Paul endured on his fateful journey by sea to Rome. Most remarkable is the courage and faith with which he braved those harrowing days on the Mediterranean.

Keep in mind, Luke is a physician, not a seasoned sailor. His account isn't a ship's log. It reads more like a journal. What begins very innocuously as a Mediterranean cruise, turns into one of the most frightening ordeals of Paul's life. Luke, having endured the same death-defying adventure, gives us his eye-witness account.

Remember, only Paul has tucked away in his heart the promise of God that he would reach Rome alive. The remaining two hundred and seventy-five passengers knew none of that, so the panic effect is understandable. There's nothing predictable about voyages on the open sea. Circumstances can change in a matter of minutes.

Let me pause here and say that too often our tendency is to focus on circumstances, especially in storms. God emphasizes the objective. At those times when life's contrary winds blow hard, we tend to hear only the creaking of the hull and feel only the buckling of the deck. God desires that we cultivate an inner life of trust that ensures a more confident, reasoned response. As we voyage with Paul across the Great Sea, we'll see with human eyes how such triumphant trust emerges.

A CLEAR AND PROMISED DESTINATION

The journey began with all the pleasant expectancy of a memorable ocean voyage as Luke writes, "We would sail for Italy." Placed under the care and custody of a Roman centurion named Julius, Paul was joined by Luke, of course, and a Macedonian companion named Aristarchus. Together they embarked on the first leg of the long voyage to Rome.

Now would be an appropriate time to put your finger in this page and flip to the back of the book and view the map titled "Trip to Rome." There you can trace the route of Paul's voyage from Caesarea up around the island of Cyprus, through Myra (where they changed ships), past Rhodes, down south below Crete, across to the obscure island of Malta, then up through the strait past Sicily and to the harbor near Rome. Paul only knew the destination ahead of time—Rome. He knew nothing of the circuitous, treacherous route that would bring them there.

Luke describes the two vessels Paul would take: One was a large vessel that had originated at Adramyttium, a harbor town on the western coast of what is now Turkey, southeast of Troas. It was a merchant ship that worked the southern coastline, eventually docking at Caesarea. They sailed on that vessel up the coast to Myra, where they disembarked, then boarded an Alexandrian cargo ship destined for Rome.

Having been on all three bodies of water in that part of the world—the Adriatic, the Aegean, and the Mediterranean—I've come to a simple conclusion. The deep-blue waters of those great seas look a lot more inviting on maps and in travel brochures than they do from the windswept deck of a ship in the middle of a storm.

The ships Paul sailed on, of course, were nothing like what I've enjoyed in my travels. Those ancient vessels were more like barges, shaped almost as squarely at the bow as they were at the stern. That, along with the single-mast outfitting rigged with one enormous sail, made the giant wooden crafts difficult to maneuver even on a clear day. Not that much wind would have caused the weathered timbers of those ancient ships to creak and groan and, if the seas got rough enough, to split and splinter at the seams.

Nothing about their crude design rendered them seaworthy by today's standards. But none of that seemed to worry Paul as he and his companions embarked from Myra in Lycia and set sail for Italy.

They most likely launched in late August, but (as we shall see) the shipwreck caused a three-month delay at Malta, forcing the final leg of the journey to fall in the dead of winter. It was not a pleasant time to travel the seas and fight the cold winds and harsh currents of the Mediterranean. I'm told there are few more treacherous bodies of water than the route below the southern reaches of Greece. It was there the storm hit full force.

In many respects, the storm Paul and his companions encountered developed along the lines of what modern meteorologists consider a perfect storm. In recent history, such a storm occurred in the waters of the North Atlantic. In 1991, volatile fronts from the north, the east, the west, and the south converged off the coast of Massachusetts, creating such a threatening combination of hurricane-force winds and towering waves that the entire East Coast went scrambling for cover. Numerous fishing vessels retreated to safer waters. Writer Sebastien Junger, in his book *The Perfect Storm,* tells the tale of that strange confluence of atmosphere and sea, and the ill-fated *Andrea Gail,* whose captain and crew vanished without a trace. Junger's dramatic retelling of that freak convergence of elements in a single storm system eerily resembles what Luke describes in Acts 27.

The entire chapter is devoted to Luke's dramatic retelling of Paul's very own perfect storm.

> And when we had sailed slowly for a good many days, and with difficulty had arrived off Cnidus, since the wind did not permit us to go farther, we sailed under the shelter of Crete, off Salome; and with difficulty sailing past it we came to a certain place called Fair Havens, near which was the city of Lasea. And when considerable time was passed and the voyage was now dangerous, since even the fast was already over, Paul began to admonish them, and said, "Men, I perceive that the voyage will certainly be attended with damage and great loss, not only of cargo and the ship, but also of our lives. But the centurion was more persuaded by the pilot and the captain of the ship, than by what was being said by Paul. And because the harbor was not suitable for wintering, the majority reached a decision to put out to sea from there, if somehow they could reach Phoenix, a harbor of Crete, facing southwest and northwest, and spend the winter there. And when a moderate

south wind came up, supposing that they had gained their purpose, they weighed anchor and began sailing along Crete, close inshore.

Acts 27:7–13

When the centurion chose to go with the majority rather than heed Paul's advice, he made a grave error in judgment. Leaving the calmer waters off Crete, the centurion put his men and everyone on board in harm's way on the open sea. The voyage changed from difficult to dangerous almost overnight. The velocity of the winds increased as did the ocean swells. All on board knew there was trouble ahead. Luke later records the desperate turning point: "But before very long there rushed down from the land a violent wind, called Euraquilo; and when the ship was caught in it, and could not face the wind, we gave way to it, and let ourselves be driven along" (Acts 27:14–15).

"Euraquilo" is the equivalent of one of our northeasterns; the combination of gale-force winds and rough seas that rage along the eastern seaboard from south to north, dumping heavy rain, snow, and ice along the way. Such blizzard-like conditions can create grave hazards. Only what Paul experienced was not on land, but at sea.

The storm grew so violent in its intensity that, according to Luke, "They began to jettison cargo," until eventually they were forced to heave overboard the ship's tackle, rendering the vessel impossible to control.

To make matters worse, the thick canopy of dark clouds blocked any view of the constellations, which normally served as a reliable navigational guide. Hope waned. Survival was now in question, especially as the battle against the winds continued relentlessly for days.

Finally, the storm-weary crew caught a ray of hope. Luke writes, "When the fourteenth night had come, as we were being driven about in the Adriatic Sea, about midnight the sailors began to surmise they were approaching land" (27:27). That led to a series of soundings that alerted the men to the danger of running the ship aground. So, "They cast four anchors from the stern and wished for daybreak" (27:29b).

More than anything, they needed a compass—a trustworthy instrument that, despite the howling winds and towering seas, in response to a fixed invisible force, could cut through the furious gale, and point them to safety. Without that, they hoped daylight would reveal their exact whereabouts. The waiting must have been maddening.

For most, a growing feeling of panic set in. Even the seasoned sailors were grim and quiet as they longed for the light of day. For now, their only hope was those four anchors thrown off the stern, resulting in a relentless tug-of-war against the powerful pull of the surging swells (27:29).

As we study Luke's data of Paul's perilous voyage to Rome, we want to look not only at what is recorded, but also between the lines. It is there we find more of the real story. It is there we witness the faithful God, who keeps His promises, and the humble servant, who clings to the anchors of His eternal Word.

It is in that story, hidden within the recorded story, we learn lessons for our lives. And it is from that unwritten account we draw the strength to face our own perfect storms head-on and stare down our own feelings of panic. The storms we endure may last for days, weeks, months, or even years. Perfect storms in life are largely unpredictable. They rage on with seemingly no end in sight. Often, they appear to be wildly out of control.

I will tell you I have been in storms like that. They are far worse than any storms I've ever known at sea. At times I questioned my own survival. I remember, during one particular storm in my life, being awake at night and awaking Cynthia to whisper, "I'm not sure we're going to make it through this one." I've been there. I know you have too. You may be there now. That intensifies your interest in this frightening story.

Where you find yourself is not the result of an accident, nor are you alone. God is neither absent nor indifferent. You are precisely where He planned for you to be at this very moment. He could have calmed your storm at any point, but He hasn't. Your situation may appear as close to impossible to you as it can get. Like the sailors and passengers of Paul's ill-fated ship, you may be wringing your hands, waiting for the light of day. I repeat, that isn't accidental.

Allow me to move from the stinging spray blasting its way across the deck of that ship mentioned in Acts 27 to the real-world storm you may now be facing. Questions emerge as fear grows within. Panic thoughts make you uneasy. How do you keep it together? What do you do, for example, when you're in the hospital, and the lights have been turned out, and you're trying to believe the news you were given? You lie there, alone. The family has left for the night. All is quiet, except for your thoughts. How do you face tomorrow's fierce blast? Right now it's just you and God . . . and alien, unexpected waves of doubt are slamming relentlessly against your soul. How do you go on? More importantly, how do you replace sheer panic with simple trust?

What do you do when your mate walks out, and you're left alone, and you're living in the backwash of months, even years, of consequences *you* caused? What do you do when life grows that bleak?

Perhaps angry, threatening storm clouds have begun to roll in at the office. The once-clear skies of long-term success now look ominously dark. You sense the worst is yet to come. The possibilities are numerous. So what do you do? I'll tell you what you do: Like the crew of Paul's doomed vessel, you throw out the anchor. In fact, you throw four of them. These anchors are sure to hold you fast.

RELIABLE ANCHORS FOR YOUR STORM-TOSSED SOUL

I offer these four anchors to help stabilize you in the middle of your perfect storm. If you're enjoying clear skies at the present, that's great, but I can assure you, you'll need these someday. Inevitably, storm clouds will roll in, and you'll find yourself groping for dry land. You will need these anchors when the news comes that someone dear to you has died, or when your teenage son doesn't show up one evening, or when you daughter runs away . . . again, or when the baby's fever won't break, or when the damage appears irreparable. You'll need all four of these anchors to keep you from drifting into despair.

First, you'll need the *anchor of stability.*

> Since neither sun nor stars appeared for many days, and no small storm was assailing us, from then on all hope for our being saved was gradually abandoned. And when they had gone a long time without

food, then Paul stood up in their midst and said, "Men, you ought to have followed my advice and not to have set sail from Crete, and incurred this damage and loss. And yet now I urge you to keep up your courage, for there shall be no loss of life among you, but only of this ship. For this very night an angel of the God to whom I belong and whom I serve stood before me, saying, 'Do not be afraid, Paul; you must stand before Caesar; and, behold, God has granted you all those who are sailing with you.' Therefore, keep up your courage, men, for I believe God that it will turn out exactly as I have been told. But we must run aground on a certain island."

Acts 27:20–26

The anchor of stability holds firm when your navigation system fails. It's easy to lose your bearings in the storm. You can't find your way through the circumstances you face. Life rolls along fairly smoothly until suddenly the seas grow rough. Unseen problems occur. They were not in the forecast. In Luke's words, "All hope for being saved" is abandoned.

Those are treacherous moments when we reach the point of abandoning hope. At that difficult, gut-wrenching moment God says, "Don't be afraid, I have a plan."

In the very early years of ministry, to my dismay, I was unable to console a distraught husband, fresh out of the hospital, whose wife and kids had walked out on him. I met with him. I prayed for him. I tried to console him. Having eventually abandoned all hope, he committed suicide. It broke my heart, but the storm was too great. Like the doomed *Andrea Gail*, the man vanished in a sea of hopelessness.

Before Paul's sailing companions reached that breaking point, he offered hope by exhorting them to "keep up your courage. The ship's going down, but we're going to make it!" That's what I call throwing out the anchor of stability.

People facing intense adversity find it difficult to focus on anything other than the towering waves and stinging winds. Paul firmly announces, "Be of good cheer . . . We've heard from the Lord that none will be lost."

We find stability in storms through what God has said. Your tendency will be to turn to another source for strength rather than the Word of God. *Don't go there!* The only anchor of stability that will hold you firm, no matter how intense the gale-force winds, is God's written Word.

All this reminds me of a statement made by one of the ancient Jewish prophets, which supports the reliability of God and His Word. The following words flow from the seasoned hand of Isaiah: "But now, thus says the Lord, your Creator, O Jacob, and He who formed you, O Israel, 'Do not fear, for I have redeemed you; I have called you by name; you are Mine! When you pass through the waters, I will be with you; and through the rivers, they will not overflow you' " (Isaiah 43:1–2).

What encouraging words! "Do not fear, I have called you by name." What a great thought!

Isaiah was not writing of literal waters or actual rivers. His figure of speech emphasized encroaching circumstances that threatened the stability of one's faith. When the waters rise to dangerous depths, when difficulties reach maximum proportion, when your ship seems to be disintegrating board by board and starting to sink by life's inevitable storms, *God is faithful.* He promises, "I will be with you."

Less than five years ago I turned to that very promise. I placed my index finger on the biblical verses and said, "Lord, I want You to know I'm claiming this for my situation, *right now.* It's the only way I'm going be able to make it. You know what You're doing. All I see are waves, and the water is rising. It doesn't make sense to me, but I know that with You onboard my ship won't sink. I'm going to make it!"

Cynthia and I were seeking to relocate the ministry of Insight for Living from California to Texas, not only a massive logistical challenge, but an enormous financial responsibility. The odds were against us. There were several who questioned our need to make such a drastic move. Most of our faithful staff had told us they wouldn't be moving if we followed through on our plans. The original cost estimation was so great it made our heads spin. Our board of directors, while supportive and convinced that relocation made sense, were naturally concerned, knowing how expensive and disruptive large and extensive relocation projects can be. We could feel the gale-force winds of pressure.

It was then that I got alone with the Lord, found and claimed this statement from Isaiah's pen, and anchored myself to His promise.

I'll save you another five pages of reading—we are now completely relocated. We have secured and hired 90 percent new staff—like before, *wonderful*, servant-hearted men and women. We shall move into new facilities about the time this book is published, and the entire project cost less than one-fourth the amount originally estimated. *We made it!* The anchor of stability held us fast.

GOD IS FAITHFUL

Second, you'll need the *anchor of unity.*

> But when the fourteenth night had come, as we were being driven about in the Adriatic Sea, about midnight the sailors began to surmise that they were approaching some land. And they took soundings, and found it to be twenty fathoms; and a little farther on they took another sounding and found it to be fifteen fathoms. And fearing that we might run aground somewhere on the rocks, they cast four anchors from the stern and wished for daybreak. And as the sailors were trying to escape from the ship, and had let down the ship's boat into the sea, on the pretense of intending to lay out anchors from the bow, Paul said to the centurion and the soldiers, "Unless these men remain in the ship, you yourselves cannot be saved." Then the soldiers cut away the ropes of the ship's boat, and let it fall away.
>
> Acts 27:27–32

The scene breathed life-threatening fears. Imaginations ran wild. Paul knew that staying together was the secret to their survival. The temptation was strong to abandon ship and let each person fend for himself. That's no way to survive a storm. As the water grew shallower, fear of shipwreck intensified. But Paul warned that allowing the men to escape meant certain death.

The spiritual application is obvious. Our tendency in dire straits is to cut and run. It's easier at the moment to walk out of a troubled marriage than to face it and work toward restoration. Human nature wants to retreat to a place where each one of us can be all alone, lock the door, and pull the blinds. Alienated, we sink further into depression. Tragically, some turn to the bottle, to drugs, or worse, to a revolver.

If that in any way describes you, you need the support of family, friends, and especially God's people. It's easier to lower the dinghy and jump in all alone. I want to warn you against escaping. Instead, I urge you to stay with others aboard ship. Don't leap and try to make it on your own. Lock arms. Stay in touch with those who love you the most, who will be with you no matter what. You need the presence of God's people surrounding you when the bottom has dropped out of your life. Despite what you think, it's doubtful you can make it on your own. In our case, we had a few close friends of the ministry praying and a unified board encouraging us. Relocating was a challenging experience, but not a lonely one. You and I are designed by God to make it together. The anchor of unity holds us close.

Third, you'll need the *anchor of renewal*.

> And until the day was about to dawn, Paul was encouraging them all to take some food, saying, "Today is the fourteenth day that you have been constantly watching and going without eating, having taken nothing. Therefore I encourage you to take some food, for this is for your preservation; for not a hair from the head of any of you shall perish." And having said this, he took bread and gave thanks to God in the presence of all; and he broke it and began to eat. And all of them were encouraged, and they themselves also took food.
>
> Acts 27:33–36

Can you imagine fighting a storm for two weeks and getting virtually no nourishment? That's what the men on Paul's ship experienced. Even more amazing, that's how most respond to life's storms. We run our tanks dry fighting the battles on our own, and we end up physically weak, emotionally drained, and unable to sleep. The anchor of renewal guards against that sort of anatomical depletion. Instead, Paul encouraged the men to eat and be renewed. But first he prayed. *They all prayed!*

Can you imagine that scene? The storm raged about them, while almost three hundred men bowed in prayer as Paul gave thanks for the meager fare, then everybody on board joined together in the meal.

Your personal nourishment is crucial during times of storm. In panic moments, you'll cut a corner on your meals. You'll also fail to get sufficient sleep. It won't be long before you will set aside prayer altogether, and you'll find yourself drained, spiritually. Increased emotional pain mixed with decreased spiritual renewal can be lethal to your faith.

Spiritual renewal comes primarily through prayer. Few disciplines are of greater importance when all seems bleak. Simply talk it out. Wrestle with the reason for the storm. Seek His direction. Don't let up until you're satisfied you've got the Lord's mind. That's what Paul modeled on the deck of that rugged ship.

For some of the men on board, I'm confident it was the first time in their lives they had prayed. Certainly, it was the first time they had prayed to Almighty God! It may have been the only time in their lives they'd ever heard a prayer offered for a meal. In the middle of a howling wind-and-rain storm, they paused and witnessed a reverent, humble man offering a prayer of gratitude to the Lord God, Maker of heaven and earth. Captain of the winds and waves. That encouraged them. It was simple, but its impact was profound.

Eventually, according to Luke's account, the vessel did run aground. And though the soldiers wanted to murder the prisoners on the spot (In Rome, to lose a prisoner meant you would later lose your head.), the centurion offered a restraining voice of reason. He persuaded his men to spare the prisoners' lives—a great idea since that included Paul—and allow everyone to abandon ship and swim to shore. Reality hit hard when their ship struck the reef.

That brings me to the fourth anchor. In the middle of your perfect storm, you'll need the *anchor of reality.*

> But striking a reef where two seas met, they ran the vessel aground;
> and the prow struck fast and remained unmovable, but the stern began to be broken up by the force of the waves. And the soldiers' plan

was to kill the prisoners, that none of them should swim away and escape; but the centurion, wanting to bring Paul safely through, kept them from their intention, and commanded that those who could swim should jump overboard first and get to land, and the rest should follow, some on planks, and others on various things from the ship. And thus it happened that they all were brought safely to land.

Acts 27:41–44

The anchor of reality says, "Jump right in. Get directly involved. Don't be passive. Be engaged in the action!" The only way they were going to get out of this storm alive was that all of them got into the water and made their way to shore. The reality included a ship that began to break apart. There were no hovering helicopters summoned to rescue them from the sea. Reality *compelled* them to take action. And that's precisely what they did.

Let's pause long enough to do the math. How many started the voyage? Answer: 276. How many were promised they'd make it? Answer: 276. How many made it safely to shore? Answer: 276. As I said, *God is faithful.*

All those going through a storm need to be engaged in the process. No one is promised a magical escape clause. Passivity is faith's enemy. It isn't an acceptable option to fold our arms and wait for the storm to pass.

For you, it may mean some hard work. (It certainly did for us in the relocation project.) It may require humbling yourself before God and others. It might mean a season of counseling where a trained, compassionate individual helps you reorder your life. You may be required to admit several wrong actions and seek reconciliation as you make restitution. Whatever the case, you'll need to be involved. Reality mandates that type of mature response. It's part of throwing the anchor of reality and trusting God to bring you to shore.

Everybody who experienced deliverance from that ship on the reef had the same thing in common once they got to the island—they were all soaking-wet.

IN CALMER WATERS

The best plan for surviving a storm is preparation. No seasoned fishermen or responsible ship captain sets across the open sea without a thorough knowledge of the vessel's equipment and without making sure all is in proper working order. They rarely leave without having first spent sufficient time going over the navigation charts—studying the weather patterns and acquainting themselves with dangerous passages.

And they never leave port without anchors. That's for certain. No one wants to be shipwrecked. But the reality is, it happens, not only on the open sea, but also in life.

The secret of survival is what you do ahead of time in calmer waters. If your life is storm-free as you read this book, I urge you to take advantage of this peaceful lull. Spend time in God's Word. Study the inspired charts He has given you for the journey of life. Deepen your walk with Him through prayer and personal worship.

Then, when the inevitable winds of adversity begin to blow, and they most certainly will blow, you'll be ready to respond in faith, rather than fear. Don't wait. Check those anchors while it's smooth sailing. You'll be glad you did.

And while you're at it, pick out a specific God-given promise you'll be able to cling to, put your index finger on it, and tell the Lord you're anchoring yourself to it. I'm sure glad I did.

CHAPTER TWENTY-ONE

Arrested, Confined, but Still Effective

I want to begin this chapter by asking you to take a quiz. No pen and paper needed. You can do this one in your head. The little mini-test comes in two parts.

Here's the first set of questions.

1. Name the five wealthiest people in the world today.
2. Name the last five Heisman Trophy winners. Too difficult? Okay. How about ten gold-medal winners from the most recent Summer Olympic Games?
3. Name the winners of the Miss America Pageant in the past five years.
4. Name ten people who have won either the Nobel or Pulitzer Prize (Okay, then just name five! How about three?)
5. Name the last six Academy Award winners for Best Actor and Best Actress.
6. Name the last decade's World Series winners. Or if that's too tough, name the most valuable players for the last five World Series games.

Well, you probably could not name three in any category, to say nothing of all of those individuals. Why? Despite their renown at the time and the significant achievements handsomely rewarded, well-known awards tarnish, and the memories of who won them quickly fade.

Now let's try the second part of the quiz.

1. Name two teachers who made a difference in your life.
2. Name three friends who were there for you during a difficult time.
3. Name a mentor or two who believed in you and thought of you as someone worthwhile.
4. Name five people you enjoy spending an evening with just because they're fun to be with and you admire them greatly.
5. Name three or four heroes, living or dead, whose lives have inspired and encouraged you.

Well, how did you do that time? I'm certain you scored an "A". Matter of fact, given enough time, you could have named more for each question. Why? Because the people who make a difference are not those who have the most impressive credentials or those with the largest financial portfolios. They are not even the folks who have won the most awards or those whose faces appear on magazine covers. Those people have little impact on our lives. That's why we've forgotten their names. The real difference makers in life are those significant others who have pulled up close. They've become dear friends and, in some cases, heroes.

Interestingly, with genuine heroes outward appearances mean nothing. Their IQs or how well they performed in school make no difference to us. None of that matters. What matters most are the remarkable qualities that made them effective.

Let me ask a few more questions, if I may. Now I'm getting downright personal. When you've passed from this earthly scene, how will people remember you? What character quality will linger in their minds, prompting them to say yours was an effective life? Why would they want to pause at your name etched in granite?

Now that we're nearing the end of our study of that great century-one man of grace and grit, what character quality made *him* most effective?

Most likely, the answer can be found in the letters he wrote to churches in Philippi and Colosse. Let's depart briefly from Dr. Luke's narrative in Acts and focus on Paul's own words of exhortation at a time when his circumstances were less than ideal.

A LEARNED CONTENTMENT

Three times in the short letter to the Philippians Paul mentions his circumstances, which amount to being confined as a prisoner of Rome.

Following an unusually affectionate salutation to the believers in Philippi, Paul writes, "I want you to know, brethren, that my *circumstances* have turned out for the greater progress of the gospel, so that my imprisonment in the cause of Christ has become well known throughout the whole praetorian guard and to everyone else" (Philippians 1:12). Later he reiterates, "not that I speak from want; for I have learned to be content in whatever *circumstances* I am" (4:11). Finally, he concludes, "In any and every *circumstance* I have learned the secret of being filled and going hungry, both of having abundance and suffering need" (4:12b, italics mine). Three times he emphasizes how his circumstances do not determine his level of contentment.

Paul offers no conditions, no restrictions, no boundaries that come to bear on his contentment. Regardless of his station in life, he lived above his circumstances. I'm convinced that's what allowed God to use the man so effectively. That's what made his impact heroic. Not once in all the stories we've observed in these few chapters on Paul has he displayed a pitiful, victim mentality. Rather, through "humble means," or "prosperity," going "hungry," or being "filled," Paul remained content. Though his circumstances were often extreme, the man's attitude remained virtually bulletproof.

Now you may be tempted to chalk all that up to temperament. After all, today's culture puts a lot of stock in temperament classifications. But contentment is not genetic. Paul writes simply, "I have learned" to be content. Contentment results from an attitude that is learned, having been deliberately cultivated over time. Attitude governs contentment. By the time Paul reached Rome, battered and bruised from the battles of his missionary journeys, including most recently, the shipwreck experience, his resolve had grown impregnable.

Through the power of Christ Paul had *learned* to encounter a broad spectrum of stressful situations without letting circumstances impact him negatively. He had *learned* how to sustain an excellent attitude. He rose above his circumstances. He had *learned* to live beyond them.

Allow me to take a peek at where he was at this point. Paul did not write those stirring words while sipping ice tea through a straw on some quiet Aegean beach. Nor was he basking in the warm sun of the Italian Alps. He didn't put his stylus to parchment while enjoying a time of much-needed solitude in a lovely villa overlooking the Mediterranean. With withered hands straining against the cold, iron chains, Paul wrote about unprecedented opportunities and joyful accomplishments. We'll soon see what made the ultimate difference.

DESPITE THESE CHAINS

Acts 28:14 finds Paul fresh off the boat and still smelling of seawater from spending days "in the deep" and months on the island of Malta. During that time on the island God used Paul mightily to heal the father of his gracious host. Then Luke states, "We came to Rome" (28:14). *Finally!*

In that same closing chapter of Acts, Luke informs us that Paul "stayed two full years in his own rented quarters, and was welcoming all who came to him, preaching the kingdom of God, and teaching concerning the Lord Jesus Christ with all openness, unhindered" (28:30–31).

Despite his chains, he faithfully and fervently proclaimed Christ. Grace and grit again in full view!

Quite likely you have never been *confined* anywhere for two years. Neither have I. But periods of lingering frustration are common to all of us. As the old country song says, "Some days are diamonds, some days are stones." It's when those days extend into months, even years, of waiting for our situations to change that our patience wears thin. Apparently, Paul remained steadfast, even though he dragged chains around his apartment in Rome for two years. And that north side of the busy city where he was held under house arrest was no Park Avenue.

John Pollock vividly paints the historic canvas:

> Paul was placed in custody in a house rented at his own cost. It was
> not in the slums, the labyrinth of narrow streets and flimsy dwellings
> from which the mob emerged for periodical riots. He would have had
> a home of reasonable size—or small but with a roomy garden—just
> within the walls near the camp of the Praetorian Guard on the Caelian
> Hill in the north of Rome.
>
> The rumble of traffic down the narrow cobbled street at night,
> when the country carts were allowed to bring produce to the markets,
> the babble of jostling pedestrians by day, the distant roars of excited
> crowds in the Circus Maximus during chariot races or gladiatorial
> combats, the stench of a great city even in winter when Paul arrived,
> and the risk of malaria in summer, did not make for ease or luxury.
> And the regulations demanded the never-ending presence of a soldier
> to whom he must be chained. But he was not in prison; he could have
> friends at his side and invite all whom he wished.[1]

The same author goes on to describe the impact a visit to Paul's quarters would have had on an unsuspecting guest.

> No one could leave that hired house untouched, if only to "argue
> vigorously." It had an atmosphere of happiness with the music and
> singing which Paul mentions in both the chief letters he wrote from
> it. His character had not been soured or hardened by troubles. To
> judge by what he thought important, he was kind, tenderhearted,
> forgiving, just as Christ had forgiven him. He walked in love, the
> element which bound his qualities together. He was still the great
> encourager, welcoming a man who was weak in faith but refusing to
> argue about secondary matters. The Romans learned that he lived as
> he had taught them when he wrote three years before: "We that are
> strong ought to bear with the failings of the weak, and not to please
> ourselves . . . Owe no one anything except to love one another."
> . . . In that Roman house, bitter people softened; anger, wrath,
> clamor died away. Paul had more than ever a sense of his littleness, his

unworthiness—"less than the least of all saints"—of the marvel of his being entrusted with a commission "to preach the unsearchable riches of Christ." He seemed to delight in the contrast between the majesty of the message and the insignificance of the messenger: such a gentle little man now, yet with what steel and strength."[2]

What John Pollock calls "steel and strength" in describing the character of our missionary hero, I refer to as *grace* and *grit*.

Few people in the first century had a deeper understanding of God's grace than the apostle Paul. Redeemed from a life of vicious brutality as a rigid legalistic Pharisee, the man turned the corner, repented, and through Christ's empowering became a gentle soul, gracious and affirming. Understanding. Forgiving. Approachable. He reached the place where he was willing not only to offer hope to the Gentiles, but to live among them, though he himself would bleed pure Jewish blood. No one that I know endured the level of hardship he did as a good solider of Christ. What makes him all-the-more amazing is this: Never once does he leave a hint of complaint over being chained to a burly Roman soldier or about the inconvenience of being confined to such cramped quarters. The man simply would not grumble. By God's grace, he lived above it all. I repeat, he had *learned* the secret of contentment.

What an enviable mental attitude! As you're reading this chapter, you may find yourself in a situation far less than ideal. Not only has life become difficult and frustrating, it is growing increasingly more miserable by the day. Truth be told, life at this time for you may be borderline unbearable.

The great temptation is to allow that to embitter you—to turn you into someone who lives under a dark cloud, where doom and gloom characterize your outlook. Life's hard. You live in a situation that resembles a house arrest. You feel chained to your past, unable to escape the restrictive circumstances. Maybe you've lived this way so long that negative thinking has become a habit. You can't imagine thinking any other way.

I've got wonderful news: There is hope beyond your circumstances. You can live above them. If a man named Paul could live above his unbelievably trying circumstances, so can you. But Christ must become your central focus. He, alone, can empower you and teach you to live above the duress of adversity. Your external circumstances may not change, but deep within, *you* will. As Christ is allowed first place in your thoughts, changes will occur. Those changes will be evident to your mate, your children, your friends, and your co-workers. Instead of seeing yourself as a victim, you will begin to realize a strength that is not your own. The result? You will make a difference because of the way you respond to the circumstances that once defeated you. To the people closest to you, your contentment *despite your circumstances* will be nothing short of heroic.

Now let's get back to Paul. He is under house arrest in rented quarters; he refuses to focus on that. He is far from home and his future is uncertain; he doesn't let that concern him. He is bound to a Roman guard every day; no problem. Because he has made Christ the object of his life, contentment has replaced frustration. He's taught himself to live *above* his circumstances. The benefits?

First, the progress of the gospel is accelerated, it's never delayed. In his letter to the Christians in Philippi, Paul passionately confesses, "I want you to know, brethren, that my circumstances have turned out for the greater progress of the gospel" (Philippians 1:12). Because of Paul's attitude regarding his predicament, his testimony spread like a firestorm through the ranks of the Roman guard. Systematically, God's Spirit leveled the towering pride of the Roman military. Like felled trees in a thick forest, the heart of one proud Roman soldier after another lay in submission to the power of Christ.

Think of it this way: Paul never viewed his confinement as a barrier to the gospel, but rather as a catalyst for wider impact. That's the benefit of a learned contentment. When you live above your circumstances, you will have little trouble spreading the message of the gospel. Everyone near you will want to know how you're able to live with such joyful abandon. Christ came into Paul's life in such a way that he claimed, "He has empowered me. I can do whatever because of His strength." Paul's contentment came from Christ, and His grace flowed from him through the barracks of Rome.

Second, when you live above your circumstances, the edge of the message is sharpened, it's never dulled. Paul exclaimed that his chains had become the reason the entire palace guard had come under the hearing of the gospel. That was no insignificant statistic. By Paul's account, the message of Christ's love permeated the ranks of the imperial guard, which some scholars suggest were as many as nine thousand. Amazingly, the revival started with one Roman soldier chained to one man, but not just *any* man. That forced union became a springtide of grace to the whole Praetorian Guard.

One disciplined soldier after another laid down the arms of his heart and surrendered to his new Commander. How thrilling that must have been to witness firsthand! The gospel was sharpened, not dulled, because Paul saw his circumstances as an opportunity to launch the message, rather than slump in despair.

There's a third benefit to living above your circumstances: *The courage of others is strengthened, never weakened.* Paul's unlikely converts were not sheepish about their new-found faith in Christ. I take it that they didn't hold back. Rather, they grew increasingly more courageous in their witness. I find that so exciting!

As the soldiers charged with keeping tabs on Paul ultimately surrendered to the Lord Jesus, he became their mentor. As they witnessed his remarkable faith, they grew in their courage "to speak the word of God without fear." They discovered the inner secret to contentment: "I can do all things through Him who strengthens me" (Philippians 4:13). How often they must have heard him say that! It was so often, they began to repeat it.

The secret to Paul's contentment did not emerge from a manual on how to live the Christian life or from a workshop on positive thinking. He didn't have access to a stack of self-help scrolls promising to shore up his sagging self-confidence. Paul's secret was not found in a program, but in a Person. Christ made the difference. He taught His servant to endure all situations, every circumstance, each difficult challenge, no matter how adverse, through His power. Paul released all rights to His Master and, in turn, He released all the strength Paul needed.

Paul wrote about his secret to contentment in the letters he wrote to his friends at Philippi and Colossae. In those letters I find at least four attitudes of a learned contentment. Because they worked for him in a situation far more confining than where we find ourselves, I'm convinced they will work for us today.

FOUR ATTITUDES OF A LEARNED CONTENTMENT

"Do nothing from selfishness and empty conceit, but with humility of mind let each of you regard one another as more important than himself; do not merely look out for your own personal interests, but also for the interests of others" (Philippians 2:3–4).

First, Paul recommends an attitude of unselfish humility.

Quite remarkably, you never read where Paul said to his Roman guard, "I need you to do me a favor. Next time you happen to be near one of the Emperor's assistants, urge him get me out of this dump. I shouldn't be here in the first place. I've been here for one year, seven months, four days, five hours, and nine minutes, and that's long enough." Paul's attitude of unselfish humility prevented him from keeping meticulous records of the wrongs done to him in Rome, or anywhere else for that matter. He asked no favors. He held no grudges. He had no expectations. He was there by divine appointment. He willingly submitted to his situation.

Our self-promoting age cries out for heroic souls, who live free of empty conceit and with humility of mind that regards others as more important than self.

Paul points to the ultimate model and exhorts all of us to have the same attitude which "was also in Christ Jesus," who willingly "emptied Himself" and became "obedient to the point of death."

Christ modeled the great emptying-out principle that permeated Paul's remarkable life. If we want to learn contentment, developing an attitude of unselfish humility is the perfect place to begin.

Start with your family or with one of your neighbors. Model it next before your employees or with your clients in the workplace. You won't believe the impact that sort of selfless mental attitude will have on the people in your sphere of influence.

You won't have to wave flags or pass out tracts. Just demonstrate an attitude of unselfish humility. The results will amaze you.

Second, Paul exhorts believers to have an attitude of joyful acceptance. Paul minced no words about how believers should relate to one another. "Do all things without grumbling or disputing; that you may prove yourselves blameless and innocent, children of God above reproach in the midst of a crooked and perverse generation, among whom you appear as lights in the world" (Philippians 2:14–15).

Paul knew the stakes were high as the secular world scrutinized the fledgling first-century followers of Christ. For Christians to grumble and dispute over circumstances put the credibility of the gospel at risk. Therefore, he sought an attitude of joyful acceptance free of petty disputes and bickering. He pled for authentic joy.

Nothing is more contagious. Paul said, "Don't complain; be joyful!" That's the ticket. Joy attracts. Grumbling repels. A choice sense of humor is wonderfully appealing. People notice it when the dark spectrum of our "crooked and perverse generation" has not jaded us.

My mentor, Ray Stedman, used to say, "We live in a world of crooks and perverts. What an opportunity to be winsomely different!" I love that kind of attitude. Joyful acceptance lights up this dismal planet!

There's a third attitude Paul commands believers to possess—the attitude of strong determination. He confesses, "Brethren, I do not regard myself as having laid hold of it yet; but one thing I do: forgetting what lies behind and reaching forward to what lies ahead, I press on toward the goal for the prize of the upward call of God in Christ Jesus" (Philippians 3:13–14).

At a time when many people in his place would be looking back in regret, wondering what life would have been like in a different profession, Paul repudiates the past and looks with confidence to the future. His strong determination kept him focused on the ultimate goal—pleasing Christ all the way to the goal, even in his chains. It's the picture of a runner running for the tape at the end of the race, straining forward in strong determination. Paul said, "I'm not looking back. I'm stretching for the prize." True grit on display.

No rusty Roman chains could deter Paul from reaching for the goal of pursuing the prize of Christ. He pressed on, determined to remain focused on his mission.

I was reading to Cynthia from *Sports Illustrated* about a 90-year-old basketball scout that still does work for the Detroit Pistons. That's right— the man is ninety years old! He still gets on a plane, checks those prospects out, and brings back a reliable report. I love it! He said he flew past sixty-two without even a thought of retirement. Strong determination.

I read somewhere, "We wonder at the anatomical perfection of a da Vinci painting. But we forget that Leonardo da Vinci on one occasion drew a thousand hands." Leonardo possessed that same strong determination Paul modeled in Rome. Thomas Edison came up with the modern light bulb after a thousand failed attempts. By the man's own admission, it was mainly strong determination that gave the incandescent light to the world, not an inventor's creative genius.

But we're not talking about college athletes or persistent, brilliant inventors. We're talking about being a determined servant of Christ. There's no easy route to spiritual maturity. It doesn't happen overnight. Remember, it's a grueling journey at times. So, don't bother to publish a pamphlet on all the obstacles you face. Don't become famous for complaining. The apostle says, "Forget the past; reach for the tape. Keep running." Develop and maintain an attitude of strong determination.

The fourth attitude comes from Paul's letter to the Colossian believers. I would call it Paul's attitude of genuine thanksgiving: "Devote yourselves to prayer, keeping alert in it with an attitude of thanksgiving; praying that at the same time for us as well, that God may open up to us a door for the word, so that we may speak forth the mystery of Christ, for which I have also been imprisoned; in order that I might make it clear in the way I ought to speak" (Colossians 4:2–4).

Here's a man in his sixties who has been preaching for years asking for prayer for a clearer delivery. There was no pretense with Paul. No degree of success or number of years in the ministry gave him a false sense of ultimate accomplishment. He knew he had not yet arrived. He was convinced his preaching could be improved. And so with a genuinely thankful heart, he entreated his fellow believers for their prayers. Can you see the power of that kind of attitude? Very refreshing.

No wonder the man had such lasting impact for Christ. His secret bled through every one of his letters. May I repeat it once more? *He had learned to be content in all things.* But we can't leave the ink of these truths to simply sit and dry on the page. We must embrace the same secret for ourselves, if we are to have the same lasting impact. Some personal reflection is in order.

AN UP-CLOSE-AND-PERSONAL ATTITUDE CHECK

Let's turn the spotlight away from the man housed in Rome back then and focus it on you and your life, wherever you find yourself right now. Are you making a difference in the lives of those closest to you by the way you respond to your circumstances? Are others inspired by your faith, or are they discouraged by your fears? Are the attitudes of unselfish humility, joyful acceptance, strong determination, and genuine thanksgiving evident in the way you respond to circumstances? Maybe it's time to make some changes. Let's see if I can help.

Start by refusing to let your situation determine your attitude. When your attitude overshadows your situation, transformation really begins. As we saw in Paul, the power to transform stubborn attitudes of fear and bitterness, anger and defeat, comes from Christ. The Lord our God stands ready to pour his strength in you. He alone has the power to deliver you from those relentless foes and send you soaring.

Author David Aikman did the world a favor toward the end of the last century. He finished his extensive research and wrote the book which he titled, *Six Individuals Who Changed the Twentieth Century.* As a foreign correspondent, David Aikman has a unique perspective on world events. He writes, "What has struck me as a reporter for most of my adult life is the capacity of individual human beings again and again to rise above their times and their circumstances to change, if only just a little, the direction of the human tide."[4]

Following a discussion of a century full of great lives of remarkable individuals who lived in the previous century, he concluded that it was *their attitude* that set them apart. Did you notice? He mentioned each individual's determination "to rise above their circumstances." As I read his words it struck me: That's *precisely* what drew me to my mentors, especially the four to whom I dedicated this book.

My respect for them only intensified when I learned the circumstances each endured without losing the heart to press ahead. Heartache after heartache, setback after setback, failure upon failure, would not deter those choice men from leaving the past behind and reaching for the prize.

Ultimately, that's what compelled me to tackle a study of the life and ministry of the apostle Paul. He modeled that remarkable quality which allowed him to learn to be content in all things. That freed him to become God's man, a man of grace and grit, who literally changed the course of church history.

And so it can be for you. When Christ is given full control of your life, His love and mercy will pierce your wounded soul and allow you to release a torrent of bitterness, anger, and resentment that has festered there for years. Blame and self-pity will disappear and give way to humility and joy. Like it did for Paul, it will begin at the foot of the cross. True transformation starts there. When you come to Him in faith, He sets you free from the things that have held you captive all your life. Like Paul, you too will be released to become a channel of grace and power.

You began this chapter by answering an important question. I asked you to name three or four heroes, whose lives have inspired and encouraged you. I would suspect you named people who refused to surrender to their circumstances. Their accomplishments were probably significant, yes, but it was their attitude that caused them to stand apart from the rest, right? They soared in their spirit.

Would you like to end this chapter with a great thought? Appropriate what you have read about Paul, and you might very well become the person someone will call their hero in years to come.

CHAPTER TWENTY-TWO

Shackled, Deserted, but Still Undaunted

Nero's nervous gavel came down hard and Paul was free. Though we know nothing from the biblical record of the details of his defense before the Emperor, Paul once again knew freedom's ring and immediately resumed his commitment to preaching. Some believe it was during this period that he made his much dreamed-of trip to Spain. Maybe so, but no one knows for sure. He certainly met up with Titus in Crete, enjoyed the gracious company of Philemon and his delightful friend, Onesimus. Most significantly, he was reunited with Timothy at Ephesus. Sweet words and warm embraces must have accompanied their coming together. Paul made the most of that opportunity to pour more of his wisdom and learning into the soul of the young man with a kindred spirit, who would succeed him in the work.

His freedom lasted but a few years. Sooner than most might have expected, Paul was arrested at Troas and dragged back to Rome in chains, landing again on the cold floor of a Roman dungeon.

Travelers to Rome today usually miss that most important sight. It's inevitably missed because it's not listed in any of the tourist brochures.

There are no original works of art that hang in the gallery at that unattractive place. No sculptured statues attract a sophisticated crowd. In fact, nothing about the old dungeon is beautiful. The place is a dark and dingy hole not fit for any human to inhabit. Not only is it unattractive, the pungent odors of sweat and dried blood common to such chambers of torture offend unsuspecting visitors. If the stones, blackened by age, could talk, what dreadful tales they could tell. The few tourists who descend into that dreary space crouch through narrow passages as they sense what it was like for anyone to spend even a few days in the dank, gloomy chamber of horrors then called the Mamertine Prison.

In that lonely dungeon the prisoner named Paul spent his last hours, during which he wrote some of the tenderest words ever penned to a fledgling young ministerial apprentice just beginning to hit his stride. Paul wrote his second letter to Timothy while alone in the shadows of that damp and dirty cell.

Hans Finzel, in his fine book *Empowered Leaders*, skillfully describes the place where Paul spent his final days.

> Any visitor to Rome learns immediately that St. Peter's Church is at the center of the city's attractions. Like magnets, the Vatican, St. Peter's Basilica, and the beautiful museums that surround it draw millions to this ancient city each year. I visited Vatican Square, toured St. Peter's Cathedral, and spent half a day in the Vatican Museum. I was especially impressed by the works of Michelangelo in the Sistine Chapel. However, what inspired me most about my visit to Rome happened after I left those great buildings and that rich history. As impressive as they are, there was something more special in store.
>
> On an obscure side street a few kilometers from the Vatican, there is a small building thought to house the prison cell where Paul spent his final days. Whether it is actually his prison cell or not is of course debatable. We climbed down into this cramped hole beneath the ground and spent about a half-hour in the dark cell. It was cold, damp, and musty. A small grate in the ceiling allowed a little daylight to shine through. Historians agree that Paul probably lost his life around A. D. 67 when Nero ruled.

As I sat on that cold stone floor, I imagined what it must have been like for Paul in those last days. If this wasn't the exact room, it had to be just like it. What a way to spend your final weeks. As we stood in the cell and talked, drinking in the story that the stones could tell if they spoke, we noticed that only a few visitors climbed down into the cell with us. This was in stark contrast to the thousands who waited in line to enter the Vatican Museum not far away. The streets above were filled with tourists who were flocking to St. Peter's Cathedral, but only occasionally did someone stop long enough even to peer through the grate down into the cell. I thought to myself, "Here is where the man who wrote the greatest portion of the New Testament spent his last days. The greatest missionary and church planter of the first century died here. Wouldn't more people want to feel what it was like for him?" Obviously the answer is no. Most people visiting Rome today do not list Paul's cell as one of their top ten tourist sites. But for me it ranked as the number-one spot in Rome.[1]

Most tourists in Rome don't even know to look for the traditional site of that notorious dungeon. The thin stream of curious lookers is more likely comprised of accidental observers rather than those who set upon the place by design.

It was there, nevertheless, in a rugged rock-walled dungeon, that Paul spent his last days. Freed by Nero's earlier decree, Paul enjoyed release from his house arrest for a brief period of time before returning to this final holding tank. Sometime later in the gray confines of the official Roman barracks you could hear the sharpening of an axe that with one swift motion, only hours after the Emperor's decree, would swing down hard and accomplish its grim objective.

SOME SEASONED WORDS TO A YOUNG APPRENTICE

Every time I open Paul's second letter to Timothy I remind myself that it is comprised of dungeon talk. That's why the words ring with such deep passion and tenderness. Bent over and scarred, yet strangely content, Paul sits shackled and deserted. Search as hard and long as you wish, you'll not find even a trace of self-pity, blame, or bitterness in the weary apostle's tone. He expresses no regrets.

Time is precious and he knows it. The imminence of his execution allows only for the penning of a straightforward letter by which he graciously passes the baton of ministry to Timothy. His tenderness, however, shows through.

I'm also impressed that Paul shows no evidence he's living in denial. He makes no less than five specific references to his suffering in the prison, not once denying the reality of his situation or diminishing its significance.

Charles Erdman writes, "Possibly no other of the New Testament letters makes so tender and so pathetic an appeal. Every paragraph is suffused with emotion, every sentence throbs with the pulse beats of a human heart. Paul, the dauntless missionary hero, the founder of the Church in Asia Minor and in Europe, is now an aged prisoner in Rome, suffering, deserted, despised, condemned, and soon to be led forth to a cruel death."[2]

Since you may never have occasion to visit that Roman dungeon, you are left to imagine the crippled frame of the man who looks older than his years, bruised from the tortures of the past, scarred from the beatings and the stonings and the shipwrecks, sitting in the darkness. His hair and beard now white as bone. He crouches under the grate which offers a few dusty rays of light from the street above.

There he writes with his own crippled hand a poignant letter to his dearest friend, his son in the faith. He would later press that tender epistle into the hands of Luke, who would make certain it found its way to Ephesus. He addressed it affectionately, "To Timothy, my beloved son."

The finality of Paul's message is palpable. Days later, Timothy choked back his tears as he read in his mentor's own handwriting, "I am already being poured out as a drink offering, and the time of my departure has come."

Charles Ryrie is correct as he summarizes the affectionate and passionate words from the most significant man in Timothy's life. "Paul knew that this time he would not be freed, and that is true. There will not be another voyage across the Mediterranean. There would not be another visit to a church that's been founded, or to a place where they've never heard the gospel. Not by Paul. His life is being poured out as a drink offering, and the time of his departure has come."[3]

Only those who've experienced the dull passing of time on death row know firsthand what it's like to await certain death by execution. No wonder Paul writes an impassioned plea inviting his beloved ministry companion to "make every effort to come before winter." No one wants to die alone, even those most sure of heaven, not even the great apostle Paul.

We don't know if Timothy made it before winter or if, upon arriving, he found a fresh grave under fallen snow. We know that Paul was virtually alone those last hours—only Dr. Luke was nearby. No one else. The once-faithful Demas had abandoned Paul, drawn too much by the lure of lesser loyalties from "this world" (4:10). The details of that are left for preachers' imaginations. Titus and Mark are occupied as well. His only requests of young Timothy were to summon John Mark and also to bring along a few personal possessions, like Paul's cloak, which he no doubt left back at Troas in the scuffle of arrest.

More than a covering for the cold, that well-worn cloak bore the evidences of his arduous efforts for Christ. Pungent with the smell of brine from the Mediterranean, and stained with his own blood from Lystra, the cloak symbolized his passionate commitment to his calling and his brave determination—grace and grit. That faithful cloak would soon be traded for a glorious heavenly robe. He made one additional request: "Don't forget the books, especially the parchments." Paul longed for his personal scrolls of the Scriptures. There must be no dulling of his handling of the Truth. The old gentleman was a student to the very end.

Paul's remarks in the final chapter of Second Timothy establish the framework for the entire letter. Rarely do you read the close of a letter before the beginning. But here it's not an unwise approach to our understanding of the man's last words.

Deserted, shackled, yet still undaunted, Paul remained strong to the final day of his life. He writes with the deepest of feeling, from his tender salutation to his characteristically gracious farewell.

A SURVEY OF PAUL'S PASSIONATE EPISTLE

In the next few pages, I'd like us to journey through a quick survey of Paul's final words to Timothy. As we walk together through Second Timothy, it will be helpful if you keep in mind that Paul did not write his letters in chapters. The words flowed continuously as the Spirit of God moved the seasoned apostle's weathered hand to transfer divinely inspired truth.

Chapter One: A Clarion Call to Courageous Living

As mentioned earlier, Timothy and Paul were kindred spirits. Paul loved Timothy as a son and confessed tenderly, "I thank God whom I serve with a clear conscience the way my forefathers did, as I constantly remember you in my prayers night and day, longing to see you, even as I recall your tears, so that I may be filled with joy" (2 Timothy 1:3–4).

Sadly, we live in a culture much too fearful of unbridled emotion. We rarely witness such an unguarded transfer of truth. Too bad. Much is lost in a context of formalities and superficial religious clichés. There is none of that in this lovely letter.

He remembered Timothy's dear mother and grandmother who had raised him in the fear and instruction of the Lord. Both godly women made certain the truths of Scripture had taken firm root in the soil of Timothy's soul long before Paul recruited him for the work. Knowing his longtime companion struggled with natural insecurities, he reminded him also of the gifts God had given him and charged him to stir them up anew. Timidity would do him no good. Fear is human, not divine. God's supernatural enablement included power, love, and sound discipline (1:7). Those qualities are the stuff of greatness. They would take Timothy the distance.

All of this and so much more Timothy had, no doubt, heard before as he journeyed with Paul through Asia and beyond. Reading them must have caused the younger man to nod with nostalgic understanding. Paul's exhortations had a fresh and urgent ring to them since they were coming from the hands of a man shaking in sickness, soon to be cold in death.

The mentor's invitation was to a joined suffering and to a life of courageous ministry (1:8–12). Timothy would, in some mysterious way, share in the sufferings of Paul, as Paul shared in the sufferings of Christ. He was neither to be ashamed of the gospel nor careless with the Truth. The stakes were too high for anything less than a sober guarding of those principles Paul had faithfully deposited into his spiritual account. Paul's words were not a mere collection of pithy statements; they were an entrusted treasure; to be guarded and retained at all cost (1:13–14). By now, Timothy hung on every word.

Paul was just getting started.

Chapter Two: A Checklist for Faithful Service

As Paul goes on, he includes seven exhortations for faithful service.

1. *Be strong in grace* (2:1). Paul writes, "Be strong in the grace that is in Christ Jesus." Paul modeled an inner strength which was drawn daily from the deep well of God's grace. That same supply of grace would steel Timothy for the rigors of ministry.

2. *Be faithful to entrust truth.* Those profound truths Paul routinely transferred into his young apprentice's account were not to be spent frivolously. They were resources to be invested wisely. Paul charged Timothy to take what he had learned and heard from his mentor's mouth and entrust it all to faithful men who would be able "to teach others also" (2:2).

I frequently refer to that as the *relay of truth.* Paul got it from another, like the passing of a baton in a relay. Paul took the baton and handed it off to Timothy. Timothy now has the responsibility to do the same—hand it off to faithful men.

And the relay would continue, unless someone dropped the baton. This process has been called by some the "ministry of multiplication"—truth transferred from one faithful individual to another. There is to be no hoarding of divine revelation. "Timothy, there is to be no keeping of those rich ministry experiences and hard-learned lessons under your vest. The whole treasure trove of truth is to be entrusted to others." Paul, in effect, is writing, "Timothy, when you've run your lap, make certain you pass the baton to the next person in line." The race must continue.

3. *Be as brave as a soldier.* There's not much use for fickle soldiers, especially in the heat of battle. Paul knew the only way Timothy would survive was by willingly accepting hardship, "as a good soldier." An untrustworthy soldier goes *AWOL (absent without leave)* at the first sign of stress. Ministry sidelines swell with weak-in-the-knee soldiers, who desired the glory but spurned the sacrifice. Paul exhorted Timothy not to join their ranks. The

young pastor would need a brave resolve that not only accepted suffering as the mantle for service, but willingly embraced it. Good soldiers do that.

4. *Be as disciplined as an athlete* (2:5). The race ahead would take remarkable discipline and strong determination. It would be too easy to turn and run from the first hurdle that seemed impossible to jump. As Paul had written Timothy in his first letter, "Discipline yourself for the purpose of godliness" (1 Timothy 4:7b)

5. *Be as hard-working as a farmer* (2:6). The ministry is no job for a lazy soul who grouses at the first sight of dawn. Paul offered no rose-colored perspective on the rigors of the calling. The task requires hard work, long hours, and at times, soul-deep sacrifice. That's all part of turning out a bumper crop. Timothy needed to know that in the early years of ministry. There would be long rows to plow, and the planting of the seed would not come easy.

6. *Be as diligent as a workman* (2:15). The task called for someone willing to pay the price to communicate accurately. That required a regular, disciplined, systematic study of the Scriptures. Nothing was to be taken for granted. Paul left no room in his graduate program of *Christian Leadership 601* for sloppy communicators or unprepared messengers. Only diligent students need apply. Stay diligent, Timothy.

7. *Be as gentle as a servant* (2:24–25). Devotion to the things of the Spirit brings about gentleness in even the hardest of souls. There's no excuse for harsh leadership styles in Christian ministries. Leading gently always pays greater dividends than pounding people into submission. Cattle are driven, sheep must be led. Paul wrote, in effect, "Timothy, be gentle to those sheep! I know they're stubborn. But they still belong to the Lord." Timothy would have his critics, just as Paul did. But there was no need to clobber saints with Truth, no matter how ornery they may be. Paul recommended a gentle, servant-hearted approach for dealing with opposition.

What a checklist for faithful ministry! That'll do it.

- Be strong in grace.
- Be faithful to entrust.
- Be as brave as a soldier.
- Be as hard-working as a farmer.
- Be as disciplined as an athlete.

- Be as diligent as a workman.
- Be as gentle as a servant.

Paul knew the ministry would not be all fun and games. Real dangers lay waiting in Timothy's path. The adversary would soon take aim. The young man needed a battle plan for victory. His seasoned mentor delivered one he would be able to review the rest of his life.

Chapter Three: A Warning List for Difficult Times

Paul then removed Timothy's rose-colored glasses and opened his eyes to reality. Possibly it was here that Paul paused and looked up through the grate in that dreary dungeon. He shut his eyes and imagined what life and ministry would be like for Timothy. Knowing humanity as Paul did, understanding depravity to the depths he had written of in his letter to the Romans, he says to Timothy, "Difficult times will come" (3:1).

With that, he launched full-bore into what the battle would look like as Timothy carried on without him by his side. Read the following slowly. It's amazing—though written in the first century, it sounds like today: "But realize this, that in the last days difficult times will come. For men will be lovers of self, lovers of money, boastful, arrogant, revilers, disobedient to parents, ungrateful, unholy, unloving, irreconcilable, malicious gossips, without self-control, brutal, haters of good, treacherous, reckless, conceited, lovers of pleasure rather than lovers of God; holding to a form of godliness, although they have denied its power; and avoid such men as these" (2 Timothy 3:1–5).

Not a pretty picture. One of my mentors used to call the days Paul described "*savage times.*" The last days *have* come! Paul's predictions are now reality. The aged apostle is warning Timothy that there will be an erosion of the standard—a departure from the Truth. In fact, for many, the Christian life will be one giant compromise with the world. Hypocrisy, deception, and a watering down of doctrine will become the norm.

Paul commended Timothy for the fact that, despite the rampant apostasy, he had remained faithful to what he had been taught (3:10–11). Still the days would grow more desperate as "evil men and impostors will proceed from bad to worse, deceiving and being deceived" (3:13).

When you write from a dungeon, you tend to see life in the raw. Words lose their diplomacy as Paul made plain that the individuals responsible for such lawless religion would not remain on the sidelines. They would not only emerge, they would invade the church. They would be brash enough to break into homes, stealing and violating all things considered valuable. Timothy must remain alert.

Only by guarding his own steps and continuing in those things which he had learned from Paul would he survive such insidious assaults from the outside. But he must not drift into battle without a plan. He must step onto the battlefield armed with a strong and well-defined defensive strategy.

Paul charged him to "continue in the things you have learned and become convinced of, knowing from whom you have learned them" (3:14). There is great protection by embracing the wisdom of others. Timothy had grown up in the Scriptures. That, coupled with reliable teaching, shielded him from error.

Let's pause long enough for some self-analysis. If you're like most Americans, you're life is being lived on the fast-track. Slow down for a question: Can you remember the teaching that was passed along to you by a godly mother or a wise father, a mentor, a teacher, a coach, a friend, a pastor or youth pastor? I can remember, as if it were yesterday, some things passed along to me, especially by my father who didn't talk nearly as much as my mother. Still he somehow connected with me. Occasionally, it was in ways I would not forget.

One warm day, I lay in bed in my room on my mid-October birthday, while my dad diligently weeded the flower garden. Realizing I was frittering away the afternoon, he called out to me and said, "Charles, you need to come out here and help me finish this."

I said, "No, not today, I'm thirteen. Today's my birthday."

That's the last thing I remember saying until about dark that evening. He flew into the house like a flash and proceeded to spank me all the way out the door, across the backyard, and into the flowerbed. Yep, he spanked this thirteen-year-old! I worked until I was convinced I'd yanked up every weed in existence. As I recall, that was my last spanking.

Toward the end of the day, just before sundown, Dad said, "Come on in and get cleaned up. The family is going out to dinner to celebrate your birthday." During dinner he passed along something to me about obedience that I remember to this day: "Always respect those who are in authority over you. Do so immediately and without question."

I *learned* and *became convinced* of something that has helped me all the way through the rest of my life. When someone in authority over you has your good at heart, you do exactly what they tell you to do. You don't even ask why. Paul wanted Timothy to stick with the truth as he had learned it from Paul. Paul knew what he was talking about. He knew that kind of resolve would serve him well. He must have convictions!

Dr. John Walvoord, longtime president of Dallas Seminary from 1952–1986, once said at a graduation commencement service, "I fear that we may be graduating students with too many beliefs and not enough convictions." What an insightful comment. Paul mentioned both to Timothy. "Continue in the things you have learned (beliefs), and continue in those things of which you have become convinced (convictions)." They go together.

Things you believe are numerous. Some you believe stronger than others. Convictions are truths for which you would die. They represent what's non-negotiable. They become the pillars on which you base your life.

This is a good time to think about your convictions. You pick up beliefs from a story like Paul's, but those truths don't become convictions until you've made them your own. Which ones have you made your own? And those deep-seated convictions find origin in the inspired Word of God (3:16–17), which is all the more reason for you to stay in the Scriptures.

No person in Paul's place, condemned to die, spending his final hours in a dark dungeon, focusing on the things that honor Christ, would bother to pass along unreliable principles. That explains why Paul pulled no punches. He took the gloves off and wrote plainly about issues that mattered most. He gave his attention to issues of life and death. As time grew shorter by the moment, he became increasingly intense.

Paul brought his exhortation to Timothy to a climax with this remarkable statement: "All Scripture is inspired by God and profitable for teaching, for reproof, for correction, for training in righteousness; that the man of God may be adequate, equipped for every good work" (3:16–17). Paul was warming to his point.

Chapter Four: An Urgent Charge to a Ministry of Proclamation

Paul wrote with urgency, "I solemnly charge you in the presence of God and of Christ Jesus, who is to judge the living and the dead, and by His appearing and His kingdom: preach the word; be ready in season and out of season; reprove, rebuke, exhort, with great patience and instruction" (4:1–2). In other words, stick with the preaching plan God has promised to bless and use. Deliver the biblical goods! Be a man of the Word!

Don't attempt to be so creative and cute that folks miss the truth. No need for meaningless and silly substitutes that entertain but rarely convict the lost and edify the saved. Preach the truth. Will you notice something here? This exhortation is not addressed to the hearer, it's for the speaker. The one who is to do this is the one proclaiming the message. He is to be ready to do it in season and out of season. Being ready implies being prepared both mentally and spiritually.

In essence, Paul says, "Don't be lazy, Timothy. Do your homework. Don't stand up and start with an apology that you didn't quite have adequate time to prepare. That doesn't wash Timothy." And do so faithfully—when it's convenient and when it's not.

If I'm not prepared to preach by the time Sunday morning arrives, it's my fault. My responsibility is to be ready to proclaim the Word of God "in season or out of season," when it is hot or cold, headache or feeling great, early or late, whether I'm emotionally up or down, discouraged or at my stride. My job is to proclaim. Not only that, but I'm to deliver that proclamation accurately and compellingly. God's Word is what reproves and rebukes and exhorts. There's to be no dumbing down of the message for the sake of a modern audience. Paul warned Timothy about that slippery slide as well. As sure as the sun would rise, people would eventually stop enduring "sound doctrine," but "wanting to have their ears tickled, they will accumulate for themselves teachers in accordance to their own desires; and will turn away their ears from the truth, and will turn aside to myths." Talk about a fitting description of our own culture! To the very end, Paul was right on the mark.

Sadly, in an alarming number of churches today, God's people are being told what they *want* to hear, rather than what they *need* to hear. They are being fed warm milk, not solid meat. A watered-down gospel may attract large crowds (for a while), but it has no eternal impact. I've not been able to find any place in the Scriptures where God expresses the least bit of concern for drawing numbers. Satisfying the curious itching ears of our post-modern audiences is an exercise in futility.

The task of the minister is to deliver Truth. Frankly, I intend to continue doing just that, by God's grace, until the day He calls me home. I think there is an ever-increasing number of believers who long for nourishing messages based on the Word of God, not human opinion.

I'm not alone. Consider these penetrating words from Dr. Walter Kaiser:

> Too often the Bible is little more than a book of epigrammatic sayings or a springboard that gives us a rallying point around which to base our editorials. But where did we get the audacious idea that God would bless our opinions or judgments? Who wants to hear another point of view as an excuse for a Bible study or a message from the Word of God? Who said God would bless our stories, our programs for the church, or our ramblings on the general area announced by the text? Surely this is a major reason why the famine of the Word continues in massive proportions in most places in North America. Surely this is why the hunger for the teaching and the proclamation of God's Word continues to grow year after year. Men and women cannot live by ideas alone, no matter how eloquently they are stated or argued, but solely by a patient reading and explanation of all Scripture, line after line, paragraph after paragraph, chapter after chapter, and book after book. Where are such interpreters to be found, and where are their teachers?[5]

Paul realized what was at stake. He wanted Timothy to be prepared for the battle. "The days are going to only get worse. But you, Timothy, be sober, endure hardships, do the work of an evangelist, fulfill your ministry" (4:5).

With that he may have heard the unlatching of the gate as a battalion of soldiers made their way across the bowed planks toward Paul's dark and cramped abode. Each rhythmic pounding of footsteps brought him closer to his brutal end. It may very well have been at that moment he wrote, "For I am already being poured out as a drink offering, and the time of my departure has come" (4:6). Maybe he heard the soldiers' boots on the cobblestones of the street as he put the finishing touches on this love letter to his son in the faith. He adds, "I have fought the good fight, I have finished the course, I have kept the faith; in the future there is laid up for me the crown of righteousness, which the Lord, the righteous Judge, will award to me on that day; and not only to me, but also to all who have loved his appearing" (2 Timothy 4:7–8).

PAUL'S EARTHLY END

His earthly end came swiftly . . . abruptly. Alone and without fear, Paul stared directly into the eyes of the execution squad. Several held rods with which they would beat him; one held the sharp axe with which he would sever the apostle's head from his shoulders. Few words were spoken. They marched him through the heavy gate and beyond the stone wall that surrounded Rome, past the pyramid of Cestius, which still stands today, and on to the Ostian Way toward the sea. Crowds journeying to Rome knew by the rods and the axe that an execution would soon transpire. They had seen such sights before. They passed it off with a shrug. It happened yesterday; it would happen tomorrow.

The manacled prisoner, walking stiffly, ragged and filthy from the dungeon, was not ashamed or degraded. The squad of grim-faced soldiers never noticed as they frowned and stared ahead, but there was a faint smile on their prisoner's face—he was en route to a triumph—the crowning day of his reward. For to him to live was Christ, to die, gain. No axe across the back of his neck would rob him of his triumphant destiny. It would, in fact, initiate it!

They marched Paul to the third milestone on the Ostian Way, to a little pinewood in a glade—a glade of the tombs, known now as *Tre Fontane*. At that place today there stands an abbey in Paul's honor. He is believed to have been put overnight in a tiny cell, near the place of his execution. At first light the next dawn, the soldiers took Paul to a stump-like pillar. The executioner stood ready, stark naked, axe in hand.

The men stripped Paul—tied him, kneeling upright, to the low pillar, which exposed his back and neck. The lictors beat him with rods for the last time. He groaned and bled from his nose and mouth. And then, without a hint of hesitation, the executioner frowned as he swung the blade that gleamed in the morning sun high above his head, then brought it down swiftly, hitting its mark with a dull thud.

The head of Paul rolled down into the dust.

In that brutal moment, silently and invisibly, the soul of the great apostle—the man of grace and grit—was immediately set free. His spirit soared into the heavens: Absent from the body he was, at last, at home with the Lord.

CONCLUSION

For over forty years it has been my joy and privilege to be engaged in an in-depth study of the Scriptures. For almost that long I have had the challenge and responsibility of communicating the results of my study. As an expository preacher, I've returned again and again to the writings of Paul as set forth in the New Testament. As a writer, I've frequently referred to the man, as well as his teachings. Much of what Paul wrote has shaped my thinking, as well as my ministry—certainly more than any other writer in the Bible.

The words of F.F. Bruce express my sentiments exactly:

> "For half a century and more I have been a student and teacher of ancient literature, and to no other writer of antiquity have I devoted so much time and attention as to Paul. Nor can I think of any other writer, ancient or modern, whose study is so richly rewarding as his. This is due to several aspects of his many-faceted character: the attractive warmth of his personality, his intellectual stature, the exhilarating release effected by his gospel of redeeming grace, the dynamism with

which he propagated that gospel throughout the world, devoting himself single-mindedly to fulfilling the commission entrusted to him on
the Damascus road . . . and laboring more abundantly than all his
fellow-apostles . . ."[1]

In spite of my many years of respect for, familiarity with, and frequent
references to the man and his writings, I had never undertaken a careful
analysis of Paul's life and ministry until last year. Gripped with that realization, I set out on a quest to mine the gold I may have missed during the
past four decades. The results were not only enriching to me, personally,
they led to a series of biblical messages I delivered to the congregation at
Stonebriar Community Church in Frisco, Texas, where it is my honor to
serve as their founding pastor.

I can still recall ending that series in tears at the pulpit, profoundly
moved over the magnificence of the man's life and teachings, the sacrificial
nature of his ministry, the full-on commitment to his calling, and the horrible manner of his death just beyond the shadows of the rugged wall of
Rome. By that time I was already engaged in a related project, having
decided to go back to the drawing board and prepare a manuscript for
publication. Any story this moving, any life this significant, I felt then and
still believe, deserves maximum exposure.

Because you have now journeyed with me through these twenty-two
chapters, you understand what drove me to write this sixth volume in my
biographical series. What I feared might have been a difficult undertaking
has not been that at all. As is true of any great life, the unfolding of the
story has a natural flow about it . . . Paul's especially.

It was he who forged so many of the doctrines still embraced by the
believing remnant who form the true Church today. It was he who first
took truth where it had never been heard before. It was he who courageously pressed on, in spite of personal infirmities, frequent rejection,
emotional distress, and bodily harm. It was he who refused to let obstacles
of any size or number stand in his way. It was he who helped us understand
the role and responsibilities of the church, who preached and modeled
grace, who confronted the enemy without fear and who reached out to the

Gentiles without prejudice. It was he who built into the lives of younger men, passionately passing the torch of truth while urging them to press on, regardless. And it was he whose writings still survive after twenty long centuries. Small wonder that such a life is still admired, such teaching is still in demand, and such resolve is still legendary. He reminds us how life was meant to be lived and how death, regardless of its cause, can have dignity and purpose.

From his obscure birth in Tarsus of Cilicia, through his remarkable conversion en route to Damascus, and along all those journeys from Antioch of Syria to the very presence of Nero enthroned in Rome, including his brutal martyrdom beside the Ostian Way, the man leaves his mark on all who take the time to pause and ponder. Left in the wake of its significance, you're unable to remain the same.

A life like Paul's translates into a model anyone would want to emulate. All who examine the Christlikeness woven through the fabric of his character are enriched. We now wave farewell to this brave soldier of the cross, forever impressed by his unique blend of brilliance and boldness, commitment and compassion, love and logic, grace and grit.

ENDNOTES

CHAPTER ONE
MAY I INTRODUCE TO YOU SAUL OF TARSUS . . .

1. John Pollock, *The Apostle: A Life of Paul* (Colorado Springs, Colo.: Cook Communications Ministries, 1985), pp. 16–17. Used with permission. May not be further reproduced. All rights reserved.
2. *Ibid.*, pp. 17–18. Used with permission.
3. John Newton, "Amazing Grace," 1st, 2nd, and 4th stanzas (1779).

CHAPTER TWO
THE VIOLENT CAPTURE OF A REBEL WILL

1. Excerpted from "The Legacy of Prisoner 23226" by Wendy Murray Zoba in *Christianity Today*, July 9, 2001 edition. Used by permission.
2. Alan Redpath, *The Making of a Man of God* (Old Tappan, N.J.: Fleming H. Revell Company, 1962), p. 5. Used by permission.
3. Warren Wiersbe, *The Bible Exposition Commentary* (Colorado Springs, Colo.: Cook Communications Ministries, 1989), vol.1, p.438. Used with permission. May not be further reproduced. All rights reserved.

CHAPTER THREE
THE MEMORABLE FAITH OF A FORGOTTEN HERO

1. John Stott, *The Spirit the Church and the World: The Message of Acts* (Downers Grove, Ill.: InterVarsity Press, 1990), pp. 175–176. Used by permission.

CHAPTER FOUR
THE NECESSITY OF SOLITUDE,
QUIETNESS, AND OBSCURITY

1. Richard Foster, *Celebration of Discipline* (New York, N.Y.: Harper Collins, 1988), p. 1. Used by permission.
2. Roy Jenkins, *Churchill: A Biography*, as quoted in *The New York Times* book review section in "His Finest Hour," by Harold Evans; November 11, 2001.
3. Leon Morris, *Galatians: Paul's Charter of Christian Freedom* (Downers Grove, Ill.: InterVarsity Press, 1996), p. 57. Used by permission.
4. Charles Caldwell Ryrie, *The Ryrie Study Bible, New American Standard Translation* (Chicago, Ill.: Moody Press, 1978), p. 1771, fn. 1:17. Used by permission.
5. James Montgomery Boice, "Galatians," in *The Expositor's Bible Commentary*, Frank E. Gaebelein, ed., *Vol. 10* (Grand Rapids, Mich.: The Zondervan Corporation, 1976), fn. 17. Used by permission.
6. John R. W. Stott, *The Message of Galatians: Only One Way* (Downers Grove, Ill., and Leicester, England: InterVarsity Press, 1968), p. 34. Used by permission.
7. F. B. Meyer. *Paul: A Servant of Jesus Christ* (Old Tappan, N.J.: Fleming H. Revell Company, 1897), n.p. Public domain.
8. V. Raymond Edman, *The Disciplines of Life* (Colorado Springs, Colo.: Cook Communications Ministries, 1948, 2002), pp. 81. Used with permission. May not be further reproduced. All rights reserved.
9. Richard J. Foster, *Money, Sex, and Power: The Challenge of the Disciplined Life* (San Francisco, Calif.: Harper & Row Publishers, 1985), p. 217. Used by permission.

CHAPTER FIVE
MISSION UNDERWAY . . . THANKS TO THE LESSER-KNOWN

1. William Ernest Henley, "Invictus." Public domain.
2. R. C. H. Lenski, *The Interpretation of St. Paul's First and Second Epistle to the Corinthians* (Columbus, Oh.: Wartburg Press, 1937, 1946), p. 1287. Public domain.
3. F. B. Meyer, *Paul: A Servant of Jesus Christ* (London, England: Morgan and Scott, n.d.), p. 72. Public domain.
4. Pollock, *The Apostle*, p. 45. Used with permission.

CHAPTER SIX
OUT OF THE SHADOWS

1. Reverend James Stalker, D.D., *The Life of St. Paul* (New York, N.Y.: American Tract Society, n.d.), p. 67. Used by permission.
2. Ruth Harms Calkin, *Lord, Could You Hurry a Little?* (Wheaton, Ill.: Tyndale House Publishers, 1983), p. 37. Used by permission.
3. Pollock, *The Apostle*, p. 51. Used with permission.
4. A. T. Robertson, *Word Pictures in the New Testament, Vol. III, "The Acts of the Apostles,"* (New York, N.Y., and London, England: Harper & Brothers, 1930), pp. 158–159. Public domain.
5. Meyer, *Paul: A Servant of Jesus Christ,* p. 72. Public domain.

CHAPTER SEVEN
FINDING CONTENTMENT IN GOD'S SUFFICIENT GRACE

1. John Stott, *Romans: God's Good News for the World* (Downers Grove, Ill.: InterVarsity Press, 1994), p. 242. Used by permission.
2. Philip Yancey, *Where Is God When It Hurts?* (Grand Rapids, Mich.: Zondervan Publishing House, 1977), p. 84. Used by permission.

CHAPTER EIGHT
THE PLEASURE OF BEING IN MINISTRY TOGETHER

1. Philip Zimbardo, "The Age of Indifference," *Psychology Today,* August 1980 issue, p. 72. Reprinted with permission from Psychology Today; Copyright © 1980 Sussex Publishers, Inc.
2. Warren Wiersbe, *On Being a Servant of God* (Grand Rapids, Mich.: Baker Books, 1993), p. 20. Used by permission.
3. John Eldredge, *Wild at Heart* (Nashville, Tenn.: Thomas Nelson Publishers, 2001), p. 200. Used by permission.

CHAPTER NINE
RELEASED IN ORDER TO OBEY

1. Eddie Espinosa, "Change My Heart Oh God" (Franklin, Tenn.: Mercy/Vineyard Publishing/ASCAP, 1982). Used by permission.
2. Charles Haddon Spurgeon, *Lectures to My Students* (Grand Rapids, Mich.: Zondervan Publishing House, 1954), p. 70–71. Public domain.
3. Eldredge, *Wild at Heart*, p. 198–199. Used by permission.

CHAPTER TEN
THE JAGGED EDGE OF AUTHENTIC MINISTRY

1. Dr. Steven Lawson, in an address to the student body and faculty of Dallas Theological Seminary. Dr. Lawson's lecture was included as part of a series in *Bibliotheca Sacra*, the theological journal of Dallas Theological Seminary; Roy Zuck, general editor.
2. Pollock, *The Apostle*, p. 70. Used with permission.
3. Barry J. Beitzel, *The Moody Atlas of Bible Lands* (Chicago, Ill.: Moody Press, 1985), pp. 176–177. Used by permission.

CHAPTER ELEVEN
A GAME PLAN FOR FACING EXTREME CIRCUMSTANCES

1. Viktor E. Frankl, *Man's Search for Meaning* (New York, N.Y.: Pocket Books, Simon and Schuster, 1976), n.p. Used by permission.
2. Pollock, *The Apostle*, pp. 70–71. Used with permission.
3. *Ibid.*, p. 72. Used with permission.
4. *Ibid.*, p. 75. Used with permission.

CHAPTER TWELVE
THE DAY TWO MISSIONARIES DUKED IT OUT

1. G. Campbell Morgan, *The Acts of the Apostles* (Westwood, N.J.: Fleming H. Revell Company, 1924), p.369. Public domain.
2. Dr. Bob Cook, source unknown.
3. Pollock, *The Apostle*, p. 116. Used with permission.
4. A. T. Robertson, *Word Pictures in the New Testament, Vol. III, "The Acts of the Apostles"* (Nashville, Tenn.: Broadman Press, 1930), p. 241. Public domain.
5. David Augsburger, *Caring Enough to Confront* (Ventura, Calif.: Gospel Light/Regal Books, 1980 rev.ed.), p. 14. Used by permission.
6. Phillip Melanchthon, source unknown. Public domain.

CHAPTER THIRTEEN
TRAVELING AS PAUL TRAVELED

1. F. B. Meyer, *Christ In Isaiah, Expositions of Isaiah XL–LV* (Old Tappan, N.J.: Fleming H. Revell Company, 1895), p. 9. Public domain.
2. Pollock, *The Apostle*, p. 118. Used with permission.
3. See Pollock, *The Apostle*, pp. 124–125.
4. Donald Phillips, *Lincoln on Leadership* (New York, N.Y.: Little, Brown and Company, 1992), p. 66. Used by permission of Warner Books, Inc.
5. Phil Cousineau, *The Art of Pilgrimage*, (Berkeley, Calif.: Conari Press, 1998), n.p.

CHAPTER FOURTEEN
PREACHING AS PAUL PREACHED

1. Martin Luther. See John R. W. Stott, *Between Two Worlds*, (Grand Rapids, Mich.: William B. Eerdmans Publishing Company, 1982), p. 24.
2. Stott, *The Spirit the Church and the World*, p. 280. Used by permission.

CHAPTER FIFTEEN
LEADING AS PAUL LED

1. Howard Fineman, "A President Finds His True Voice," *Newsweek*, September 24, 2001, © 2001 Newsweek, Inc.; p. 50. All rights reserved. Used by permission.
2. John R. W. Stott, *The Message of 1 and 2 Thessalonians*, from *THE BIBLE SPEAKS TODAY* series (Grand Rapids, Mich.: InterVarsity Press, 1994), p. 47. Used by permission.
3. Dwight Eisenhower, in *Quote/Unquote*.
4. Hans Finzel, *Empowered Leaders: The Ten Principles of Christian Leadership* (Nashville, Tenn.: Word Publishing, 1998), pp. 40–41. Used by permission.
5. Source unknown.
6. Finzel, *Empowered Leaders*, pp. 41–42. Used by permission.
7. "I Met the Master Face to Face," author/source unknown. Public domain.

CHAPTER SIXTEEN
RESPONDING AS PAUL RESPONDED

1. J. Sidlow Baxter, *Mark These Men* (London: Marshall, Morgan & Scott, Ltd., 1949), p. 41. Used by permission.
2. J. B. Phillips, *The New Testament in Modern English* (New York, N.Y.: The MacMillan Company, 1960), p. 385. Used by permission.
3. J. Oswald Sanders, *Paul, the Leader* (Grand Rapids, Mich.: NavPress, 1984), p. 173–174. Used by permission.

4. Florence White Willett, public domain; as quoted in V. Raymond Edman, *The Disciplines of Life*, p. 196.

CHAPTER SEVENTEEN
THINKING AS PAUL THOUGHT

1. Don Miller, *The Authority of the Bible,* as quoted in Earl D. Radmacher, *You & Your Thoughts: The Power of Right Thinking* (Wheaton, Ill.: Tyndale House Publishers, 1977), pp. 11–12. Used by permission.
2. Pollock, *The Apostle*, p. 257. Used with permission.

CHAPTER EIGHTEEN
DEALING WITH CRITICS AS PAUL DID

1. William Henry Ward, (1886–1966), source unknown. Public domain.
2. Finzel, *Empowered Leaders*, p. 71. Used by permission.
3. Charles Spurgeon, as quoted in David Roper, *A Burden Shared* (Grand Rapids, Mich.: Discovery House, 1991), p. 58. Original source in public domain.
3. Pollock, *The Apostle*, p. 261. Used with permission.
4. *Ibid.* Used with permission.

CHAPTER NINETEEN
STANDING TALL AS PAUL STOOD

1. Mother Teresa, 44th National Prayer Breakfast, Washington, DC.

CHAPTER TWENTY-ONE
ARRESTED, CONFINED, BUT STILL EFFECTIVE

1. Title of Dick Feller song, "Some Days are Diamonds (Some Days are Stone)," Tree Publishing, BMI, Sony/ATV Songs.
2. Pollock, *The Apostle*, pp. 286–287. Used with permission.

3. *Ibid*, p. 289. Used with permission.

4. David Aikman, *Great Souls: Six Who Changed the Century* (Nashville, Tenn.: Word Publishing, 1998), p. 10. Used by permission.

CHAPTER TWENTY-TWO
SHACKLED, DESERTED, BUT STILL UNDAUNTED

1. Finzel, *Empowered Leaders*, pp. 161–162. Used by permission.

2. Charles Erdman, *The Pastoral Epistles* (Philadelphia, Penn.: Westminster Press, 1921), p. 82. Public domain.

3. Ryrie, *The Ryrie Study Bible*, fn. 4:6. Used by permission.

4. Walter C. Kaiser, Jr., *Revive Us Again*, (Nashville, Tenn.: Broadman & Holman Publishers, 1999), pp. 166–167. Used by permission.

CONCLUSION

1. F. F. Bruce, *Paul: Apostle of the Heart Set Free* (Grand Rapids, Mich.: William B. Eerdmans Publishing Company, 1977), p. 15. Used by permission.

THE DARKNESS AND THE DAWN

The two most significant events in human history are the death and resurrection of Jesus Christ. And no one can uncover their meaning for today quite like Charles Swindoll. From the poignant interactions of the Last Supper, through the despairing events of Gethsemane and the seven last words of Jesus on the Cross, Dr. Swindoll challenges readers with a new perspective on the atoning work of Christ.

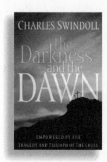

DAY BY DAY WITH CHARLES SWINDOLL

Condensed from the *Finishing Touch,* this devotional provides 365 daily readings, which highlight Swindoll's masterful story-telling ability, his insights into Scripture, and his down-to-earth style. *Day by Day with Charles Swindoll* will inspire, challenge, comfort, and even humor readers as Swindoll chats about the many facets of the Christian life. Packaged as a convenient, small-sized, carry-along devotional, this is a great gift for those who want an uplifting, not-too-heavy devotional.

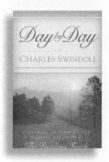

DROPPING YOUR GUARD

Charles Swindoll unveils a biblical blueprint for rich relationships in this life-changing classic. In this updated version of his best-selling book, Swindoll poignantly and honestly portrays the need for authentic love and transparency.

THE FINISHING TOUCH

When the going gets tough, most people just quit. This daily devotional challenges us to persevere and to finish well the race set before us as God finishes in us the good work He began. This popular volume is Swindoll's first collection of daily readings.

FLYING CLOSER TO THE FLAME

Best-selling author Charles Swindoll explores the void that exists in many Christians' lives due to a lack of understanding about the Holy Spirit. In *Flying Closer to the Flame,* he challenges readers toward a deeper, more intimate relationship with the Holy Spirit.

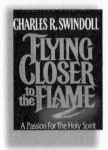

THE GRACE AWAKENING

In this best-selling classic, Charles Swindoll awakens readers to the life-impacting realities of God's grace, the freedom and joy it brings, the fear it cures, the strength it lends to relationships, and the ever-increasing desire to know God. A modern-day classic from Charles Swindoll.

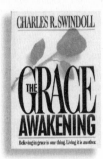

THE GREAT LIVES SERIES

Throughout history, people have faced the same challenges and temptations. In his Great Lives Series, Charles Swindoll shows us how the great heroes of the faith offer a model of courage, hope, and triumph in the face of adversity.

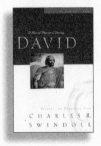
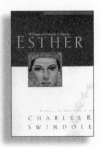
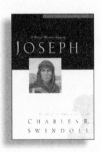
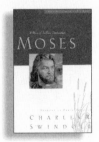

GROWING UP IN GOD'S FAMILY

Growing older doesn't necessarily mean growing up or maturing in Christ. Using the stages of physical growth—birth and infancy, childhood, adolescence, and adulthood—to describe the phases of spiritual maturity, Swindoll encourages Christians to pursue spiritual growth.

HAND ME ANOTHER BRICK

Most of us could benefit from wise advice on how to be a more effective leader at work and at home. Charles Swindoll delves deep into the life of Nehemiah to show how to handle the issues of motivation, discouragement, and adversity with integrity.

HOPE AGAIN

Combining the New Testament teachings of Peter and the insights of one of the most popular authors of our day, *Hope Again* is an encouraging, enlivening, and refreshing look at why we can dare to hope no matter who we are, no matter what we face.

IMPROVING YOUR SERVE

In this classic volume, Charles Swindoll uniquely shows the important aspects of authentic servanthood, such as: What it takes to serve unselfishly, why a servant has such a powerful influence, and what challenges and rewards a servant can expect.

LAUGH AGAIN

Discover outrageous joy in this modern classic. Charles Swindoll shows how we can live in the present, say "no" to negativism, and realize that while no one's life is perfect, joy is always available. Applying scriptural truths in a practical way, Swindoll shows readers how to laugh again.

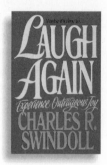

LIVING ABOVE THE LEVEL OF MEDIOCRITY

Charles Swindoll tackles the problem of mediocrity in one of his most popular books. With his trademark stories and practical insight, he boldly confronts the issues of self-discipline, laziness, and our tendency to accept less than what we deserve, drawing clear lines between the pursuit of excellence and the pursuit of success in the eyes of the world.

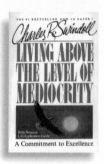

LIVING ON THE RAGGED EDGE

Here is an intimate glimpse into Solomon's ancient journal, Ecclesiastes, in which the young king's desperate quest for satisfaction—in work, in sexual conquest, in all the trappings afforded by his fabulous wealth—was as futile as trying to "catch the wind." For those struggling with the anxieties and frustrations of our modern era, the good news is that you can find perspective and joy amid the struggle.

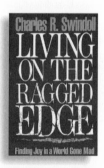

THE ROAD TO ARMAGEDDON
Various Authors

The end of a century. A new millennium. For Christians everywhere, there is little doubt that these are the last days, as we move down the road to Armageddon. This book features six of the most respected scholars and teachers on Bible prophecy and coming world events. An important tool for understanding the future.

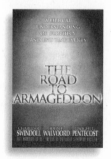

Simple Faith

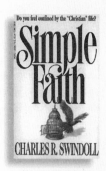

Must we run at a pace between maddening and insane to prove we're among the faithful? Is this really how the Prince of Peace would have us live? In this book, Swindoll answers with a resounding, "No!," showing how Christians can break free from exhausting, performance-based faith, back to the simplicity of the Sermon on the Mount.

Start Where You Are

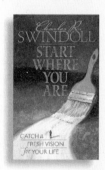

"To start fresh, to start over, to start anything, you have to know where you are," says Charles Swindoll. "Seldom does anybody just happen to end up on a right road." In *Start Where You Are*, Swindoll offers upbeat and practical advice on creating a life worth living, no matter what the circumstances are now or where they may lead in the future.

Strengthening Your Grip

As only he can, Charles Swindoll combines biblical insights with unforgettable stories that inspire readers to strengthen their spiritual grip on issues such as family, prayer, integrity, and purity.

Suddenly One Morning

Through the eyes of a shopkeeper on the main street of Jerusalem, readers experience the life-changing events of a week that begins with a parade and ends with an empty grave. This Easter gift book combines an original Swindoll story with beautiful full-color art.

THE TALE OF THE TARDY OXCART

In *The Tale of The Tardy Oxcart*, Charles Swindoll shares from his life-long collection of his and others' personal stories, sermons, and anecdotes. 1501 various illustrations are arranged by subjects alphabetically for quick and easy access. A perfect resource for all pastors and preachers.

THREE STEPS FORWARD, TWO STEPS BACK

Charles Swindoll reminds readers that our problems are not solved by simple answers or all-too-easy clichés. Instead, he offers practical ways to walk with God through the realities of life—including times of fear, stress, anger, and temptation.

YOU AND YOUR CHILD

Best-selling author and veteran parent and grandparent Charles Swindoll believes that the key to successful parenting lies in becoming a "student" of your children—learning the distinct bent and blueprint of each child. Here's practical advice for parents wishing to launch confident, capable young adults in today's ever-changing world.

Notes

Notes

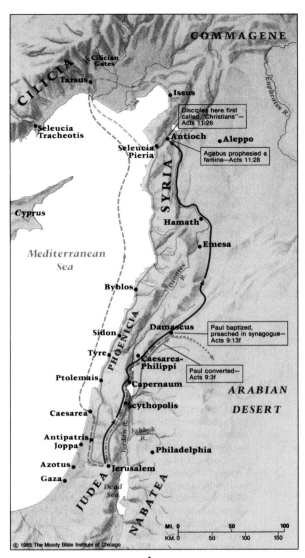

Disciples here first
called "Christians"—
Acts 11:26

Agabus prophesied a
famine—Acts 11:28

Paul baptized,
preached in synagogue—
Acts 9:13f

Paul converted—
Acts 9:3f

© 1985 The Moody Bible Institute of Chicago

MAP ONE: PAUL'S EARLY TRAVELS

- **●**   city

- **≍**   mountain pass

_____ Paul (Saul) commissioned to journey to Damascus
and seek out Christians (Acts 9:1f)

- - - - Paul spent time in Arabia (Gal 1:17)

─ ·· ─ Paul returned to Jerusalem and was received by
disciples (Acts 9:26f)

─ ─ ─ Paul fled from Hellenists (Acts 9:28f)

─ ─ ─ Barnabas journeyed to Tarsus and returned to
Antioch with Paul (Acts 11:25f)

_____ Paul & Barnabas sent to Jerusalem with aid for
believers amidst famine (Acts 11:29f)

▬▬▬ Paul & Barnabas returned to Antioch, joined by John
Mark (Acts 12:25)

MAP TWO: PAUL'S FIRST AND SECOND JOURNEYS

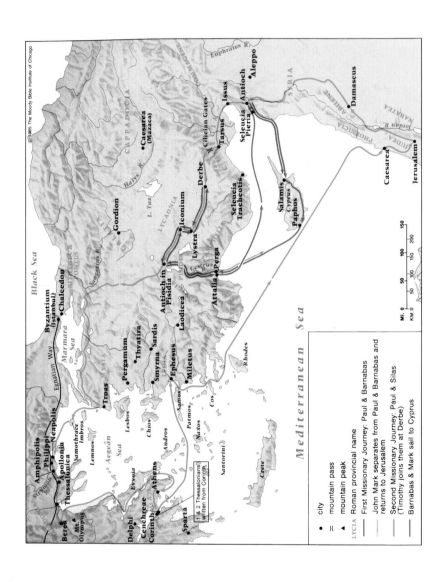

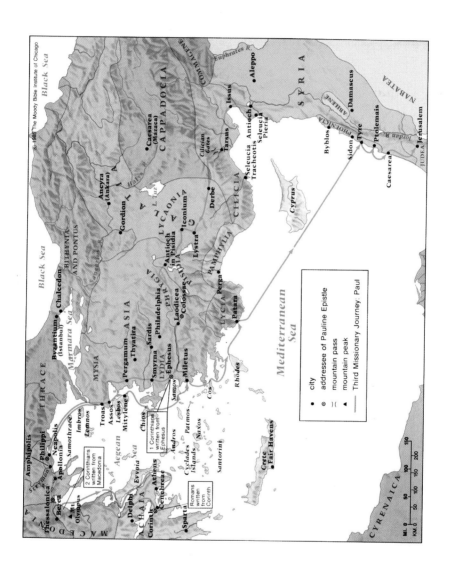

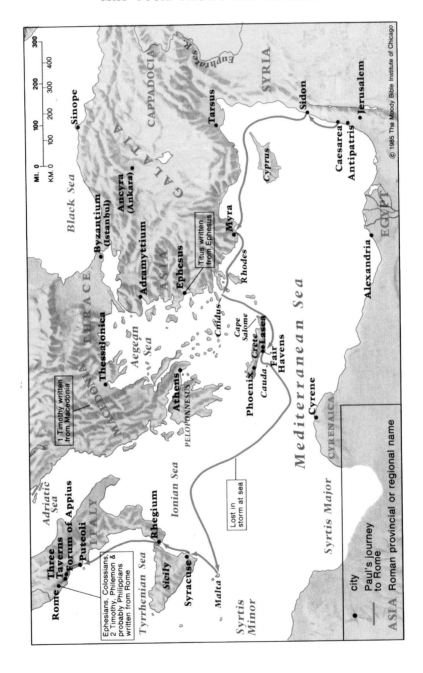